FATHER
DID WE KNOW YOU?

PREFACE

During my lifetime, I have read many books, and quite often thought that an educated person should leave something behind, his or her own mark, thoughts, or ideas, for others to learn from.

I cannot include myself in that category of people because I only reached the fourth grade at school, but I am sure that the countless ups and downs I have lived through in my long life will be of some interest to many such people.

These ideas were given to me by Mrs Maria Chajkiwska, the wife of my old friend Lewko. I used to visit them very often and would recall events from my arduous life. Maria would listen to my stories very attentively, then tried to talk me into writing my exploits down on paper, as she felt it would be a shame not to have a written record.

I gave her idea much thought and would tell her that my Ukrainian grammar was poor, that my writing was also illegible, and on top of that I had never undertaken such a project. True, in the past when I had more free time, I would often scribble down a few poems, but these were solely for my own pleasure.
In the end I agreed with Maria that I would write something down in prose, and she would then correct the grammar, editing what I had written into a story. The main object was for me to write the truth, no matter how painful and this is what I did.

When I reached three hundred pages, Maria advised me to show my manuscript to a professional body of people for their advice. Four people read these pages and all of them agreed that I should continue, which you will see I did.

ACKNOWLEDGEMENTS

I would like to express my gratitude to my dearest and oldest friend, Alex Kirichenko, for the time he spent proofreading and correcting my many grammar mistakes.

I would also like to thank my friend and neighbour Grahame Johnston for all his technical and photographic expertise. To my Cypriot friend Mario Louca for his work navigating Amazon's minefield of questions and requirements in publishing this book. To my wife Roksanna, for her patience and understanding. Finally, I extend my thanks to Google Translate and Google Maps for providing invaluable information at my fingertips.

DISCLAIMER

I have taken all necessary steps to ensure that every aspect of this book is as close to my father's original work in Ukrainian. I am not responsible for any spelling mistakes of persons, places, villages and towns.

DEFAMATION OF CHARACTER

I cannot be made responsible for any liability caused to any person, organisation or other body mentioned in this book, either dead or alive, nor about their character, religion or race.

CHAPTER 1
CHILDHOOD

Bitter times

Thoughts of capture

That's a son growing without a father

I was born in Ivano Frankivsk (formerly Stanislaviw), Western Ukraine, on the 10th of June 1916.

I have no recollection of ever seeing my father who, I was told by my mother, worked on the railway as an engine driver and was seriously injured, from which he died shortly after, during the First World War.

My mother, Maria, was from the village of Kaminne. From a young age my mother worked as a maid for wealthy families. I lived with my mother in the city until I was six years old. The first time I left the city was to go to my young aunt's funeral, which was held in a village nearby. City life was very hard, my mother would find work whitewashing houses, doing laundry, often leaving me alone at home for the whole day. My mother would come home, often to find me asleep, it would take her a long time to wake me, and when she finally did, I would be fed leftovers from where she worked. Once I finished eating I fell back into slumber. In the morning my mother would wake me, make breakfast then leave a little for lunch. On the days my mother had no work, she would allow me to play outside with the other children. It was great fun playing during the summer as there was no need for shoes, but during the winter I never had shoes, so I had to wrap my feet with rags, or do without.

On Saturdays I would go around the Jewish households to light their fires, for which they would give me a piece of bread, or bread made from yellow maize. Saturday was the best day of the week for me because my mother didn't work, she would have to buy a bundle of firewood or a bag of coal. My mother would only light a fire twice a week, on a Saturday and Sunday when she was at home. In the summer, I would run around the house, on the bench, the bed and on the table, but most of the time I sat on the window sill staring outside, the only thing visible was the garden. During the winter months when work was scarce, my mother had no money for a candle or a fire, so I would get a piece of dried bread, which I would eat in bed to stay warm, whilst sometimes my poor mother would go to bed hungry. There were days when I awoke, to find my mother had already left. One of the first things I did was to try to see if my mother had forgotten to lock the door, but she never forgot.

During the summer months, especially in the heat, I found it difficult to wait the whole day long for my mother to return from work. One day I thought of checking the window panes, to see if any of them were loose, so that I could take one out, and that way create an exit for myself. I tried to move each pane of glass, but they were all fixed solid, there was no way I could loosen them using my hands, I needed a tool or knife, which my mother would always lock away in a box, so that I wouldn't accidentally harm myself. During the next few days I found an old screwdriver, so I again checked every window until I found one which I thought would be the easiest. In those days the glass on windows was held by thin strips of wood, not putty. It took me the whole day to scrape the wood, the bottom strip was easier as it was a little damp, but the sides and top were hard going. At the end of the day I cleaned and tidied everything, not leaving any traces of my work for my mother to see. That evening when my mother returned from work, I was already asleep and no matter how hard my mother tried to wake me I wouldn't get up to eat, so she told me to eat my supper for lunch the next day.

The following morning I got up early so as to carry on with my work. It took me most of that day to finish the work, the sun at this time was in my eyes, and then suddenly the whole glass pane dropped onto the floor and smashed into pieces. Frightened at what my mother would do to me, I climbed out of the hole that I had made and jumped onto the ground running into one of the neighbouring gardens. The garden offered a cornucopia, an abundance of cucumbers and red berries which I couldn't eat enough of. That evening I don't remember how much I ate, I even picked fruit which I stuffed down my shirt sleeve to hide for the following day. At nightfall I found a deep furrow surrounded by potatoes and corn where I quickly fell asleep. During the night I awoke several times to the sound of barking dogs.

The following morning, the sun was already hot when I was woken by a strange girl. Startled, I quickly jumped to my feet and tried to run. The girl saw my red face, thinking it was blood she cried 'Oh Mother of God, help him' then stood frozen to the same spot for what seemed like ages. I ran as fast I could until I reached some bushes where I hid until the girl disappeared.

In a short space of time, I had learned the layout of all the gardens, where the ripest fruit was grown and where the best spot was to sleep. I now became more frightened of being caught by the neighbours than by my mother. I was also too afraid to sleep close to home and the stray dogs.

I spent three nights and two days wandering in the gardens until a thorn entered my foot whilst rummaging around the tomatoes. I was bandaging my foot with a piece of rag, when suddenly in front of me was stood a very large woman, holding a bundle of long twigs. She asked 'What are you doing son, all dirty and bedraggled in someone's garden?' I was petrified and didn't reply. She then quickly grabbed me by the arm and said 'Now you won't run away from me, I know whose child you are'. I tried to struggle free from her but she was too strong, we walked through the gardens until we reached what was her back yard. She sat me on a bench by her house and told me not to move, otherwise her dog would bite me. Looking around I could see a tall hedge, her dog watching me menacingly, not taking his eyes off me for a single second. The lady entered her house, returning with a large basin of cold water. She told me to take off my shirt and torn trousers and step into the water. The lady called to her daughter, telling her to throw my clothes away as they were covered in fleas. The lady washed me herself, from head to toe, whilst her daughter went into the house to bring a long nightdress for me. When I was washed, the lady combed my hair, put on the nightdress and escorted me to a hut where wood was kept, then locked me inside.

There was nothing inside the wood hut besides splinters and a very large melon. The melon was covered in blood, which, on seeing it, frightened the living daylights out of me and made me cry. I went into a corner and squatted until I fell asleep. I can't remember how long I was asleep for, but when I woke up I could see standing above me the same lady with my mother. There was no need for my mother to ask any questions, for the lady had already filled her in. My mother thanked her for catching me and apologised for the damage I had caused, promising the lady she would repay her in kind.

Once we arrived back home, my mother didn't lay a finger on me, she merely walked around the house muttering to herself, with tears running down her cheeks. I noticed the window I broke hadn't been repaired, the hole was just covered with an old sack. That evening we had no lighting or cooked meal, my mother gave me a piece of dried bread with a cup of cold milk.

The next morning my mother woke me, gave me a different shirt, washed me, and for breakfast I had a nice fresh roll. After breakfast my mother showed me what she had prepared for me, then said 'Son you have left me with no alternative, so I must now tie you up when you are left alone in the house'. My mother took a rope which she had previously prepared and tied it to a hook on the wall, then taking my left leg, she firstly wrapped it with a cloth, covering it with the other end of the rope. Once tied, the rope length was too short for me to get onto the table, so I could only sit on the bench. The future looked bleak for me now, I could no longer sit at the window sill because the rope was too short, I could only stand on the bench if I wanted to see through the window. The following morning, my mother would gently tie the rope to my other leg, alternating each day.

One day we had a visit from my 'good uncle' who argued with my mother that she should move to the village and that it was time for me to start school. My mother didn't work on Sundays and feast days; those were the days when I could play outside with the other children. I loved my mother very much although she beat me frequently. I know I caused her a lot of problems, that's why she walked around with a long face. I spent more days 'imprisoned' days than being 'free'. When I turned seven, my mother did what my 'good uncle' asked and together we took a train to the village where my grandfather lived.

CHAPTER 2
LIFE IN THE VILLAGE

I fell in love with the village of Kaminne from the very first moment, every orchard I walked by attracted me, I saw many different plants and fruits. My mother now had her own father to look after me. My grandfather was a good builder, but at that time was not working because he had damaged his back. Grandad, when he had money for tobacco, would tell me stories about his life, the war, the battlefront and when he was held in captivity in Italy. When he had no money for tobacco, he would sit by the house singing, making wooden spindles and rakes with his knife, later selling them for tobacco and alcohol. Grandad didn't have any possessions, only seven chickens. He would check their nests two or three times a day for eggs. Sometimes the eggs were still warm, and both of us would go to the Jewish shop to exchange them for tobacco. My mother would also wait for the eggs, so that she could buy matches, salt and paraffin. Because my mother had very little of her own land, she had to go out in search of work to the local manor house where she would milk their cows, mornings and evenings, while the remainder of the day was spent working the land.

After that first summer the school term started and I went to school for the first time. My school teacher was called Mr. Tymczyna. I was an average pupil, but one day I overheard the school teacher telling my mother not to bring me into school too early, because I spent my time swinging on the school gate.

Life in the village improved my mother's life, she began to receive a widow's pension for my father, so with the extra money she would spend it on clothes and drink, which resulted in her receiving many male suitors. My grandfather couldn't stand looking at the transformation in her, so he left the house, found some old widow and lived with her. When my mother had the extra money, villagers advised her to send me to a school in the city, otherwise I would revert back to my old ways in the afternoons, now that grandfather no longer lived with us. In the afternoon, mother would take me to the fields with herself. I was responsible for feeding the chickens, until one day a duck went into the paddock with the chickens. I wanted to scare the duck away so I threw a stone at it. Unfortunately, the stone broke the duck's leg, it sat and wouldn't get up, so I picked it up, then threw it into the nearby weeds. That evening my mother went into the garden to collect vegetables and heard a duck quacking, so she went to the duck, picked it up and brought it home. At home, my mother took an axe, chopped the duck's head off, then plucked it and was overjoyed there would be a good meal on the table. That Sunday, my mother and I had a good dinner, after which I went to play outside with the local children, where I was approached by a lady, the owner of the duck. She asked me if grandfather had been round, what my mother was doing and what we had for dinner and what we'd be having for supper. Once she discovered from me that we had meat, that was enough for her, she later marched over to our house, saying she knew what happened to her duck because I'd told her so. My mother didn't know which way to turn, so she eventually told the lady that she didn't have the money to pay her, but would work for her to compensate her for the loss of her duck. Once again my mother was furious with me; she then took me into the fields to help her carry the local harvest, and fetch water from the stream for the other workers.

In the middle of my summer holidays, one Sunday afternoon it was raining quite heavily, my mother went to a neighbour's house, we didn't go to church service because my mother didn't have the money to buy me any decent clothes. My mother would wash my shirt every Sunday, then hang it out to dry, so that I could wear it later in the day. This particular Sunday, I climbed a pear tree from which I fell and broke my left arm. Word soon got to my mother what'd happened, so she rushed home where she found me holding my heavily swollen broken arm. My mother tried in vain to stretch it, but the pain was too severe, she decided to take me to the local hospital.

CHAPTER 3
IN HOSPITAL

On arrival at the hospital, because it was a Sunday we were told to come back the following day, so my mother left me alone in the hospital and she went back home without me.

The broken arm incident had happened just before I was to start my new school in the city after the summer holidays. My uncle had already arranged for me to start at the new school, though this was now impossible as I had a plaster cast put on my broken arm, which needed to stay on for six weeks. Hospital life was a holiday for me, I was allowed to walk around the gardens, other patients sent me out to local shops to buy tobacco and cigarettes. The nuns gave me as much to eat as the adults, the only downside was that we had to remain in our beds until mid- morning. To one side of my bed lay an elderly man who taught me how to pray morning and night. My mother would visit me every Sunday, and since she had a little money now, she would bring me a treat once a week. It was in that very hospital where I had my first orange.

Every morning the old man next to me would take me to the hospital chapel before breakfast, we would both sit together in the same pew. During visiting times, nobody ever visited him, while my mother would only come on a Sunday, because on weekdays she would have to work.

One morning a nun approached me to tell me that the doctor wanted to see me after breakfast. He told the nun to remove my cast, and after doing so he examined my arm by twisting and turning it, and then said I could go home.

On this occasion I did not return to the village, but my uncle had arranged with my mother that he would pick me up from the hospital, then take me to his house for a couple of days so that he could find a school and suitable accommodation for me. When my uncle came to collect me from the hospital, he had brought me a new set of clothes. Once I was dressed we both set off on foot to his house, situated on the edge of the city.

CHAPTER 4

BACK IN THE CITY OF STANISLAVIW

My uncle's house was so small that I had to sleep in the kitchen. I was taught how to eat, how to hold my cutlery, wash my hands before and after meals. I wasn't allowed into the garden, I could only admire and eat its contents with my eyes, from the path. I was later to find out that my uncle's wife and daughter had been instructed to ensure that I only look and not touch.

Living at my uncle's I found very hard going, just sitting in his small yard staring, yet doing nothing. At lunch time, whilst sitting at the table, I wasn't even allowed to swing my legs. This went on for two days, while my uncle was running around the city trying to find a school for me. He found it difficult, as the term was already six weeks old. He tried to find me a Ukrainian school, but they were all full and could only accept me the following year, so in the end he had to settle for a Polish school. I was at that time eight years old and was expected to re-take my first year, because it was taught in the Polish language, whereas in the village I was taught in Ukrainian.

At the Polish school I had to sit at the back of the class. The Polish language wasn't difficult for me, I had already picked up a little in the streets.

As luck would have it, at one of the Ukrainian schools that went by the name of Shashkevytch, one of the teachers, a priest, was sent to a different parish after the first term. This priest had a son at the school, which opened up a vacancy for me. Even better, the school allowed me into the second grade.

Living at my uncle's house was made worse by his wife. She was always on my back, picking on me needlessly. My uncle could see this, so he found me accommodation in a hostel run by nuns.

Living in the hostel was much better, I had more freedom, I knew a lot of the boarders, there were about forty in total and eight of them attended my class. The nuns would escort us to school every morning. After school every child made their own way back, since everyone finished at a different time. The only thing I missed was the food at my uncle's. The nuns would invariably prepare a thick buckwheat porridge, whether you liked it or not.

I loved being there in winter after a large snowfall; the nuns couldn't take us to school on foot, so we were transported on a large sledge, big enough for twenty children.

At Easter my mother wanted to take me to her village, but the nuns advised her not to, as they said I was a little behind with my lessons and staying at the hostel would give me the opportunity to catch up.

I finished my second grade, albeit with very poor marks, because I had too much freedom. We would sometimes be punished by the nuns, but never physically. The hostel had its own orchard, where there was an abundance of apples and pears. In front of the hostel grew several large acacias, on which crows nested. I would throw stones at their nests destroying them, the nuns would tell me off, despite the fact that the crows stole small chicks from the paddock.

The nuns would always conjure up a punishment for disobedient children, making them water the garden in the summer, cut down weeds, or pump water from the well, whereas for the very mischievous like me, they would send us to the meadow to keep an eye on the cows so that they could graze undisturbed. They would always send us in twos as there were five cows. There were also horses and pigs in the hostel grounds, but they were looked after by a worker, as it was too much work for five nuns. There was also a section of the orchard were only flowers were grown. These flowers were taken to the Cathedral every Sunday and the nuns used to dress the altar with them. During school holidays, the nuns used to take us to church every Sunday, though during term time we attended the chapel inside the hostel.

For my third year, I had to attend a Polish school on Tranitara Square, that had four Ukrainian classes and four Polish classes. One Sunday we would pray at the Ukrainian Church, the second at a Polish one. Although my form master was Ukrainian, called Krochmaliuk, he was also the director of the girls' Ukrainian School. He was a tough nut, often he would give me detention, as a result I would invariably miss dinner. During the first term I found lessons difficult, and although all my teachers were Ukrainian, they demanded a lot from me. To cap it all, the nuns would set us additional homework. If somebody returned to the hostel late because of school detention, they were given a 'cold dinner' then made to sit by their books until their work was finished.

At school, there was only one teacher who liked me, he was called Kutyj, he taught us singing and because I had a good voice he took a shine to me.

Whenever the nuns for my punishment sent me to herd the cows in the pasture, this pleased me no end, because there was an open area nearby called Sokola, where gentlemen played tennis. I would act as their 'ball boy' for which they would reward me with money. The pasture where the cows grazed was quite secluded, so it only took one of us to keep an eye on them, while the classmate collected the tennis balls.

There was another 'punishment' I enjoyed. Twice a week the nuns would select four of the stronger boys, who would take a small handcart on which were placed four large metal urns, and would then sent to the local butcher on Hluchowsky Street. The butcher would pour water and then boil sausage meat in them. By the time we returned back to the hostel along the uneven roads, half of the brine had spilled over. The nuns would use the liquid from this brine as starters for an assortment of soups. When the metal urns were brought back to the hostel, they were placed by the kitchen under the veranda and, after standing overnight, the top layer of the brine would turn into lard, which the nuns used to baste our boiled potatoes for dinner.

Day after day, this is how I lived in the hostel. I was now ten years old, still misbehaving and was constantly being punished by my teachers and nuns. I finished my third year at school abysmally, my uncle would sometimes check on me at school and he too would scold me verbally after my teacher Mr. Krochmaliuk reported my misbehaviour to him, never having a good word to say about me. My uncle would pull me aside, usually into the orchard, where he would lecture me about my conduct, saying things like I was the first to cause mischief, but the last to learn anything. My uncle's words were soon forgotten, and by this time my mother showed very little interest in me, as she was planning her second marriage.

At one point my mother tried to take me out of the hostel because she had acquired a cow and needed someone to take it out to pasture, but my uncle stepped in and forbade her.

A year later my mother married Vasyl Fedorovytch, who worked all his life on a homestead looking after horses, and where my mother worked as a dairy maid. I remember vividly my mother's wedding day when I carried my new baby brother; I was by then ten years older than my brother Vasyl.

I spent only one vacation in the village before my mother's second marriage. My uncle forbade it, he spent all his efforts in trying to give me a good education, which meant more time at school and less time in the village, though at that stage I didn't realize or appreciate his help.

Back at the hostel I was up to my old tricks, nobody could control me, even after the parish priest had often chastised me. To their disappointment, no amount of punishment had any effect.

In my fourth year I met up with the local hooligans, most of whom were former hostel children.   These hooligans were a couple of years older than me, but still remembered the goings- on at the hostel. I used to bring them bread which was easy for me to steal or I would take them soup into the orchard. In the summer months, we usually ate outside in the hostel grounds, and in the garden there was a loose piece of wood in one section of the fencing, so I could easily get myself into the outside world through the gardens and orchard, as the main gate was usually closed, unless the maid who we called 'Auntie Anny' sometimes forgot to close it.

The first duty the nuns had in the mornings was to go to the chapel for prayers. This gave us the opportunity to raid the orchard of the apples and pears which had fallen to the ground.

In the hostel we still had a problem, namely an old codger had bequeathed all his fortune to the hostel, giving him the right to live there until his death. He would always keep an eye on us, day and night. He slept next to our dormitory and one of his tasks was to wake certain boys in the night who wet themselves, we had a few of those.

Winter months were the worst in the hostel, for after school the whole time was spent with our books, the only consolation being during the Christmas holidays, when we would go carol singing with the nuns to certain houses. These people would always give us biscuits, nuts, apples and sweets. I always used to go carol singing because besides singing I would be the one who made a little Christmas speech to the hosts. Our first call was always to Bishop Chomoshyn and once we happened to call on his birthday when I recited a poem.

We would also look forward to St. Nicholas's Day, when we would visit a different hostel on Hluchowsky Street, occupied by girls. There we would receive presents and sometimes tree cuttings or twigs, a symbol of punishment bestowed on naughty children.

In my forth year, I gained a better understanding about the hooligans , they still wouldn't leave me alone, demanding less food and more clothing and footwear. I could see where all this was leading to, so I tried my best to avoid them, there was never a shortage of soup in the hostel and this was the easiest 'gift' I could pass onto them.

One day my partner in crime was late coming for his soup, so I had to leave my own bowl of soup hidden in the bushes. At that time, one of the nuns who was permanently ill, and had no official duties, would pass the time walking through the orchard and gardens, praying and clutching her rosary beads. It was she who noticed an empty bowl in the bushes. All bowls had their own personal identification mark, so every bowl was accounted for. When the bowl was displayed in front of all the other boys, they all said it belonged to Prytulak.

Later that day, when I returned from school, the Mother Superior called me into the dining room, then asked why my bowl had 'spent the night' in the orchard. I couldn't lie, nor could I twist my story, obviously because of the identity mark on my bowl. I told the nun the truth that I'd left my bowl of soup to a former resident of the hostel because he was hungry, I even gave his name, as he was known to the nun.

In the hostel it was customary for boys who didn't pass their exams to be admitted to enter the grammar school after their fourth year, the nuns would try and pass on the 'failed student' to a tradesman to learn a profession. Many of these 'failed students' would leave their 'new masters' because they were often nasty, exploiting and beating the boys, many of whom ended up on the streets, turning to petty crime and hooliganism.

This is how the local hooligans lived, during the summer months they didn't suffer too much. However, during the winter months I would often come across them in the market. They wore torn clothes, looked dirty and unkempt, and were easily identifiable. They would sleep in Jewish-owned stables, where they would find work chopping wood, fetching and carrying water for a crust of bread.

On Maundy Thursday, I made arrangements with one of my friends that I would bring him some food to the orchard, even reminding him not to be late. I put together a plan, that my homeless friends wouldn't go hungry over Easter. In the hostel, bread acted as the main currency, with bread I could exchange it for crayons, pens, exercise books etc., and because I was friends with the hooligans, I wasn't scared of anybody in the hostel. On the contrary, they were all scared of me.

On Good Friday, I didn't take my own bowl, but found an unmarked bowl, filling it to the brim with a coarse barley soup mix and left it in a prearranged spot. The nuns were in the chapel praying, so as I was walking fearlessly to the spot I heard somebody whistling. My friend had warned me beforehand that there would be a nun in the orchard and she heard the whistling, I couldn't see her as she was screened by the trees and didn't notice her until she was almost on top of me.

Later that day, the Mother Superior packed all my belongings and sent another nun to fetch the resident priest. On his arrival the priest said that I was to be expelled. He gave me my train fare and asked a nun to escort me outside. At the station the nun bought me a ticket to Tysmenychany. I thanked the nun, kissed her hand, and this was how I unexpectedly ended my education in Stanoslaviw (Ivano-Frankivsk).

CHAPTER 5

BACK IN THE VILLAGE

On arrival in the village, everyone was surprised to see me, but it was not unusual for pupils to come home during school holidays, especially if they had family. I found a new lease of freedom, since nobody questioned me why I was in the village, even though I only ever came back to the village twice during the school year.

After the Easter holidays my stepfather kept trying to talk my mother into allowing me to stay in the village, as he needed someone to take the cows to pasture during the summer months. My mother didn't need much persuasion, so during the spring months I spent my time on communal land with my cow. I was very happy there, not a care in the world, quickly forgetting my schooling days. Because I still wore my school uniform looking after the cow, fellow boys gave me the nickname of 'pupil' which I didn't mind, as it was quite common for villagers to give someone a second, more descriptive name.

After harvest cows were taken to other fields, usually gulleys where wild vegetation grew. I didn't like these new pastures, because sometimes cows had to be constantly led on a rope in case they were to fall and injure themselves. I looked for wider gulleys, and it was in one of these places where I found other boys doing the same. One day my cow started to fight with another and lost one of its horns. I tried to repair the damage sticking the horn back, but the cow would just shake its head and the horn would fall off. I got scared that my stepfather would beat me, so I brought the cow home, left it by the house and ran off.

CHAPTER 6
BACK IN THE CITY

Hungry, petrified and dirty I arrived in the city by nightfall. I was too terrified to wander the streets alone, so I headed for the familiar place I knew, the hostel. I climbed through the broken fence, the dog knew me so he didn't bark, allowing me to wander at will through the orchard finding pears and apples plentiful supply. After my feast on fruit I sneaked into the stable, spread fresh hay in a corner, curled up an immediately fell asleep.

I was awoken the following day by the laughter of children, it must have been noon or even later. I couldn't do anything until nightfall, when I again headed into the orchard, this time taking two days' supply of fruit, some of which I hid in the barn.

The following morning I was the first to rise, all the nuns and servants were still asleep. I went over to the water pump, washed myself, then slipped out of the grounds to the market. After loitering around the market all morning, I found nothing of interest, so I walked to the park where the gentlemen were playing tennis, at least I knew I could earn some money. With the money I bought half a loaf, went back to the hostel were I filled myself on fruit, then crawled into the stable to sleep.

I carried on with this routine for a couple of months until it began to get colder, even too cold to sleep in the barn. In the meantime, I couldn't find any form of work. Once whilst I was wondering the streets, I got caught out by heavy rain close to a building site. I found a shelter where I could safely fall asleep. When I opened my eyes to familiar voices, I realized that they were from a couple of my hooligan friends, and it was they who helped me land a job on the site, fetching and carrying lime and bricks for the builders.

The building site became my next home together with my two old friends until Christmas. In the evenings we would carry suitcases at the railway station for gentlemen travellers.

Shortly after Christmas, while I was working at the railway station, my uncle spotted me. He called me over, grabbing me by my arm so that I couldn't escape. He then started lecturing me on my appearance and the kind of life I was now living. My uncle escorted me to his house where he had a houseful of guests. On seeing me they shouted scornfully, berating me for the state of my clothes or the absence of those that my stepfather had provided me for the winter. The guests' comments were ignored by my uncle, who grabbed me again and marched me to his kitchen. He poured water into a small iron bathtub, told me to take off all my clothes and shoes, and threw them outside, because he was afraid they were full of fleas. After scrubbing me from head to toe, I dried myself, put on a shirt of my uncle's, then fell asleep on his sofa until morning.

When I awoke the next morning, my uncle's wife gave me a blanket to wrap myself in, then I stayed as I was until my uncle returned after lunch. I was given some food, got dressed in the new clothes and shoes my uncle had bought, then off we went into the city.

My uncle took me to see a joiner on Galeria Street where they negotiated my immediate future. I was to work for four years without pay, all I would get in return was board and lodgings, my uncle agreed to pay for my clothing.

After a week, I left the joiner, the skin on my back had broken and was sore due to carrying heavy planks I was expected to haul all day long. During the daytime I helped the joiner in his workshop, in the evenings I helped in his home, doing the work of his maid and cleaning up after the pigs. On Saturdays the joiner's wife brought me into their house for lunch, after which I had to wash all the floors. On Sundays I was allowed to go to church, so I would wake up early, have breakfast, get dressed in my new clothes, and then run of to church.

The church was full of people, in the middle aisle stood soldiers and children, I pushed my way to the front were I recognized some children. I was no longer embarrassed as I wore my new clothes with great pride. No sooner had I reached the front, knelt and began to pray than I heard a commotion, whereupon the soldiers marched out of the church, followed by the children and me behind them.

In the churchyard I recognized many children, some from the hostel, but they all ignored me, only Mother Superior came up to me and enquired what I was doing. I respectfully bowed to the nun and kissed her hand, after which she invited me back to the hostel for lunch.

After lunch I explained to the nuns about all my exploits once I had left the hostel. They couldn't believe that I spent all summer in their barn, without so much as a growl or bark from the dog. To prove my story, I went outside with the nuns, then when they saw that the dog didn't bark at me, but recognized me, they believed my story.

Once they felt fully convinced, I was called back into the dining room and it was proposed that I should work for the local shoemaker on Lupovi Street, who did a lot of work for the hostel. I knew him quite well, since I often used to take him shoes from the hostel to be repaired.

Before we left to see the shoemaker, I was asked if I had fleas, especially after my story to them about sleeping rough. I explained that I had just been at my uncle's where I'd been thoroughly scrubbed, washed and dressed in new clothes. Nevertheless, the nuns still peered over my shirt and were shocked to see my red raw back, thinking I had developed some sort of growth. When I explained what I had been doing the previous week, they took pity on me.

At the shoemaker's after the customary Christian greetings, the shoemaker invited the nun to sit down. She explained what my recent job involved, that it was too difficult and strenuous for me and between them they soon came to an agreement, and I stayed.

Alas, my life with the shoemaker also came to a swift end. Life at the shoemaker's wasn't bad, the only task I couldn't stand, was that his wife would send me to the market every morning for vegetables. On my way to the market I would always bump into some of my old school friends, they'd be carrying books in their satchels while I'd be carrying shopping bags. They would pull my leg, saying things like 'What kind of shoemaker are you to become? All you do is carry potatoes and cabbages from the market'. At the shoemaker's there was plenty of work, but all I did was clean up after a day's work. One of my jobs was to take repaired shoes and boots twice a week to the Christian Seminary as well as to my old hostel. On Sundays I wasn't allowed to attend church, I was always delivering shoes and boots to people's houses.

After a couple of weeks, I began to put together a plan of how to leave the shoemaker. I was sick of hearing that I was a slave, not a student. To leave would be easy, but winter was now upon us, the cold had already set in, and to sleep in a barn wasn't in the least bit appealing. In all the time I worked for the shoemaker, he never gave me a penny, the little money I had was from tips that some customers had given me,, so I pondered how I could pay myself.

One Friday I was to take a beautiful new pair of boots to a gentleman, a pair that fit me like a glove, but on my return I told the shoemaker that there was nobody at home and that I would return on the way to the market the next day.

On the Saturday, I made my own breakfast, put on two shirts and my new clothes. The shoemaker's wife gave me a shopping list, the shoemaker gave me money. I put the cash into my pocket, the boots into the shopping bag and left, but not to the market though, but straight to the train station instead.

That morning the snow was falling heavily in lumps, making it very difficult to see. I held the bag with the boots under my armpit, put both my hands into my pockets, my head down to shield me from the blinding snow, and eventually made it to the train station. Once under cover, trying to sweep off the thick snow, I spied a policeman and suddenly fell into a cold sweat brimming with fear, thinking maybe I should get rid of the boots, but there was nowhere to hide them as the station was full of people. I quickly headed for the ticket office, where I was told there was no train for another three hours. I thought of having some lunch to kill time, but then the thought of the shoemaker sending somebody to look for me forced me to change tactics, so I decided the best option would be to walk.

In the summer months, I would easily walk to my home village in three hours, but not on that day in the heavy snow. The wind didn't help matters, blowing in all directions the snow covering the roads, making it difficult to see where I was going. It took me ages to reach the first village, my shirt was wet with sweat, the fear that I had stolen a pair of boots and money had taken over my whole body, relentlessly thrusting me forwards.

At the edge of the first village, my mind was racing at breakneck speed thinking of where to go, stressed by the fear of losing the boots. I had to be equally careful of walking towards a house with a ferocious dog, but when you are hungry and desperate, adrenalin gives you an injection of strength. I walked past house after house, recognized the train station and the nearby Jewish shop closed because it was Saturday. I grew more and more desperate, so I knocked on the door of the first house I saw. The owners of the house invited me in to sit by the hot stove, then gave me something to eat and drink. They asked me all sorts of questions, what I was carrying, whether I had anything to sell, so I lied to them, saying that I didn't have enough train fare, and that was why I had walked so far. Shortly afterwards, I left and headed to my village of Kaminne. It must have been after three o'clock when I finally arrived, but not to my mother's house, as I was still afraid after my last escapades. I went to my aunt's house instead. My auntie had four children, they lived in a small house, her husband, a Pole-Mazur, (a Slavic ethnic group with historic origins in the Polish region of Masovia), a good man but couldn't speak Ukrainian, even though he had lived in the village for many years. He worked in a sawmill in a small town called Nadvirna.

When I arrived at my auntie's house, she at once started to talk about my mother, how much she was worried about me, that I was a lost soul, there were stories circulating that I had become a thief, stealing from various stalls in the city market. Once settled in, my auntie said that I had grown in the last six months and that I looked well. She added that I had done the right thing to leave my stepfather's house, because he would never have bought me new clothes, as he didn't have anything decent to wear himself. She went on to say that she'd often reassured my mother that I wouldn't starve, because I'd be able to look after myself.

I began to look at my auntie in a different light. In the past I'd always thought of her as a spiteful person, but now she came across as very sympathetic and accommodating. She didn't question me about where I had been or what I had done, she simply placed all my belongings by the fire to dry. After supper I went to sleep and so did my cousins, whilst my auntie said she would wait up for her husband, as today was pay day.

The next day, word soon got out in the village that I had spent the night at my auntie's. My mother, too, got to hear the news and it didn't take long for her to come round, she knew I wouldn't have the guts to call upon her. She hadn't even closed the door properly when she started laying into me 'Why didn't you come home? Haven't I heard enough embarrassing comments from my neighbours? Everybody is saying that because of your stepfather you are wandering the city streets, unfed, unkempt, dressed in rags, and now you have come to your aunt's house, expecting her to feed you for nothing. I suffered all summer without anyone to look after my old hornless cow, which I had to sell at half price. I have suffered so much shame that only God knows, everybody is saying to me that you are you are a delinquent and your only friends are hooligans like yourself '. Whilst my mother spoke, I just stood quietly by the fire, motionless, occasionally my auntie would say something in my defence, 'Don't take any notice of what people are saying, they are lying, and besides he didn't steal from a poor man, because a poor man has nothing, he only took from a rich man and God won't punish him for that. Don't believe everything you hear, you have your own wisdom, don't go and throw your own son out onto the street, wait two or three years and he will leave himself. Now you best go home, bring him some cornflour and beans if you have any, then tomorrow he will go with my husband to the sawmill'.

CHAPTER 7

THE SAWMILL

That evening I got ready again to pursue a new trade, this time I put on my new boots, poured a little flour and beans into a bag, then set off near midnight with my uncle towards Nadvirna and the sawmill.

It was about five in the morning when we arrived, my uncle kept off the main open roads, as the windswept snow had made them difficult to get through. We made our way straight to my uncle's barrack. On entering, I heard them speaking in Polish-Mazur, some people were making breakfast and others barbequing deliciously smelling chicken.

A little later when the offices were open, my uncle escorted me to see the person in charge and on the strength of my uncle's standing, I was given a job operating a circular saw. On my first day of work, my fellow workmates assumed that I was my uncle's son, so I worked inside the workshop, but when they found out that I was a nephew, I was sent outside to tie ready sawn planks into bundles. My first two days inside, I only wore my shirt, but outside, in the snow, the only cover was overhead, leaving the sides exposed to the elements. My hands were so cold that I had to wrap them with rags, as I didn't have any gloves. My immediate supervisor, a Mr. Shulo, never allowed me to go inside the workshop to get warm.

I slept in the barrack with my uncle. There I learned how to make a broth, I would buy bread and lard, and soon I became accustomed to my new way of life. Every two weeks I would return to the village with my uncle for clean clothes and leave my mother some money, with very little left for myself, just enough to buy food.

In a way I was pleased in a way that I had this job, all thanks to my uncle and his connections. He met my auntie in Austria were they worked together picking beetroots. Although my uncle lived in Halychyna with my aunt and had three children with her, he never spoke Ukrainian. Their children, who went to the local school in the village, all spoke Ukrainian, though what happened to them in later life I do not know?

My employment in the saw mill soon came to an end, after six weeks of work, not that I didn't want to work there, but because there was no more wood to be cut, the season had come to a close.

CHAPTER 8
WHAT NOW?

On my return to the village this time round, I didn't live with my auntie but with mother. There was nothing for me to do, except occasionally chop some wood and bring some water into the house for my mother, or I would look at her peeling potatoes one day, grating them the next, so as not to make the same kind of soup every day. My stepfather would come home religiously for lunch every day, sometimes it wouldn't be ready because the fresh wood was difficult to burn. My mother would always feed her husband first, then us, the three boys, myself, Vasyl and Peter who was my stepfather's son.

I sat around the house with nothing to do all winter, until the last snow had melted. One day a strange man from a neighbouring village was accompanied to our house. He had been told that I was bored and had nothing to do, whereas he needed to take his cattle to pasture. The man discussed terms with my mother and that same day I left once again for another village.

On our way to the man's village, one that I knew well by the name of Kryplin, very close to the city, he told me that he didn't have children of his own, and if I behaved myself, he would treat me like his own child.

The first week I chopped wood most of the time, I removed all the manure from the stable and feed the two cows. I began to enjoy my new surroundings, these people were not poor, my bed was over the fireplace, I could eat bread every day, not like at my mother's, where bread was baked only twice a year, at Christmas and Easter. The lady of the house would get up very early each morning, and then take fresh milk to sell in the city. Two weeks later the lady took me into the city, I took one large milk urn, she took the other and a bundle of cheese and butter onto a small cart. Within the hour we made our first call, and I immediately went into a cold sweat, we had just pulled up outside my good uncle's gate. The lady didn't take any notice of me, she was concerned to sell all her dairy products. I looked around, not recognizing any known faces, I suppose it was still very early in the morning. The lady approached my uncle's gate, I was following with an urn of milk, still looking around, wiping the sweat off my brow, more from shame than fright, getting closer and closer to the gate. All of a sudden I accidentally dropped the milk, panicked, turned and ran as fast as my legs could carry me. I didn't hear the lady shout after me, so I kept running until I reached the next street. The lady was quite old and I knew she wouldn't catch me.

Heading briskly towards my 'home village' the sun was now above my head, it felt nice and warm, I was quite a distance past the city. I soon passed the second village when, all of a sudden, along the road I knew very well, a man on a horse and cart shouted out to me. He asked me where I was going. I never told people the truth, so I lied to him that I had been in the city looking for work, and was now returning home to my village. He told me to jump on but warned me not to stand behind the horse or he might kick me, so I entered the cart from the rear. I noticed the man was carrying an iron plough and a large bundle of dry straw, on it an old blanket and a small bag. During the journey, the man questioned me what kind of work I was looking for, then asked if I was willing to tend to his cows. It didn't take me long to decide as there was no work for me in my village, so I said yes to him. No sooner had I agreed than the horses turned off the road into an unploughed field.

We ploughed the field until sunset, only stopping once to eat a piece of dried bread with a spreading of garlic, for water we drank from a nearby pond, as did the horses. The house and stables the man owned was a little bigger than my previous one in Kryplini, his village was called Yiatkim near Kaminne, but I only worked there for two weeks, because my stepfather needed me to look after his own new cow.

This time I looked after my stepfather's cow on a homestead owned by a rich Jew called Fuchs. I was to look after a herd of forty cows with another youngster called Vladyk Yiashkiw. The both of us would look after the herd of cows, the Jew would pay my stepfather for my work, but in return I would only receive my food. The work was quite easy as the pastures were flat and wide, the only difficulty I had was to clear the manure from the cowshed, but as Vladyk was a couple of years older and stronger than me, he would help me out.

During the summer months all the milk was transported to the dairy. Every evening our job was to take the milk urns to the well to be washed. Once everyone had gone to sleep, Vladyk and I used to scoop off the cream and drink it. Mr. Fuchs would always drink fresh milk in the mornings and we would drink fresh cream in the evenings. Mr. Fuchs used to send us early to bed, then early to rise. I used to go home for my meals, but slept in the stables with Vladyk, and by the end of the summer even Mr. Fuchs was surprised how well I looked. Little did he know that it was thanks to all his cream.

One day Mr. Fuchs sent me to his son with one cow, which he said was old and didn't yield any milk. He wrote a letter to his son and with a piece of rope he tied it to one of the cow's horns, then after lunch he sent me to the village of Vovchynets. At the start of our trip, the cow walked well, then after a while it kept stopping, so I allowed it to graze and take a drink from a stream. I wasn't in any rush, it was still hours away to nightfall, so I took it at a leisurely pace. As I approached the town limits, the sun was beginning to set, some people were already using lights and the village was on the other side of the town. The cow kept stopping, wanting to graze and no matter what I did it wouldn't budge. Out of the blue I was approached by a Jew on a horse and cart, in which I noticed a calf. The Jew asked if I were allowed to sell the cow without my father. I said 'Give me fifty zloty (Polish currency used at that time) and the cow is yours'. The Jew replied 'Don't try and be so clever son, the cow is old, I will give you half'. I didn't want to negotiate too long, so the Jew turned into a side road then asked if I could count. He took my rope and tied it to his cart, then took out some money, a mixture of notes and coins and we parted. I quickly walked to a nearby park to recount the money and realized that the Jew had underpaid me by two zloty.

Undeterred, and with the money from the sale in my pocket, I decided to go to the cinema, something I only dreamed of in the past, now I could really go. Outside the cinema someone stood on my toe, that's when I realized I had no shoes. It was an old acquaintance who had no money, so I treated both of us, which cost me the princely sum of one zloty. Afterwards, we went for a good meal and then went to sleep in the barn at my old hostel.

For three nights and days we stayed together until my money ran out. On the fourth day I said goodbye to my friend and we parted. I tore up the letter Mr. Fuchs had given to me and headed back to my village. I didn't go straight home. Instead, I went to see Mr. Fuchs and lied to him that the cow had been walking at a snail's pace, so slow that I had to spend a night in the woods, then a gang of strangers who were passing by took the cow and tied me to a nearby tree. I didn't dare shout in case my voice attracted some wild animals. 'Aren't you the clever one' he said 'Now for the one hundred zloty you have lost me, you will work three years for me'. When I told the story to my stepfather on my return home, he went to see Mr. Fuchs and said, 'Who sends a young boy with a sick cow to the town? It's your own fault, don't blame the boy'.

I carried on looking after Mr. Fuchs's cows until the winter came, the work was getting too hard for me, so I had to leave. Again, it was back to the old routine of sitting at home with nothing to do. My only pastime was to skate on the frozen pond, even though my boots were now wearing thin. I just wished that I could get work again at the sawmill. Then one Sunday morning, near Co-operative shop, stood a baker holding a basket of bread, calling Mr. Palamar to open the shop. On my skates I quickly called in at M r. Palamar's home, then returned to help the baker unload his bread. When we finished, the Jewish baker asked me if I would like to help deliver bread. It took me all of two seconds to say yes, I gave my skates to one of the local boys, and without even saying anything to my mother, returned to the town.

CHAPTER 9
IN THE BAKERY

It was a Sunday, which was why the Jew worked because Saturday, the Jewish Sabbath, was his day off. He counted the money from the shopkeeper, we both sat on the horse-drawn wagon and slowly made our way along the snow-packed road towards the next village. We stopped at every Jewish shop, they bought bread from him because he was Jewish, as did all the Ukrainian shops because he worked for a Ukrainian bakery owned by a Mr. Veshnewsky. That was the first time in my life that I'd seen a Jew working for a Ukrainian. I spent most of my time running after the wagon because it was too cold to sit there, and whenever I sat up front the Jewish driver gave me an old sack to wrap around my feet. Once we past the last village, the Jew told me to sit in the back of the wagon. The wagon was constructed from metal and was very cold, but I was glad that nobody would see me in the town. The Jew locked me in the wagon like a dog under padlock, but amongst the empty boxes I found an old roll, a sweet one at that. Unexpectedly, we came to a halt, then I heard the rear of the wagon opening and took fright that someone would recognize me, but it was already dark and we were safely in the bakery yard.

My first task was to walk the horses to the stables, they knew the way well, so I just followed them. In the stable the Jew showed me where everything was kept, the hay, oats, water and instructed me to give what and when. I was shown where the dog slept and where I would be sleeping. He locked the stable and we proceeded through the yard, then stepped into the bakery. I was staggered to see people half naked, outside it was freezing, yet here in the bakery people were working without their shirts on, merely wearing white hats and aprons.

We both walked upstairs to the kitchen on the first floor where the Jew told the cook to give me a good supper because I hadn't eaten all day. I don't remember what time it was, probably about nine, but I saw on the table I saw rolls and white bread as if it was a feast day. One of the girls showed me to a seat, then brought me a large bowl of hot soup, inviting me to eat as much bread as I wanted. Whilst I was eating the girl started to inquire whether I was from the town or from a village. True to character, I just replied by giving her a pack of lies. After supper I thanked her kindly and made my way to the stable and slept.

Early next morning the Jew woke me and told me to water the horses, seven of them altogether, but I only gave water to two. I shovelled some oats into a trough and went to the bakery. The bakery was a beautiful sight, people walking around only in their shirts, whereas I felt so cold in the freezing barn and it would take me ages to fall asleep. We both quickly loaded the wagon with bread and rolls, then climbed upstairs for breakfast. There were other people like myself, sitting talking and eating. I picked up some of their conversation and found out that they all slept in the bakery behind the ovens, in a changing room on planks of wood, while in the summer months some slept in the stable and others in a storeroom for flour. For breakfast I had sweet coffee with fresh rolls and butter, but this morning I noticed a different girl in the kitchen.

Outside it was still dark when we set off, that day we took a different route to other villages. We delivered to a variety of shops, mostly to Ukrainian Co-operatives, as it was expected that shops bought from their own, 'each to their own' we were taught. We also supplied many Jewish stores, because they knew the Jewish driver and they also helped each other. As we passed through each village, everyone could see the Ukrainian lettering on the side of the wagon.

What surprised me most was seeing for the first time in my life a Ukrainian gentleman and a Jew tending his horses. Mr. Veshnewsky was very fond of his Jewish driver who he trusted implicitly. I worked as a delivery- assistant six days a week, we alternated our drop-offs so that each shop had a delivery three days a week. On Saturdays, the Jewish Sabbath, I worked inside the bakery. I had to pump water from the well into a large container, sweep, fetch and carry, I was even sent out to the shop to buy cigarettes and aspirins. I became very useful to the bakery on Saturdays, as it was a busy day. Once the production cycle had finished, the experienced bakers would go home, leaving apprentices like me to clean the bakery, which would take us until late.

Mr. Veshnewsky was from Chodorow and wasn't a baker by profession; he had bought the bakery from a Jew, but to own a bakery, he needed a certified baker to run it. The bakery manager was called Mr. Tyhaniuk, a very nervous person who always got cross if things didn't go his way. I often saw him taking five or six tablets during each shift.

Mr. Veshnewsky employed many of his family to keep an eye on the business. One such person was called Romko, who never went to bed at night but slept on a chair in the shop. During the day he would deliver bread in the town, using only one horse. Another was called Yuszo, who worked in the bakery at night on the so-called 'white shift' making white bread and rolls. Mr. Veshnewsky placed great trust in Yuszo, who would go around the shops collecting money and he would also pay for the flour at the mill. One day

Yuszo set off on his routine errand, taking a large amount of money to the flourmill. He was never to be seen again.

Mr. Tyhaniuk, who had seen me working in the bakery every Saturday, was impressed with me and noticed that I was a quick learner. He had a word with Mr. Veshnewsky and requested that I leave the delivery job and work in the bakery instead.

This happened in the spring as it was beginning to get warmer and pleasant enough to be able to sleep after lunch in the sunshine. The horses too, needed their rest. On our rounds, my Jew always ate at familiar Jewish homes while I would have to guard the wagon in case anybody tried to steal bread. On Sundays our run took us to my home village, which gave me an opportunity to see my mother, give her a white loaf and she would give me a clean shirt.

I remember one Friday we had a large snowfall, the roads were very heavy going, so the run took us longer than normally. On our way back, because we were late we'd entered into the 'Sabbath'. It wasn't permitted to ride a wagon on the Sabbath, so my Jew walked and prayed, whilst I drove the wagon all the way back to the bakery, I wasn't even allowed to speak to him, which was why he always asked for a helper. These 'helpers' worked for almost nothing, they merely received food and lodgings, so the turnover was high, two or three months was the average span, I was one of his longest-serving 'helpers'.

Mr. Tyhaniuk didn't give me a moments rest. I used to run like a headless chicken round the bakery, passing rolls onto a wooden peeler, (an instrument, shaped like a wooden spade, used for inserting bread and rolls into an oven) a fellow-worker would then load them into the oven, a job had to be done quickly and accurately. If I happened to drop a roll onto the floor, Mr. Tyhaniuk would promptly hit me with the peeler anywhere he could connect. Despite his irascible temper, Mr. Tyhaniuk taught me many things and from him I learnt a trade, for which today I am eternally grateful. Nobody could work with Mr. Tyhaniuk, much too nervous and demanding, but I jumped to his every command for two years.

In the bakery, discipline was very strict, everything had to be done on time, nothing could be put aside for another time, everything has its own time. A cobler or tailor, on the other hand, can go back to their work, but once a baker's dough is mixed it cannot rest, a dough cannot stand longer than necessary because an old dough loses its strength, and when bread is in the oven, it cannot stay in longer than it has to. There is a saying in the bakery trade 'time doesn't push the baker, the work does.'

One of the earliest terms I had to learn in the bakery was the name of certain 'tools of the trade' in German. Although we didn't have any to speak of, many machines came from Germany, so I had to remember these words.

The hardest day for me was Saturday night, firing the ovens, cleaning them beforehand, and then insuring they would remain lit for the remainder of the week. By the end of the night I was glad it was over so that I could fall sleep, even food at this point was of no interest. My sleep usually came to an abrupt end when I was woken up and told to load Romko's bread onto his wagon.

The bakery where I worked was called ' The Ukrainian Motorised Bakery' even though we didn't have any bread mixers. To mix dough in a trough for two hundred loaves of bread would take two strong people over half an hour. The bakery employed two shifts, during my shift I had to run to and fro between two ovens without a break, quite often I was at my wits' end, which automatically meant being hit on my back with the peeler. I lived through my punishments, listening and doing everything I was told, like it or not. Whenever he wanted me to go into the town with him, Romko never gave a second thought that I might need the day to sleep. Meanwhile, the other bosses didn't take any notice either, because young boys like me were in abundance. Many of them didn't last the pace, but I persevered, even though they all took advantage of me.

After six months of 'schooling' under Mr. Tyhaniuk , he shouted less at me and stopped people like Romko taking advantage of me. After a year I gained in strength and height and didn't allow people to boss me around.

During winter I slept behind the oven with others, and as it was warm and snug there, nobody got changed or covered themselves. The Jewish driver used to bring me a clean shirt from my mother every Sunday. To have a bath was unheard of, perhaps in summer in the river, but in summer I slept in the store room on the flour bags, covering myself with an empty flour sack. When I awoke, I looked like a rat that had just come out of a sack of flour.

I had also learnt how to make a ferment dough and a starter dough for rolls. I also mixed doughs for plaited bread. Mr. Veshnewsky would often buy in old butter and eggs, then make me mix the dough because it stank, but once it was mixed and baked, the taste was good.

The first year went by without anyone knowing much about me, not until one Saturday afternoon Mr. Veshnewsky sent me to the local seminary with some rolls. When I arrived I was recognized by Father Palyvoda, who asked me to show him my hands. 'Any idiot can put on a white hat and apron, but to be a good baker you must have clean hands, a good nose and delicate taste buds'.

Two weeks later, on Sunday, I was mixing a sour dough ferment, when I noticed my 'good uncle' walk into the bakery. Mr. Veshnewsky took my uncle upstairs, so I quickly finished my work, then went upstairs to the kitchen for my lunch. The kitchen door was slightly ajar and I could hear the whole conversation. My uncle explained my whole life story to Mr. Veshnewsky, about the hostel, my various jobs, all the trouble I had caused him with the nuns and priests. After I finished my lunch, I crept downstairs to fire the oven, my uncle and Mr. Vashnewsky carried on talking for another hour. They both descended the stairs and Mr. Vashnewsky called me into the shop, then said 'You have already worked for me for a year, you will work for another three years, for which you will receive food and lodgings, on top of that you will receive one set of clothing and a pair of shoes each year. Every Friday afternoon I will allow you to bake for the Jews, for their Sabbath, Challah (a special Jewish ceremonial bread, from which a small portion is set aside as an offering, usually braided, and eaten on Sabbath and Jewish holidays) and whatever else is required. The money you receive in tips will be yours'. It later turned out that I earned ten to twenty cents from each customer, in total I could earn two zloty, which was enough for me to go to the cinema.

Everything my uncle told Mr. Vashnewsky, he repeated to Mr. Tyhaniuk, then at the first opportunity he would start to 'pull my leg' about the hostel, my jobs with the shoemaker and joiner, afterwards the other workers would join in on the act. One night I was sent to another bakery with an empty flour sack for some 'steam' which is needed when baking bread and rolls, for without it, the products will crack.

One night Mr. Tyhaniuk tried to play the same joke on me, I didn't let on that I already knew about it, so I played along with him. I slowly walked three streets away to the Jewish bakery and said that my boss had sent me for some 'steam'. The workers just looked around at each other, when one of them took my empty sack and told me to follow him outside. He then half filled the sack with logs and stones put them on my back and off I went. As soon as I left their gate, I emptied the sack, leaving just one log, then made my way slowly back to the bakery. After about an hour, I reached the gate of the bakery, filled my sack with fresh stones, until I had enough to be able to carry, then knocked on the bakery gate. Within seconds two bakers came running to me, picked up the sack and went into the bakery, whereupon everyone started to laugh, but when they tried to pick up the sack, they were left puzzled, convinced that it was impossible for me to have carried such a weight. They soon realized that their joke had backfired. The following morning when Mr. Vashnewsky heard about the joke, he laughed loudly, called me over and gave me half a zloty. All the workers present had 'long faces' on them and didn't try to pull another stunt like that again.

One day in spring I found myself a secluded spot on top of the flour bags in the storeroom for a well-earned nap. That day the flour millers brought a fresh batch of flour. They saw me sleeping, so they carefully covered me with fresh bags of flour, without waking me. When I woke, there were three layers of flour bags on top of me, almost to the ceiling. I couldn't manage to wriggle myself out, so I cried out. I usually didn't like to lie on the side of the pile, but on this occasion I buried myself in the middle, using the empty sacks as covering. My cries went unheard until one worker came into the storeroom for a sack of flour and heard my voice and called the other workers, who promptly uncovered me. For this stunt, I got a good hiding from Mr. Tyhaniuk, although it wasn't my fault, because the millers knew very well that I was there. On top of my hiding, I was made to work all day with the 'black shift' meaning the workers who made black bread.

In my third year at the bakery, Mr. Tyhaniuk moved me to work at the table where I would weigh the dough into pieces and mould them into bread. By then I knew most of the work in the bakery, more so than many of my peers, probably because I was one of the longest serving youngsters in the bakery. Mr. Vashnewsky also trusted me, especially when he was busy, he would ask me step in for him working in the shop, or count bread and rolls for the orders. At times, when there enough staff in the bakery, I would deliver large baskets of fresh rolls by horse and cart to the railway station. At the station, porters would already be waiting for me, they would help me unload, weigh the rolls, then load them back into the baskets, for their help, I would always give them a white loaf. I was told to wait for the train coming from Lviv, on its way to Vorokhta and Yaremche, to ensure the baskets were correctly handled, otherwise the rolls would invariably be damaged.

On my way back to the bakery, I would often be stopped for a lift by people who I had grown to know, for whom I gladly obliged, and from whom I was always given a few coppers. There were also the unwelcome passengers, the local hooligans, who would sometimes force their way onto the wagon, taking my whip, then needlessly striking the horse and making me take them wherever they wanted to go.

There were other incidents too, where I would see 'ladies of the nights' loitering around the station. The local police would try to arrest them, the 'ladies' would seek refuge in my wagon. I would lock the wagon, wait for the train to depart, before making my way back, dropping off the 'ladies' one by one. One or two of them would sit at the front with me, and although I was seventeen years old at the time, I was still scared of them. Back at the bakery I would brag to my fellow workers about my nightly exploits, saving three 'ladies of the night'. The next morning I was called into the shop by Mr. Veshnewsky and called a big idiot for boasting to my fellow workers. Somehow, even my uncle got to hear about this story, and then he too gave me a good telling off. I was deprived of my 'nightly deliveries' and, instead, I helped 'crooked Joseph' a distant relative of the boss with his own delivery route, to load his delivery wagon.

There was also a driver called Peter, who only delivered within the city. There were always six or seven horses in the stable, who were looked after by 'another faithful servant' called Vasyl, he would gather stale bread from the bakery, usually a week old, and returned bread from the Thursday market, which was old in the first place, and whatever was left, then he would cut all this bread into pieces, before feeding them to the horses.

That summer, I once again occasionally delivered rolls to the station, but would put on a black jumper, as the memory of the dirty 'Belvedere' was still fresh.

Towards the end of my apprenticeship, Mr. Tyhaniuk prepared me for my exams. I passed them very easily, as I knew all the questions inside out. Mr. Tyhaniuk was also one of the examiners, though he didn't ask me any questions.

Once I became a fully qualified baker, Mr. Veshnewsky was supposed to pay me fourteen zloty per week, but he only paid me seven, saying that I made money on the side on a Friday from the Jewish customers and on Saturdays from the neighbours. If the truth be told, I never made more than three Zloty a week on the side, from which I had to buy my shirts and shoes. Luckily I didn't smoke, but I liked chocolate and going to the cinema, once a week on Saturdays, because I was the first to start work on a Sunday at three in the afternoon.

Mr. Veshnewsky liked me very much, but other bakers insisted that I join the bakers' union, since I worked for half of my entitlement while many old bakers were now without work. I told my boss and he laughed, yet the bakers warned me that if I didn't join the union, they would beat me up and I wouldn't be able to work at all, but I just took it as a joke.

Not all the bakers liked me; some of them resented me associating with my 'hooligan' friends. They would constantly badger me about the hostel and my friends, threatening to work me over if I continued my friendships with the hooligans. I just laughed this off, I wasn't afraid of them. At that time I could easily carry a sack of flour weighing one hundred kilos, I was eighteen years old, felt no fear, knew plenty of people in the city and if I wanted somebody to get a good walloping, it was easily arranged.

My boss liked me because I was a good worker, I always slept in the storeroom, except in the winter by the ovens, I had plenty to eat, enough money in my pocket, to go to the cinema once a week, didn't drink or smoke, though my only downfall were my friends, who were always short of money, didn't work, but all liked to go to the cinema, one of them begged me to pay, and naturally I couldn't refuse them.

Returning from the cinema, I used to soak my shirt in a bucket, then would sleep until noon. On awaking, I would wash my shirt, mix the sour doughs, then climb upstairs for lunch. Once finished, it was downstairs to be the first in the bakery, doing my job to the best of my ability.

One day I was bopped by one of the mixer's, who accused me of adding salt to the sourdough, which prevented it from rising. This wasn't my doing, somebody had put salt into the trough were I mix the sourdough. I couldn't hit him back, as he was much stronger and taller than me.

This episode angered me and I couldn't allow it to pass unopposed, so one day I had a word with a few of my 'hooligan friends' and when Mishko was going to work on a Sunday, my 'friends' lay in wait for him. He came into work late, black and blue, he thought I'd played a part in the beating, but I was in the bakery moulding bread on the table. Admittedly, my mistake was that I laughed at him, so the rest of the workers cottoned on that I'd instigated the beating. The following day after Mr. Veshnewsky was told, he sacked me.

CHAPTER 10

UNEMPLOYED

I left the bakery, having worked there for four years, with just the clothes on my back and a couple of Zloty in my pocket. I never expected such a thing to happen, for when Mishko hit me for no reason, nobody leapt to my defence, they simply laughed, then when I avenged myself, even my boss was against me, he refused to give me my certificate.

The first thing I did was to return to my home village and see my mother. It was the start of spring. There was no work for me in the village, firstly, I didn't like to work in the fields and, secondly, I didn't want people laughing at me. I spent three days in the village, then I went 'rajzuvaty' which is a term used by out-of-work bakers, an unemployed baker would visit other bakeries, the workers there would make a small collection, usually a few coppers, while the owner would donate a loaf of bread. This tradition was repeated in every bakery. In my day, there were twenty-eight bakeries in the city; twenty-four of them were Jewish-owned two Polish, one Ukrainian and one German.

I didn't bother looking for a job in Stanislaviw, so for the first time in my life I caught a train to Lviv, where there were many bakeries, but none would give me a job because I didn't have my 'unemployment papers'. I wasted two or three days, didn't find a job, only fleas from sleeping in a communal hostel, where all the city layabouts congregated and stayed overnight. I never expected to be refused by so many, I only received a little sympathy from some, though nobody would give me money, or a place to stay. In all honesty, I didn't starve in the city, I could always get a piece of bread, and once or twice a Jew would give me a few coppers, so that I could buy some milk. The worst and biggest problems in the city were the hostels, everyone single one stank to high heaven, was filthy and ridden with fleas.

When I realised there was little hope of me finding work, I decided to move on, not to Warsaw, but in the direction of Ternopil. I started walking through small villages, where I would sleep in communal hostels, as there were very few privately owned. Everywhere I went, I would say that I was looking for work. There were no bakeries in the villages, so circumstances forced me to call on wealthy-looking households and beg for something to eat or money. If I was lucky and landed on a generous household, I would sleep there, be given supper and breakfast, and if I was really lucky, a piece of bread for my journey.

I was in no rush to reach Ternopil, as the people in villages were mostly generous. It was only after my third night on the road, early in the morning, that I was in the city. But Ternopil was not a patch on Lviv or Stanislaviw. I walked around the whole city in a day, calling on every bakery and found nothing. I was so disappointed with the city that I didn't spend the night, but carried on walking towards Chortkiv. On reaching the village, it was the same old story, but at least I was given hope when I was told to head to Borschiv, where there was a Ukrainian bakery.

I reached Borschiv that same evening found the bakery and was offered a job there and then.

CHAPTER 11
WORKING AGAIN

At the bakery in Borschiv, all the workers were Ukrainian, and I admitted immediately that I had been on the road, sleeping rough in communal hostels, and probably had fleas. The owner told me to take off all my clothes, soak them all in water, then when the last batch of bread was baked , whilst the oven was still hot, to place all my clothes into the oven, which would kill all the fleas. The following day I did this, and found that the fleas were no longer residing in my clothes, but my hair was full of them. Without further ado, the bakery owner took out a pair of clippers and shaved off all my hair, and that's how I got rid of those wretched fleas.

The work in the bakery was good, I was now experienced in everything, so I could put my hand to all the different tasks. In the beginning everyone was quite sympathetic, I said very little, just listened to what was said. They all knew my circumstances, then after a while they started to tease me, so after three weeks I left that bakery in Borschiv.

From Borschiv I walked through Skala Podilska, then onto Koroliwska, where I got a job in a Polish bakery, under the name of Lozy. Koroliwka was a small Jewish town with two small bakeries. My new boss rented one of these bakeries, he was married to a Ukrainian who originated from Skala, where they had in fact both met. Her parents helped them finance the bakery. A lady I met in the previous village told me that this couple were desperate for a baker. I took the lady's advice and made my way to Koroliwka, arriving just before nightfall. I found the bakery easily, but when I arrived Mr. Lozy wasn't there, only his young wife carrying a child in her arms. When I told her I was looking for a job, she was very happy as they were desperate for a baker.

When Mr. Lozy finally arrived, his wife quickly ran outside to greet him, not giving him time to stable the horse, excitedly boasting to her husband that she had found him a baker. He entered the bakery, introducing himself in a formal manner, spoke in broken Ukrainian, and also addressed his wife in the same way. He told me that as things stood he worked through the night himself, and then would deliver the bread to the neighbouring villages in the morning, and that the work was becoming too much for one person. We didn't banter for long, he offered me fifteen Zloty per week and full board. No sooner had I given him my prompt answer than his wife made us supper, after which we both started work in the bakery.

The bakery was small, as was the oven, only accommodating sixty loaves of bread in total. The oven was fired by wood, just like the bakery in Borschiv, so I had knowledge of cleaning the burnt cinders before relighting them. Once we'd finished baking at four in the morning, Mr. Lozy sat on a chair and fell asleep, in the meantime I cleaned the bakery. At six, Mrs Lozy called us into their home, where all three of us breakfasted at the same table. The breakfast was excellent, I had only seen such a breakfast at my old boss Mr. Veshnewsky's table. Afterwards, I was shown into my own room, where I at last slept on a bed, not on flour bags in a storeroom.

Mrs Lozy woke me for lunch, which only the two of us ate as her husband was still delivering, and often on his return he would stop at the millers to collect five or six bags of flour. Mr. Lozy didn't have a covered wagon, only an uncovered one that farmers would use to transport potatoes in. Every day he would sell in the neighbouring villages, between approximately a hundred and twenty to one hundred and fifty loaves. They also had a small shop inside the bakery, run by Mrs Lozy. I had the afternoons off, until the evening, but I would often stand in for Mrs Lozy, selling bread and rolls, apart from which nothing else was baked.

On Thursdays, the small town held a market where Mrs Lozy had a stall. Mr. Lozy didn't do his usual run on these days; instead he delivered bread to the market. The bread was usually bought by Ukrainians, and there were also Jewish stalls selling their own bread.

Mrs Lozy was known to everybody as Nastya, but I only called her 'madam'. She never dressed like a lady, though she was a beautiful woman. After a couple of weeks, Nastya asked me if I would help her on the 'Thursday' market, as her husband spoke Ukrainian poorly. I agreed with pleasure, so after breakfast instead of going to bed, I would put on my white hat and shirt, and help Nastya on her stall. I had already learned from the Jews how to banter with people, how to joke with them and how to sell bread. We began to run out of bread, which naturally pleased Mr. Lozy, so he began paying me extra for my 'overtime'.

Mr Lozy was a young man, with very little free time, not only did he have to worry about bringing in flour, but would also have to prepare chopped wood for the oven. I began to take on more responsibilities and would start work earlier. I took Nastya with me into the bakery to help me load the bread into the oven, as it was difficult for one person alone. By the time Mr. Lozy had returned from his deliveries I would have the first batch of bread in the oven, and then the three of us would have supper together. Afterwards, Nastya would put the child to bed and Mr. Lozy would also have a couple of hours sleep.

I liked my new surroundings, my work and my new employers who looked after me very well. They paid me adequately, my food was better than the meals even Mr. Veshnewsky ate. Four weeks into my new job and I was able to buy myself new clothes and a pair of new shoes, the first brand new pair I had ever bought in my life, previously they had always been second-hand. Nastya gave be a nice embroidered tie that made me look better than Mr. Lozy, who was already bald, while I had by then grown back the curly black hair I had to shave off because of those damned fleas.

During our working hours I would tell my employers about my travels, how I became unemployed and about the people I met in various hostels, how one group of people would leave their fleas for another group to collect them. In those days life was hard under Polish rule, people were constantly looking for work and would stay overnight in the villages. I met many unemployed people in these hostels, single, married, and some would even take their wives on their travels. On my travels I met Jews, sometimes Gypsies, but most of all Poles, even nobility from as far as Warsaw. The Jews would only stay with their own, whereas I and the Poles would sleep in communal hostels, where there was plenty of old straw and fleas, brought from faraway Warsaw, the Poles even made up songs about the travelling unemployed carrying fleas. To survive, the unemployed men would send their wives out with blankets covering their stomachs, giving the impression they were pregnant, and no person would dare refuse an expectant mother food. They would beg at large households and seek out priests, teachers and wealthy Jews. The people single people who travelled didn't find it as easy, many had to resort to raiding homes where a woman was known to be on her own, and they would take what they could find.

I described my earlier time in Lviv and Borschiv , the numerous nights spent in the communal straw beds. This time Mr. and Mrs Lozy listened attentively to each word, especially Nastya, who would later ensure that I always had a clean shirt to wear. She took pity on me and would wash all my clothes, iron them, and place them neatly in my room.

I was enjoying my time more and more, my employer liked me, and his wife too. During work I would often sing, because I liked to sing, I knew plenty of songs and with my songs I began, in a manner of speaking, to 'undress' Nastya. She too liked to sing, so we would often sing together, but only when her husband was away.

I was in my twentieth year, Nastya was only twenty-three, a mere couple of years separated us and we shared similar thoughts. Nastya was ten years younger than her husband, and he was bald to boot. Nastya understood my songs, but I didn't realise that my songs were breaking her heart. She would say 'Your songs are strong, because you chose them so; you know my weakness and plight, yet every day with your words, my heart is becoming weaker'. In the mornings, I would see her through my window, washing her eyes with her tears.

I was a stranger to Nastya, by the name of Ivan, she was the wife of my employer, but when I sang, I brought back memories of her parental home in Skala. When she had enough of my singing, she would shout 'Ivan stop singing, you are tearing my heart out. I am not at fault, your mother is at fault, yet you keep reducing me to tears'. My songs reminded her of a warm summer, a slow flowing river, where she collected wheat in a nearby field, and how she yearned for those years to return. I reminded her of her paternal home, of her mother and sister, in her dreams she would cry out for her father to take her away from the place she didn't want to die in. She would resent her father for selling their best corral and she would question the curse that had befallen her. 'Why am I being punished?' she would utter repeatedly. Her husband wasn't aware that his wife had been weeping for three long years, pining for her childhood home.

Summer soon passed, winter was around the corner. My room was above the bakery, and across the road lived my employers. The days were becoming shorter and colder, so I closed my window, I didn't want to torture Nastya with my songs. Nastya would always come to my room to wake me for lunch, and at times when I didn't get up straight away she would playfully throw water over me.

I had a good life in Koroliwka, I was turning into a prestigious young man, with a different outlook on life, but had decided that my time there had to be brought to an end. Before I left, I bought myself two new suits, a pair of boots, a pair of shoes and a few shirts. I had enough money in my pocket and felt a gentleman, no longer was I tortured by those fleas. Nastya did my washing, ironing and cooking and generally looked after me. By spring I confirmed to myself that I had to leave Koroliwka, even though I knew full well I wouldn't have a better life anywhere else, but I didn't want to sin.

CHAPTER 12
ZALISHCHYKY

I left Koroliwka as the last winter snow was melting and made my way again into unknown pastures, in the direction of Zalishchyky. I had many opportunities to leave earlier, but the thought of leaving a good job and all the attached luxuries kept holding me back. Once I set my mind to something, I didn't change course in search of an opportune moment. My best option to 'escape' was in the morning when my employer was out delivering and Nastya would be busy indoors. After breakfast I would go up to my room to sleep, and through the window I could see what she was up to, later she would come up and wake me for lunch. The day I left I couldn't sleep, I simply packed all my clothes into a sack so that nobody on the road would question me, put the sack into a bakers' bread basket, then to make it appear genuine, I placed two loaves on top, as if I were taking the bread to a shop.

On my way into Koroliwka, a couple of times I walked along the river bank of the great river Dniester, (Danube) and would look at this fast- flowing river and the beautiful surroundings that God had made of the countryside. After walking a few hours, I passed the village of Dobrivlyany which translated means 'beautiful nature'. The village stood at the foot of a hill, below it a road, and the river Dniester. On the other side of the river was Rumania, I could see people there looking after cows and women washing clothes on its banks. In Dobrivlyany , the south- facing hill was almost all filled with grape vines, basking in the afternoon sun, I could see why the village had been given its evocative name.

The small town of Zalishchyky could only be reached by one of two roads. Inside the town all the houses were immaculately kept, all I could hear was the musical tones of the great river. On looking around this small beautiful town, I came to the conclusion that it was a place for wealthy people, not a pauper like me, who wore patched trousers. Nevertheless, I carried on walking, taking in the beauty of the town, until I came across the smell of fresh bread. I followed my nose into a side street, and then sure enough there was a little bakery. Without further ado, I walked straight in. I was told that the 'mistress' wasn't home, but the accountant was upstairs. On entering the small room above the bakery, I saw a Jew wearing a black hat, sitting at the table. When he saw me, he took off his hat and asked me what I wanted. When I told him that I was looking for a job he said, 'Good, the season is starting and we need a baker, the 'mistress' isn't at home, but if you like, go downstairs and wait for her return'. I went downstairs, looking around how the work was done, but nobody took any notice of me, everyone had their hands full. I didn't have to wait long, before the 'mistress' arrived, who was at once told by one of the boys that I had been waiting for her.

The 'mistress' introduced herself to me politely, and then invited me to go back upstairs to the office. This time when we both entered the room, the Jew stood up to offer his seat to the 'mistress'. She ignored his offer and, still standing, got straight to the point. I was asked if I was a qualified baker, or was I just looking for casual work, the Jew interrupted and asked if I had a certificate. I replied that I didn't have a certificate but knew all the work, and if he didn't believe me, I could show him straight away. The Jew believed me, whereupon we started negotiating, saying that there was work only for the season, for which I would receive twenty five Zloty per week plus food, but if I wanted a permanent job, then I would only receive twenty Zloty. In my stupidity, I agreed to a permanent job for twenty Zloty, and was told I would start work the following afternoon at three. Without entering into too much bargaining, I had landed myself a job, but one important point I had forgotten to raise was if I could spend my first night in the bakery. I remembered this when I returned downstairs but couldn't be bothered to go back up.

I emerged from the bakery and went in search of a bakers' uniform. I had money in my pocket and it was still early. Once I had bought my uniform, I started to look for accommodation. I knew the town prices would be expensive, so I headed for the nearest village of Zvenyachyn, which was about four kilometres away. Not content, I carried onto Dzvynach instead, in the opposite direction. I approached the village decently dressed, without a hat, within the hour. My first task was to find where the Soltys lived, he was the person who liaised with the local government, and without his approval no one would give me lodgings. I was already very familiar with this procedure. What's more, we were close to the border, so you had to be very vigilant. I found the government house but unfortunately the Soltys wasn't in his office. As luck would have it though, a gendarme, a form of policeman, with jurisdiction in villages, appeared out of nowhere and started asking me various questions, and when I told him I was looking for work, he asked for my documents. He spoke to me respectfully in Polish, then after a while he offered me a job, driving his children to school. I politely tried to refuse, saying I was about to start work at a bakery in Zalishchyky the next day. Despite my reluctance, he was very persistent, saying that it would only be for two or three weeks before he found another boy. Then, when I continued to decline he informed me that he knew the owner of the bakery very well, in other words, I had little choice but to accept his offer, otherwise I wouldn't get the bakery job.

I didn't have the strength or dare refuse his offer of work, so he quickly wrote a letter to his wife, then showed me how to get there, but kept my documents. I took the letter from him angrily, but only had myself to blame for falling into this sticky mess from which I couldn't escape. How could I possibly go anywhere without my documents?

I walked through the village, asking a passing boy where the Commandant lived; he quickly escorted me to the right house. As I approached the gate, I saw a young girl who was about to feed a cow, and when I asked whether the lady of the house was home, she retorted cheekily 'Why do you want the lady? Why should I bother the lady if we can sort what you want ourselves'. I replied, 'I have a letter here from the gendarme for the lady'. She asked me to wait a moment whilst she finished feeding the cow. A couple of minutes later, she escorted me into the house where I met the Lady Commandant. She politely asked me to sit down whilst she read the letter. In the meantime, the girl started to wipe down the table, constantly throwing her gaze at me.

'Oh! What good fortune the Good Lord has brought us today, I've been so worried not having a servant, and here I see such a nice young gentleman, and who speaks such good Polish'. The young girl quickly threw in 'Will the young man be staying with us?' The lady replied to her that I would be, then turned to me and asked my name, to which she replied, 'Oh that's very nice, but we will call you Yanek' (John, in Polish). Then the mouthy girl exclaimed 'Oh! Won't it be wonderful for us now, Madam will have Franek, and I will have Yanek'. The lady turned sharply to the girl saying, 'Stop your joking Carol, I am going to collect the children, you go and get supper ready, as I am sure your Yanek is hungry'. What kind of a mess had I got myself into, in the midst of these two rather garrulous women? I was rescued from this embarrassing situation by the two children who came running towards me, on being told that they had a new servant. The children started asking me questions, while, luckily, mouthy Carol was told to keep her mouth shut in front of the children. They were very inquisitive, wanting to know everything about me, asking where I'd been to school, if I could read Polish. Whilst I was with them, I found my nerves settling a little, I even found the courage to ask the lady a few questions. The children soon left for their own room, to finish their homework. I was left in the kitchen, all in a sweat and red-faced, waiting for the children to return. I ate with the children at the same table, but the moment they left was when my problem really began.

Carol had been waiting impatiently for this moment; she could now start on me. She was probably four or five years older than me and claimed to know everything, she wanted to know everything about me and asked me all sorts of stupid questions. When the lady returned after putting the children to bed, she asked if I wanted something to drink, milk or tea, then turned to Carol and ordered her to get my bedding ready and show me where I was to sleep. I was shown to the barn and was told to sleep with the horse and cow, but I wasn't having this. I built up enough courage to say that I wouldn't sleep in the barn and made my way to the kitchen to collect my sack, ready to leave, then angrily turned to the lady, 'I didn't come to your house as a slave, I only listened to Mr. Commandant who said you were desperate for a boy. I only agreed to work here for three weeks, and I am certainly not sleeping in a barn with a cow and a horse'. Fate had taught me many things, I knew how far I could go with certain people, but I was determined not to sleep in a barn over the summer months.

At once both women stopped joking with me, escorted me to the kitchen and asked me to remain seated. Then, holding on to the words I had uttered which were like a thorn in her side, the lady put on her coat and left to seek her husband at the government office.

She soon returned with her husband, I was convinced they must have discussed on the way back how best to handle the situation. When the Commandant confronted me, I noticed for the first time that he was bald as he took off his cap on entering the house, and he then announced 'Mr. Yanek went to school, he can read and write and has never slept in a barn. The Commandant then took me into a room, sent Carol upstairs to fetch a blanket and a cushion, and within half an hour I had a bed ready in what was to be my bedroom. Carol had made the bed together with his wife from a pillow and a quilt. I couldn't expect anymore from them, so I thanked them all and went into my room.

I was pleased with myself that I had overcome the problem of my sleeping arrangements and had found enough courage, so much so that they all kept quiet and respected my decision. Both ladies soon changed their tune and became very quiet, seeing before them not the stupid boy they had first thought.

I later found out that their previous servant had slept in the barn in the past, this was the normal done thing. He apparently didn't last long, having left because of Carol, and Mr. Commandant wasn't going to forget too quickly.

Lying on the bed, I began to think of how in such a short space of time my life had changed, I had never ever dreamt that I would one day become a servant. The only positive outcome that I was pleased about was that I didn't have to sleep in the barn. Nevertheless, I was still angry with myself that I had allowed myself to be talked into staying there, and I was particularly concerned that I might lose my job in the bakery. That night I lay awake for a long time before I fell asleep. I kept thinking about the servant who had to escape from that wretched girl. I thought about Nastya in Koroliwka and my long adventure. Once I fell asleep, I remember sensing somebody in my room, shining a lamp. I turned over and slept soundly until I woke in the morning, only to find 'the devil' standing over me laughing. I rubbed my sleepy eyes and could see Carol standing over me provocatively, 'I thought you were dead, I jerked your body several times, and even kissed you twice, and thought I would never wake you'. I was seething at this wild bitch for her inappropriate behaviour, and then launched into a tirade of choice words which hurt her deeply.

I got out of bed, washed myself in the yard from a standing barrel of water, and then went into the barn to feed the horse and cow. I noticed my new pair of shoes on my feet; careful not to step into any manure. I had just finished feeding the horse and cow when the mistress shouted in my direction, urging me to bring some water from the village well because the barrel was empty. Fortunately, the horse knew his way to the well, where I saw other people drawing water and then pouring it into barrels. It was about five hundred metres from the house to the well, there were always plenty of people there, and nobody went short. Several people came to the well on horses, some people using small handcarts, the remainder carrying buckets by hand.

As to the well, so too back to the house, the horse led the way, and we soon returned. In the yard, Carol began bossing me around, ordering me not to stable the horse but to harness it to the carriage, because the children needed taking to school. The mistress helped me strap down the horse. In the meantime, Carol insisted I should go to the kitchen for breakfast. The household was bustling, only Mr. Commandant was still in bed, his wife reminding their children to be quiet because their father was still asleep. During breakfast, my face was burning with embarrassment because of Carol, who was constantly grinning at me, and for the third time in a row asked me how I'd slept, and if I'd dreamt of her. I replied that I slept badly, feeling my face burning and becoming redder, to which she replied, 'Don't worry, you will feel better after I have kissed you again'. I quickly finished my coffee and dashed outside, I was again very angry at the witch, but she just looked at me like a wild beast. I didn't have time to dwell, as the mistress called me to the carriage, reminding me it was time to take the children to school. The mistress sat at the front with me whilst her two children sat in the rear. On the way through the village we stopped twice to pick up another three children. From Dzvynach to Zalishchyky was close and the road was straight, as the saying goes 'you could roll eggs along it'. We first stopped outside the government offices in Zalishchyky, where a boy collected a briefcase, then we stopped outside a school, and a little further on was the second school.

From the school we rode to the bakery where I was supposed to start work later that day. I could see the bakery workers were pleased to see me, they already knew that I would be starting that very day. I followed my mistress upstairs to see the bakery owner, a Mrs Shaferova. I could tell immediately that both women new each other by their mutual warm welcome. Mrs Shaferova was about to say something to me, but my mistress interrupted and explained everything that had happened the previous evening, then she apologised for the fact that I had been forced by her husband to work for their household. Furthermore, she promised that as soon as they found a replacement for me, they would release me from my duties, enabling me to work in the bakery. Mrs Shaferova listened to everything, agreed and said she would take me on if I was needed at a later date.

I made my way downstairs, leaving the two ladies alone. As it turned out, I stopped by at the bakery every week to collect bread to take back to Dzvynach, where the Poles had a shop called 'Kulka-Rolniche'.

From the bakery we rode to the Commandant's home in Zalishchyky on the banks of the Dniester. There I released the horse from the carriage, let him loose and admired how he made his own way nonchalantly through the orchard to the stable. In this house lived a retired Polish colonel who occupied the whole of the first floor, and the ground floor was left empty for occasional holidaymakers from Poland. By this house lay a large orchard, which was rented by a Jew. The mistress explained one or two things to me, then went upstairs to see the colonel, who greeted me warmly, asking me one or two questions. The mistress left me with the colonel in the orchard, whilst she went into town. The colonel explained many things as he showed me around the house, the laundry room, the attic, where all the fishing equipment was kept and where they even stored a kayak and a rowing boat. The old colonel soon got tired, excused himself and went into the house. I walked around the orchard, taking in the natural beautiful surroundings, even allowing myself the odd smile, thinking that maybe what had happened might turn out for the best. After all, I had money, it was spring, the scenery was spectacular, especially in the orchard, I felt as if I was in paradise. With the birds twittering, the trees budding, even the smell of the grass was sweeter, while in the background roared the Dniester.

I looked thoughtfully for a few moments at the hill on the other side of the river, wondering whether it would be possible to swim across to the other side. I was sure it could be done, the rowing boat was even waiting on the bank, as though beckoning me to jump in. My daydreaming soon came to an abrupt end when I heard the mistress return from town and call me for something to eat. She held a insulated flask, and from the bakery she had brought a couple of freshly baked rolls, then invited me into the house, where we negotiated my pay. The mistress said discreetly that she didn't want to discuss money in front of Carol, adding that she was paid twelve zloty per month, but because I could speak Polish, which was certainly good for the children, she had decided with her husband, to give me fifteen. I didn't want to agree to this amount, so I took the opportunity to press for more, not for the amount they proposed, but it was not easy to get my way with the mistress, for she kept 'sweetening the pot' by adding three Zoloty of her own. This was to remain between me and her she said, nobody was to know, neither Carol nor her husband. As I still wasn't won over, she promised to buy me a present every month; this again was to be between ourselves. We carried on bartering, until I knew I had reached my peak, so eventually I agreed, thinking to myself whether or not I had made the right decision.

Once an agreement was reached, she began to explain my duties after noon. I was expected to feed the horse and cow, fetch water twice from the well, prepare firewood for Carol, ride to a homestead once a week to collect straw for the horse and cow, then if I wanted, although it wasn't compulsory, to help her and Carol in the garden, tending the tomatoes. She finished by saying that as soon as they found a replacement, she would keep to her word and even go with me herself to the bakery.

As we finished talking, the children returned from school, the mistress poured them coffee from the flask while I watered the horse, then harnessed him to the carriage. We rode to a warehouse where the mistress stocked up for her shop. We bought half a sack of sugar, salt, paraffin, cigarettes, rice, matches and a few other items. From there we called at the bakery, collected a few loaves of bread and rolls, and finally headed home. On this occasion, the going was slow as it was all uphill. We dropped the children off at home and I accompanied the mistress to her shop with the goods. I carried everything into the shop, the mistress locked up, for the shop was unattended, then proceeded back home for lunch. The mistress ate with her children in their own room, whereas I ate in the kitchen with Carol. Chatterbox Carol, was both maid and cook, she also cleaned the house, milked the cow in the afternoons and worked in the garden with the mistress, and now they had an extra helper in me.

A week soon passed, then the second, yet still no replacement was found. It was obvious that the Commandant wasn't in a hurry, they were clearly happy with my service. April and May soon passed, in June the tomatoes had begun to ripen, I was still driving the children to school, and helping the

Commandant's wife with the tomatoes in their two gardens. Once the tomatoes were ripe, I delivered them to Zalishchyky, where the mistress had regular customers, and every day I would also deliver some to the town. This was how the mistress would make extra money to buy me clothes every couple of weeks, a shirt, working trousers, even working shoes. I didn't see why I should ruin my good shoes shovelling manure.

Quite often I would travel into town on my own with the tomatoes, collecting the money, then onto the bakery for bread. By then the bakery workers knew me well, poking fun at me, saying how easy it was for the Commandant to make me work for him. Others would say in jest that I probably didn't know how to bake and was easily frightened on seeing how much work they had to do.

My favourite time was usually after I dropped the children off at school, I had the morning to myself to spend in the garden, where I could read the books the old colonel would lend me. I could also fish and swim when the water was warm. Very often the colonel would reminisce about his life exploits to me, talk about all the trees in the orchard, which apples were early and which late, which pears were sweet which were hard, and he even talked about an old army friend, Marshall Pilsudski who loved fruit from this orchard. 'He often came to visit me in the summer. We knew each other very well from our army days and stayed best friends until the end. We used to catch fish in the river, we would sit on this old bench drinking wine, but that was a long time ago, all in the past. I remember this beautiful garden and orchard, this enticing river, but everything is now lost and these times will never return'. I listened to all his stories, about the Marshall, the house and orchard; he reminisced about his family tragedy, why his brother had died. He even told me about the Commandant, who had married his former servant. 'They are both from Poznan in Poland, that's where they met, they moved here when the Commandant received his new posting, but don't tell anyone, not many people know this'. The colonel told me many interesting things; he sometimes liked to listen to me sing, because I would often sing to myself whilst walking through the orchard. He would listen attentively to everything, and when we sat together on the bench he would ask me to sing, he was especially fond of a couple of folk songs I knew by heart.

Back at home, 'as bitter fate would have it' chatterbox Carol became seriously ill, so we had to drive her to hospital in Zalishchyky. As a result, the mistress turned me into a maid. Until then I had never had to wake early in the mornings, it was always Carol who woke me, and although I was angry at her, she always did her own thing. Mr. Commandant quickly noticed that Carol was always sniffing around me, and whenever he was on night duty in the police station, he would sneak home and enter my room, checking to see if Carol was there. She had a reputation, and the Commandant was aware of this, though I didn't because nobody had ever told me. Whenever the two women were together, they would often tease me while we worked by the tomatoes, I sometimes would go red in the face with embarrassment, not understanding everything they asked me, but they were both very experienced, and as I didn't know what to say about these subjects, I would often turn red as those tomatoes. The mistress was ten years older than me, but that didn't stop her joking with me.

Whilst Carol was in hospital, the mistress asked me to mix a bread dough, which I did with pleasure, after mixing and moulding, I baked the bread in the oven. When the children had gone to bed that night, the mistress and I spent a couple of hours chatting. I once noticed the Commandant coming home one night and checking my room, when Carol was still in hospital. I was interested to know why the Commandant looked into my room, so I confronted his wife, and asked if she knew why, and she said 'Oh Janyk, aren't you stupid, you see I am a young woman, and my husband is old, he is eighteen years older than me, surely you can see his bald head. He knows very well that Carol wakes you, obviously he doesn't trust me, and is frightened that I might fall in love with you'. I began to go red in the face again, but she laughed and said, 'Don't be afraid, we are not children, Janyk you no longer suck your mother's milk, surely you must realise that you're a grown man by now, but the snag is you're a coward.' She went on to say, 'You must understand that rarely does a man trusts his wife, you are in your twentieth year, and my husband knows this well'. I couldn't listen to anymore of her silly talk, so I went outside, fed the horse and cow, then left to spend the evening in the village.

The following morning, on my way to the well for water, I was thinking of how best to avoid this dilemma, how I could leave this job as soon as possible, there and then. Carol was in hospital for two weeks, and it that time I took the children to school every morning, when we could see Carol standing by the hospital gate in a white nightdress waving to us. In those two weeks, the mistress visited her twice and when she eventually returned my workload slowly diminished.

Shortly afterwards, I experienced an unpleasant situation that happened one day as I was taking the children to school, I was guiding the carriage at a steady pace downhill, now and then having to apply the brake, when all of a sudden a cartful of young lads heading downtown caught up with me on the road. The boys had been drinking and were quite boisterous, determined to overturn my carriage with the children aboard. I pleaded with them profusely, telling them that the children belonged to the police commandant and that there would be trouble, but they weren't in the least bit convinced. Two of the older children could see what was going on, so they jumped out of the carriage, yet three remained inside when the carriage overturned. The children burst into tears, but after consoling them, they marched off to school. In the meantime, I stayed by the carriage waiting for somebody to help me turn it over to its upright position. It wasn't long before another cartful of boys, this time from a different village stopped. We quickly put the carriage back onto the road, and I managed to catch up with three of the younger children a few minutes later. The elder two had walked onto the police station to see their father. I dropped the three younger children at school, then as usual went to the commandant's house on the river. A couple of hours later, the commandant arrived in tow with the two older children and a couple of burly policemen. The commandant took us all to where the drunken boys had descended upon us. The children and I pointed the culprits out. Needless to say, the boys received a good hiding from the commandant and his men.

This incident finally resulted in me leaving the commandant's employment, on friendly terms I should add. It was now July, I had wasted three months, it was the school summer vacations, and we all parted amicably.

It was now the beginning of harvest time, when I finally started work at the bakery, the weather was stifling hot, the holiday makers were in town, so the bakery had become busy and I was needed. I started work on my previous conditions, earning twenty Zloty per week. I started work at six in the evening and worked until eight in the morning, six days a week. The food was very good, my only problem was the accommodation, for the room over the bakery was impossible to sleep in during summer, so I slept in the attic, where more air circulated, though the roof was covered with a sheet of metal, which made it unbearable to sleep. When I finished at eight, I had breakfast, drank my coffee, then went to sleep until one. When I woke for lunch I didn't have much of an appetite, and I felt very tired. After lunch I had to make a starter dough, then I was free until six, so I could either go back to sleep or go down to the river for a swim, which I often did.

The beautiful town of Zalishchyky soon became just a dream, though it wasn't Koroliwka, the town I'd really been yearning for. In Zalishchyky I slept very little, in twenty- four hours I managed to get maybe two or three hours' shuteye because of the intense heat, nor could I get any sleep in the light of day. For the entire month of July, the sun didn't just warm the air, in the attic it was hotter than hell. August was even worse, the sun not allowing no-one any sleep whatsoever. On Sundays, since I had some free time in the afternoon, I wanted to take advantage and see something. Sunday nights were a nightmare for me, I just wanted to sleep, so to refresh myself I would put my head into a bowl of cold water. I still felt tired, I once forgot to salt the rolls, and this lost us an hour in production time. This forgetfulness of mine got round the whole town, for the rolls arrived one hour late in the town, all because the baker had forgotten to add salt to the dough. Mrs Shaferova, forgave me the first time, but my head remembered that mishap for a long time. Mrs Shaferova, a widow, originally from Chornivka, on the other side of Dniester, was an elderly lady, but a very good one, paying her bakers well, and everyone who ate there ate well. She employed a lady who just cooked and another one who cleaned the bakery and rooms.

By September it wasn't as hot, so I slept better, but then I had another problem, namely Carol. She started to come and see me on a Sunday, telling her mistress she was going to church in town, but instead of going to church, she took joy in endlessly doing my head in. She tried to encourage me to leave my job and marry her, she claimed to have a small holding but nobody to look after it. I tried not to listen to her, I tried to avoid her, I knew more or less at what time she would come in, so I left the bakery, but she would spend all afternoon looking for me. Failing that, she persisted and wrote me letters, which I totally ignored and never replied, and I wasn't remotely interested.

At the end of September, I developed an eye problem, my eyelids became red and sore. My body temperature increased so much that I was admitted into hospital. I spent three weeks there, my only visitors being Carol, who came a few times and the commandant's wife. Nobody from the bakery visited me, most of the workers were Poles and Jews, their manager was a Jew.

When I left the hospital, I didn't have the inclination to return to the bakery. The hospital doctor advised me to rest, sleep more, preferably during the night, when I slept in the attic in daylight. To make matters worse, I was in a permanent state of sweat from the heat, and that's why my eyes were red, for lack of sleep.

As the saying goes, 'you know who your friends are when you are in trouble'. I soon began to warm towards Carol; it was a hardship for me being in a hospital full of Poles, I always felt like an orphan, nobody visited me except for Carol, always bringing me something, so I felt a little more sympathy towards her. When I left hospital, she was waiting for me. We both went to see the commandant's wife, who by then had taken on another servant. Whilst I was in hospital, Carol had filled the commandant's wife with all sorts of stories that she believed. Carol announced she would be leaving her job, and I would be accompanying her to her village to be married. This is how Carol dressed the story, and her mistress believed her, even helping her to pack and prepare food for the journey. Later that afternoon we set off towards Carol's village, stopping a couple of times on the way for a bite to eat.

It was late by the time we reached the village, Carol wasn't in the least in a hurry, and she just repeated she was happy to be close to me. On the way she told me many silly things, mostly lies about her house, yet she neglected to tell me that she used to work on a homestead.

On our arrival she only showed me her house, but no matter how hard she tried to convince me, I didn't enter. She also showed me the Soltys house, the head of the village, where I was to spend the night. He showered praises on Carol to me all evening and advised me to marry her, as her household needed a good man to run it. To me everything sounded worryingly unreal. I didn't want to listen but I had to endure the pain for the remainder of the evening.

The next morning I woke early, I didn't even want to wait for breakfast, but soon heard Carol's voice around the house. She was talking to the Solty's wife, insisting she didn't want me to breakfast at their house, but at her own. On the way to Carol's house I tried to explain that I felt embarrassed going to a stranger's house, but she replied that I wasn't going to a stranger's, but to my own.

She had forewarned everybody at her house about me, so everybody knew what to say. In the house, there was an old lady, Carol's mother, a ten year old girl, who I was told was the daughter of Carol's sister, in Argentina at the time, a young boy of four, her other sister's boy, who lived in the house with his mother. Without any exaggeration, the house was completely topsy-turvy, a mess everywhere you looked, dust and dirt in every corner, a haven for flies, a place where you certainly wouldn't want to eat. Carol's mother would just be shuffling around the house, constantly complaining about her children.

For breakfast Carol had made what looked like an omelette using the bread we had been given the day before. The dining table on which the food was served was as filthy as the floor, it was obvious it had never been cleaned, it was fairly evident that the small boy had walked all over it, just as I had done when my mother used to lock me up in our house. I now felt sorry for the old lady who in her old age had to put up with such a household, one daughter working as a maid, the other rumoured to be in Argentina. I realised I wouldn't get to the truth here, or at the cousin's. Outside in the yard too, there was dirt up to your knees, while everything was overgrown in the large garden with old hay thrown onto a pile in the orchard. This place definitely needed a hard- working person, to bring everything to some order. Following me was Carol's mother, repeating that she would only be looking after grandchildren if she had decent children, and she wouldn't need to suffer herself.

All day long I was led everywhere, shown everything, forced to listen to boastful remarks, but nothing interested me, I was just looking for an excuse to leave everything and return home. They still managed to talk me into having lunch with them, after which I packed my belongings ready to go. Carol wouldn't leave me alone for a minute, escorting me to Zolotyi Potik, her village was the neighbouring one, but I don't remember its name. Along the road, Carol would not give up repeating that I should quickly return to her, so that we could get married. From Zolotyi Potik to my village was quite a distance, so I had to make an overnight stop, then on the second day I arrived at last. Home sweet home!

CHAPTER 13
BACK IN THE VILLAGE OF KAMINNE

This time my mother was very pleased to see me, although I wrote to her and on a few occasions enclosing a couple of Zloty. My mother commented that I had grown, dressed well, and that I looked like a proper young gentleman.

I arrived into the village just when the villagers were digging up their potatoes, and I joined in the work, proving to be of much needed help to my mother. I hadn't completely settled when the postman delivered a letter from Carol, then another on the second day and still a further one the third day, by which time the postman was visibly angry at me, as he had enough work to do without me.

When the opportunity arose, I related to my mother all the exploits I had got up to since last leaving home. My mother immediately set about convincing me that I had thrown away a golden opportunity to get married, that I wouldn't suffer needlessly, it didn't matter that Carol was a few years older. After all, I wouldn't be cooking for her, my mother continued 'It's better to marry young, for if there's a good homestead, you'll be able to earn a little money'. When she noticed that Carol had written so often, Mother commented that it didn't seem a joke at all, even though she never read any of my letters. The poor woman was illiterate, but could understand Carol's plight, and slowly tried to convince me to go back and marry her. As my mother remarked, there were no suitable girls for me in the village, for who would want to marry a pauper like Ivan. In her view, I needed a woman with her own house, one who would have me, for the women around here with their own houses had many suitors. In the end, my mother finally convinced me to return to Carol and marry her, because if I left it too late, a woman with her own home and large homestead would have many takers, and I would later regret not having acted sooner.

I was in no hurry to leave the village, as it was a happy time for everyone there, people gathering at each other's houses, always playing music and singing. Although I didn't know many villagers, they knew me, especially the ones that had been to school in Stanislaviw. They now avoided me but there was no reason to, and when I once asked Anna Boychuk for a dance, she refused for the second time, saying 'Once is enough for you'. My mother observed everything that was going on, and understood fully, so she was more and more determined to send me to Carol, especially as there was nothing for me in the village. To work for a stranger in his field digging potatoes for one Zloty wasn't worth getting dirty for.

Whilst I worked in Zalishchyky, I had earned myself a little money, not a lot, but enough for a couple of suits, shoes and shirts, I also bought my mother some winter clothes, as my step-father showed little interest. My mother and step-father were pleased, to have me help them, but once the work was done, I was only a hindrance. I understood their dilemma; there just wasn't the room in the house for an extra person. I finished helping my mother to gather the last of the potatoes, leaving her to see to the light duties. I packed my belongings, and said goodbye to my mother and the village once again.

CHAPTER 14 CAROL (KAROLKA)

The morning I left, I was accompanied by a drizzle all the way to Otynia. By the time I got there my shirt was soaked through, though at least on this occasion I didn't have to beg for food. I came across a shop where I bought half a loaf and a piece of meat. I ate my food, rested for about half an hour, then continued along the road. It took me two days to reach Zolotyi Potik, I didn't want to spend the night at Carol's house, so I found somewhere to sleep, then carried on to her house in the morning.

Carol's mother explained that she was digging potatoes for the Solty's, where I had slept before. Since I didn't care to sit in the house all day, I asked where she could be found. Her mother gave me directions, so off I went. I walked along the given route, until I saw a group of people digging potatoes, but there was no sign of Carol. I noticed an old man, digging alone, at the same time looking after his cow. I muttered to myself 'God help me' then approached the man, asking if he knew of a girl who was digging potatoes for the Solty's. The old man pointed to a group of people about half a kilometre away. I could see the group of people, but didn't recognise anyone.

So as not to stand around idly, I took off my jacket, then told the old man that I would help him, I couldn't face walking to a group of total strangers. The old man passed me his hoe, his wife standing nearby, pleased that her husband had a digger. As I was digging, I explained to the old couple the reason for me being there to marry Carol. The old lady couldn't believe her ears, they happened to be her close neighbours. For the next hour or so, they filled me in on everything about Carol, so much so that my hair stood on end.

To begin, they told me that she worked as a cook for an economist, in a local homestead. Then I was told she was married to a very quiet squeamish man, she used to do what she liked to him, even leaving him to live with the economist. People said, that one day the owner of the homestead came for an inspection. Out of sheer fright the economist locked Carol in a wardrobe. Later, Carol poisoned her husband; he spent three days and nights in a stable before he died. Since then people avoided Carol like the plague, and that's why she sought her fortune elsewhere, where nobody knew about her. Now she had returned to the village, bragging that she had found a new suitor, and that soon there would be a wedding. As the old couple were explaining me their story, I began to feel hot and cold.

The conversation broke off temporarily. While the old man saw to his cow, I took the opportunity to straighten my back and have a short rest. For lunch the old lady spread out an old sack onto the ground on which I sat, she then gave me a piece of dried bread and a couple of pears. We later carried on until evening, packed everything, at the same time as the nearby group of workers, then made our way to their home.

I was lucky that I had come upon this old couple, who knew everything about Carol, not like the Soltys, a relative of Carol's, who only had good things to say about her. I asked the old couple if I could spend the night in their house given that it was Sunday the following day, and I would leave to go back home in the morning,

As was often the case, my plan didn't materialise. The Soltys had many people working for him. In that particular field, the Soltys had two wagons, one of which was driven by his son, who noticed a stranger working for the old man, and on his return he told this to his fellow workers, describing more or less how I looked, and even recognising me from the previous week when I had slept in their house.

We arrived at the old couple's house, as nightfall began to settle. I had a wash, cleaned my shoes and trousers, then waited for the old lady who was preparing supper. I needed a call of nature, so I stepped outside, only to see Carol standing by a wall. I stood frozen to the spot not knowing what to do. Without more ado, Carol quickly grabbed me by the arm, then started scolding me and asking why I had been to those bad people. Why had I not waited for her at home but gone into the fields instead? I wanted to say something in reply but stood speechless, whereupon she pulled me towards her orchard, out of earshot of her neighbours. When I was able to break away from her grasp, I found Carol to be very obstinate. I felt intimidated, as though in fear of her, as if she were possessed by the devil. She tried hard to convince me to enter her house but I managed to refrain. We sat on her porch until late at night, and I told her everything I had found out from the old couple, but she flatly denied everything. She insisted that the neighbour had blatantly lied, because they'd once had a dispute over a boundary line, and that's why he was angry at her family, and what he had recounted was all lies. By then I didn't believe a word she had uttered. In my mind's eye I saw the poor husband she had poisoned because of the economist. When I asked her if was true that she was married, she denied this firmly and unequivocally. From time to time, the little four year old boy kept running in and out of the house, referring to Carol as 'Nene'. When I asked why she was called 'Nene' by the child, an endearing name used in those parts for 'mother' she replied that he was her nephew, that's why he called her 'Nene.'

Carol's mother also tried to persuade me to come indoors, as it was time to sleep, but I stood my ground and ignored all their pleas. It was getting very late, and I didn't want to trouble the old couple next door, so I went to sleep in Carol's barn, where four years previously her husband met his violent death. Carol didn't want to leave me alone, but in the end I forced her out, promising her that I would spend the whole night on my own. It was probably after midnight when Carol finally left me alone. In the barn I found plenty of hay, and a blanket made out of a sack was brought to me, which I couldn't see anyway, as it was dark. I didn't bother to undress, just took off my shoes, and lay on the hay.

This was the first time in my life that I had lain awake all night, not getting a wink of sleep, just thinking, what that woman had told me. She wasn't even twenty years old when she married one of our Ukrainian boys, she'd been working for the economist as a maid for a while when she met her husband. Although they had their own small homestead, Carol carried on working for the economist, leaving her husband, mother and her sister to work their own land. Carol had a child, and everybody said it was the economist's, and not by her husband. The village knew what the economist got up to with Carol, once locking her in a wardrobe, whilst showing the owner of the homestead the fields. This took a long time. Cooped up inside the wardrobe, Carol started to scream because it had been locked. Eventually, it had to be smashed open, giving the village plenty to talk about. She had poisoned her own husband because of the economist, then out of shame escaped to the city in search of work. Her poor mother had to look after not only Carol's son, but also the daughter of Carol's sister who had gone to Argentina. Carol was away for four years, neglecting her own homestead and leaving it to fall into ruin.

I lay awake all night, each and every one of these thoughts turning over and over again in my mind; I could run away, but I couldn't really since I had left my coat at the old couple's house. At daybreak I prayed for the moment I could go and collect my coat, then return home. As I lay there I could hear somebody coming into the barn and moving towards me. I pretended to sleep, until I felt Carol kiss me on the cheek, she then lay next to me and demanded what I'd dreamt about. I quickly replied that I'd dreamt about her husband, at which she immediately turned pale, moved away from me and heard her son calling 'Nene'. She didn't make a sound until her son had left the barn, again trying to convince me to go into the house, because strangers could see that I had slept in the barn. I promised that I would, as long as she went first, which she did, but a couple of minutes later her mother entered, and she too tried to persuade me to go into the house, as breakfast was ready, but I fell silent.

Carol's mother returned to the house, probably to warn her that I was no longer there. A few moments later Carol came running back into the barn, but this time I told her firmly that I wouldn't go into the house, as I wasn't hungry and didn't have an appetite. Carol again strutted out of the barn, went to the house and returned with some victuals. I threw away all the food she brought, covering it with hay and leaving her with an empty plate, which she was pleased to see.

After breakfast, Carol took my trousers and shoes into the house to be cleaned. Considering it was Sunday and a feast day, Carol proposed that we went to Zolotyi Potik. I saw this as a good opportunity to escape from her clutches, knowing the town was on the way to my village. I washed myself in the barn, then asked if I could go next door to collect my coat. At the old couple's house I shaved, thanked them kindly for their invaluable information, said my goodbyes, and returned through the orchard to Carol's house. When Carol noticed me, she asked me to wait a couple of minutes, she wasn't quite ready. I could see eyes peering at me from all directions, her mother's and the little girl's. Carol came out wearing her Sunday best, the day was sunny, so they urged me to leave my coat behind as it would be too warm, but I ignored their pleas and carried the coat over my arm.

To reach Zolotyi Potik, we took a footpath through a wood. On the way I stopped a couple of times by a bush, giving the impression that I was being sick, which Carol disliked. We proceeded at a leisurely pace, a few people passed us, some people would greet us, others didn't bother. I gave Carol the impression that I wasn't feeling well, instead I was calculating how I could best escape.

Once we arrived in Zolotyi Potik I felt hungry, telling Carol the scrambled egg she'd made me that morning wasn't to my liking, which is why I'd brought it all up. She believed me, so we stopped at the first open cafe where she ordered me a breakfast. I polished it all off and we then carried on to the church. We didn't spend very long in the church, we were bickering every God-given minute, and she was winning all the arguments; a crafty and cunning little witch, she always had an answer at the ready.

On our way back towards Carol's village we crossed the river Stripa, at which point I became rather anxious not to fall into her web again. I asked if we could find a quieter route so that we could talk, as I still had plenty to discuss. She didn't agree, saying that we could discuss everything once we got back to her home. At this point I stood my ground, insisting that I wouldn't take one more step until she told me the whole truth. I first asked about the little boy and, without any hesitation, she said he was her son and we would soon have a shepherd. After this I didn't have any inclination to pursue the matter, so I quickened my pace in the direction of her village. This time we passed by other people, I quickened my pace leaving her behind. As soon as she was out of sight, I changed direction and headed for the thick wood, running as fast as my legs could carry me, away from this nightmare.

I stopped behind a tree, listening for any sign of her. When I was convinced that I'd shaken her off, rather than walk through the wood at dusk, I headed back to Zolotyi Potik, where I subsequently spent the night, at the same place, on my way to 'get married'.

The following morning the weather had turned, it was miserable with rain. The road back to my home village was now well- known to me, but people recommended me to take the road to Tlumach. It was heavy going, but in my soul I felt joy and happiness at the thought that I hadn't allowed myself to be manipulated by Carol, and that I was now many miles from her house. My shoes were covered in mud, but I was in no hurry, I had two overnight stops ahead of me before reaching Tlumach. I inquired about work in the town, but it was difficult at the end of the summer season when most households made their own bread.

I went around all the bakeries, the few that where there. Each one I went into I saw the beautifully shaped fresh rolls and loaves of bread, bakers working without shirts, though by then I felt tired of the journey, even more so of the frightful experience I had just escaped from. I felt safe and fortunate, proud of my profession. In one bakery I dried myself, after which I was given some food. I didn't need to hurry home as there was no one expecting me.

Before nightfall I left the town and headed towards a village, to find overnight accommodation. On the road I came across an old lady who asked me to read her a fortune ticket she'd bought in the town. She herself was illiterate yet very keen to hear what her fortune had in store for her, and she wanted to know everything before reaching home. The fortune ticket was written in Polish, but the lady was dressed in peasant clothing, she spoke Ukrainian, but in a very broad dialect. The old lady said she was Polish, though she couldn't speak the language, she'd lived there in the village since birth, speaking in the same way as everyone else. I gleaned from our conversation that she had a daughter of my age, and we carried on talking and joking, until she invited me to spend the night at her house. I said that one day I would call upon her, but today I had to find a cobbler to repair my shoe as it was beginning to let in water. We soon came to her village, and on arriving at her house she invited me inside. I had not yet got over one shock, and I certainly didn't want to start another relationship, so I gave her my address, promising I would call in the future. We said our goodbyes, and I went looking for a cobbler. The cobbler has easy to find, he proceeded to repair my shoe, and I ended up staying the night in his house. The cobbler also told me many interesting stories about the old lady who I'd met earlier and her daughter. I set off the following day before noon, and by nightfall I was back home.

On seeing me return so soon after our last parting, my mother thought I'd come home for my birth certificate. Once I'd related all my woes to her, and only to her, I could see from my mother's face that she was disappointed. Clearly, it was not what she wanted to hear.

I spent a few days at home with neither a deed to fulfil nor a purpose in mind. The work in the fields was coming to an end, so I spent my days sitting around the house, looking through the window, watching people pass by and wondering what to do next.

In the evenings I would go into the village where the local girls and boys would meet, the girls would do some washing and embroidery, whilst the boys would talk and joke with the girls, ending up with everyone singing together. I knew a vast amount of songs, some of which the villagers had never heard. I was liked for my melodies and I was often invited to tell them a story and sing them a song. I had plenty to relate, and I had a sense of humour to boot, so the boys insisted that I came. On one such evening, as I approached the group, there was one boy who was reading a book. After about half an hour, he asked me if I would read for a change, which I agreed to gladly, although the last time I had held a book in my hand was when I was doing my exams to qualify as a baker. I was reading the *Kobzar* by Taras Shevchenko, some of the girls were doing chores and listening, others sat around. It was almost midnight when the group dispersed, some boys would escort their girlfriends home, the rest walked along singing happily, this was the village custom.

One evening, my stepfather returned from the co-operative, that's where he delivered milk, and was told that there was work on the railways, near Mykulychyn. The following morning I caught a train to Mykulychyn, and that same day started work. I found the work very hard, never having worked with a crowbar, and I soon developed blisters on both hands. The worst problem was where to sleep, some people slept in the homes of local villagers, others in a warehouse with no roof.

The work in Mykulychyn was seasonal, local people for some reason didn't work there, most workers came from Stanoslaviw and Lviv. Every worker had an 'open ticket' and could return home nightly, returning the following morning, but in my case it would take up a lot of time, so I went to the local village, in search of accommodation.

As I was walking towards the village I noticed an old lady carrying a bundle of wood on her back. I walked up to her and asked if she knew of anywhere I could get accommodation for a couple of weeks, since I was working in the local rail yard. The old lady looked me up and down, and then said 'Carry the bundle of wood on your back for me and you can come and stay in my house'. The remainder of our journey to her house wasn't far, just the other side of the meadow. I suddenly felt a glow of warmth through my body and thanked God that I'd asked the old lady.

The old widow, I found, had a very pretty daughter called Anna. Unfortunately, I also found out later that she was prone to suffer from haemorrhoids. Nevertheless, she was very pretty and knew many Hutsul songs, and we often sat on the porch singing, and from her I learnt many new songs.

Hutsul's are generally good people, but tend not to trust strangers, they won't allow anyone into their homes at night, cursing strangers for bringing diseases into their midst. It took a while for me to win over their trust, even though we were fellow Ukrainians.

I was very happy with my new surroundings. Some fellow workers, however, were envious, for I came home from work to find my supper ready. I didn't pay for my lodgings, though I would always bring something from work and would make sure Anna had enough firewood.

I soon learnt all the Hutsul ways, their special dishes, the way they spoke, soon becoming one of them. On a Sunday I would go to the library with Anna, once I even escorted her to a Hutsul wedding. When we arrived at the wedding, we had to go through a gate which led into a yard, the whole homestead was surrounded by a large wooden fence. Inside there was a very popular band called the 'Legends' playing. I found the spectacle very interesting I just stood at the side watching, forgetting about my hunger, until I saw Anna approaching me, as beautiful as a rose, who took me for something to eat, followed by a generous portion of strong alcohol which, after drinking, gave me courage to ask Anna to dance. She was well known locally, but nobody knew me, so I received plenty of stares as we danced. Anna's mother returned home earlier, warning us not to stay too late for after midnight wolves prowled through the woods.

Anna and I walked back home, we passed the spot where I'd first met her mother. Then, lo and behold, we saw wolves nearby. We quickly entered the house, and two minutes later we saw two wolves in front of the window, not so surprising as the house was situated, by the edge of the wood.

Anna was a very honest and happy girl who had a good sense of humour and liked to sing. Her only problem was her ill health, she was quite weak, unable to pick up a bundle of wood.

Unfortunately, my work in Mykulychyn didn't last long, I only received three pay packets, but my stay there continued. Christmas soon came, I joined the local choir and drama group, and every evening I was occupied with one thing or another. I had a decent bass voice, black curly hair, and soon I became the talk of the village, especially among the single girls.

On the whole, life in the village during the winter months was very happy for me. I lived for the evenings but during the day I was bored. I always helped my mother financially whenever I could, I would buy her boots and clothes, for her husband had nothing to give her. He spent all his working life working in the homesteads, but often he wouldn't have two pennies to rub together.

The old lady I met on the road to Tlumach didn't waste much time, she persuaded her daughter to write me a letter. I had received two letters from her, whether they were written by herself, I didn't know, maybe she had somebody clever enough to write them for her. If she had written the letters herself, then she couldn't be as stupid as the cobbler told me. I had a great deal of time on my hands, so I thought why not try. Outside the snow was deep, up to your knees in parts, but this didn't bother me. My mother was under the impression I was off to Stanislaviw, I'd mentioned to her before Christmas that I might try my luck there.

As soon as I awoke the next morning I got dressed and left. It took me all day to get to the village of Oleshi, where I spent the night. The following day was spent in the village, I didn't want anyone to know where I was going. That evening I left again, I had another seven kilometres to walk. On the way, I was planning in my mind how to approach the house and what to say; after all, calling unannounced on a young lady would have caused much embarrassment to those concerned.

CHAPTER 15
ANNA

The door was opened by the old lady, who immediately recognised me and invited me in. She helped me take off my coat, then asked me to sit down, apologising for her daughter's absence, since she was at one of the neighbours, but assured me of her imminent arrival, as it was already dark. Her husband was not at home either, he was seeing to the cattle, in the meantime she was lighting the paraffin lamp. As the lamp began to burn, Anna entered the house. The light from the lamp was slowly becoming brighter, Anna asked her mother 'Who is in the house? Is it the man I am waiting for? Because my heart is telling me it is'. I sat quietly on the bench, not saying a word, feeling my face as red as a beacon from shame, I'd never have expected such an introduction. The old lady brought the lamp closer to me, I saw Anna for the first time with her goofy smile. She approached me and introduced herself, saying she was upset with me, because I'd only written her one letter, whereas she'd written four.

Shortly afterwards, the man of the house entered, introduced himself, then told the women to prepare supper, commenting that I must've been hungry after my long journey. While the women were busy in the kitchen, the old man started to explain everything about his household, how he had to do all the work because the women spent most of the day chatting and gossiping. He had to take care of the cattle, Anna only helped him to cut the straw, he even had to clean the manure in the stable, adding that he often thought of hiring somebody to help him, but Anna kept delaying his decision, reassuring him that I would be soon coming, yet she didn't expect me to arrive in such severe weather. He finished by saying, he was glad I'd finally made it and hoped that I would be of help in his old age. The old lady would often jump into the conversation, always changing the subject, then Anna would correct her mother, giving me the impression that she knew best. The old man went onto talk about his future plans for spring, what he intended to sow and plant, then he said 'The most important task is how to talk Anna into our future plans'. I listened very attentively to every word because it was very difficult for me to understand, he used such comical words that I'd never heard of, twisting every word from Polish to Ukrainian, or the other way around. I was dumbfounded, wondering where these Poles were from? Their language was neither Ukrainian nor Polish, because I knew both well. I later found out that it was from the Mazur region, a dialect that I'd never come across.

When supper was ready and we sat at the table, I was surprised to see pickled cucumbers served with milk. I ate the food forcefully, not having the courage to refuse it. I suffered that night in bed, listening to my stomach rumbling. I had to relieve myself twice during the night and, on hearing me shuffling around the second time, the old man shone a light at me, whereupon I turned red with embarrassment.

The following morning I told them that I wouldn't be eating breakfast, owing to the fact that I had an upset stomach from the previous day's food. The old lady then started to praise her food, describing the various herbs she added, her food couldn't possibly have been at fault, it must've been because I was so hungry and had eaten far too much of it. Anna nevertheless, carried on making breakfast but I insisted that I couldn't eat so early in the morning, which indeed it was, because they needed a light on in the house, and they also required a light to see into the stable to feed the cattle. The old man inadvertently came to my rescue as I saw him struggle with a large tub, so I dashed out of the house and gave him a hand in the stable. They kept five cows and a horse, and surprisingly it wasn't cold despite a sharp frost outside. The old man prepared some chaff for the cows, adding beetroots and potatoes, then mixed a few oats with chaff for the horse. The old man mentioned that he used to own two horses, but now that he was older he had no need for two, especially since his daughter wasn't up to looking after horses. As we were talking Anna came running in, saying that breakfast was ready, that she had prepared it herself, and that she was sure I would like it. She placed a large bowl of scrambled egg, half a litre of steamed milk and a large three kilo loaf of bread, with a side bowl of butter. When I saw this mountain of food in front of me, I politely said that I didn't drink milk, only black coffee. Anna replied that they didn't have coffee but could only offer me tea and that I would have to wait a while. The old man advised me to eat the egg whilst it was hot, then the old lady added that I wouldn't gain any strength from coffee, only townsfolk drank it.

After breakfast I saw that the parents were preparing to leave for town, leaving Anna at home with me, this showed how naive and simple they were, throwing their daughter onto a total stranger. The old man instructed me to keep an eye on the horse and cows, Anna was supposed to feed the pigs and I was also to help bring in a tub of weeds. I noticed the old lady whisper something in Anna's ear, which I wasn't bothered about, I just made a mental note whilst observing my new surroundings. I wasn't happy with being left alone with their daughter, quite the opposite, I was embarrassed that the old couple allowed their daughter to be part of their crafty scheme.

Before they left, the old man carried a small basket in his hand, whilst his wife ran from corner to corner, trying on various headscarves and furs, even Anna was giving a helping hand, prompting which looked the best. In the end, when everything was decided, the old lady stopped on the threshold and warned me that Anna was still young.

I'd had enough problems with that leech Carol, who'd taken me for an idiot, so now I decided to play safe and keep my distance from goofy Anna. I could see their game and understood their goal, so I acted as the simple village boy, keeping my thoughts to myself, just observing and waiting for the final outcome.

Once the parents had left, Anna, who was quite crafty, and also two or three years older than me, began to thrown herself at me. She sat down beside me, then said in an outspoken tone 'Now we have the opportunity to be more open with each other because my parents left intentionally so that we could be alone, I certainly couldn't say what I think of you in front of them'. She knew very little about me, only what she had been told by her mother, but she certainly wasn't so credulous as to believe everything, quite the contrary, she waited for my arrival so that she could be convinced for herself.

Now I could see her feeling happier, she was close to me and wanted me to say how I felt about her. I didn't want to embarrass her, I could see she was being naive, so I decided to let her suffer a little and wait until noon at least. She explained everything about herself and her family and promised me that she would make me a happy person. I only had to say that I would marry her, and from that moment I would be made and wouldn't ever need to worry about anything. Besides, the homestead was big, it only needed a strong willing person, whereas her father was too old to take care of the land and look after the cattle by himself.

I seized the opportunity to take advantage of the situation and not to allow her to have her own way. I thought it best to remain in this warm house through the winter rather than look for a job, so I lied, saying that we could get married, but only after Easter. On hearing this, Anna jumped with joy, kissed me, then exclaimed 'I 've been waiting for you to say that so that I could kiss you. It's not long to Easter, you can live here carefree, just help my father with the cattle, and we can plan our wedding'.

The first few days were difficult, sitting day and night with the same people and engaging in the same conversation. Occasionally, when the sun shone I helped the old man in the stable with the cattle, cleaning after them, loading the manure onto a sledge, then transporting it to a field. This was done, the old man said, because it was impossible to take a cart into the field in spring, when the road was very bad. We would pass the odd villager, they would glance at me thinking that the old man had found himself a servant, because there were no takers for his goofy daughter, even though she came with 'land'.

Mother and daughter were busy preparing for the wedding, Lent was half way through, the wedding was five or six weeks away. For me to be married I needed my birth certificate, which was back in Stanislaviw. When I mentioned this to them, I could see they didn't trust me, so they suggested that I travel to Stanislaviw with Anna.

The nearest train station was in Tlumach twelve kilometres away. Walking in thick mud through the village was impossible, so we had to walk through gardens and orchards. Anna had her own boots, the old man was willing to lend me his, I declined, they were too big, I wore my own shoes instead.

Our journey, tough as it was, took us over two hours. Anna soon broke out in a permanent sweat since we didn't stop to rest, only when we reached the station. The old lady had packed food for us so we wouldn't go hungry, and slipped us a few Zloty.

The train journey didn't take long to Stanislaviw, we walked towards the church where I'd been Christened. Finding the church was easy, though I was certainly in no hurry. I'd had enough of her leading me by the nose, and all I wanted from her was a couple of Zloty so that I could tuck into a good lunch. We both reached the Cathedral, where I told her to wait outside. I entered alone, immediately remembering every nook and cranny of the building; I had spent many hours there in my childhood with the nuns. After about half an hour I walked out and saw Anna waiting, I lied through my teeth saying that I'd seen a priest, who told to return in an hour with five Zloty.

I could have easily lost Anna in the city, I knew it well, but I didn't want to walk around with her, so I led her to a restaurant I knew. We had a good lunch, I even had a glass of beer. Afterwards, I counted the money Anna had left, but as luck would have it she only had enough for her rail ticket. I was in a dilemma and had to think on my feet how to get out of this situation. I approached the Jewish restaurant owner, lying to him that I was collecting Anna's mother. In the meantime, I didn't have the heart to leave Anna penniless in a city so far from home. I told Anna I was going outside to find a toilet. She had no reason not to believe me, so she waited.

I strode leisurely out of the restaurant because I didn't expect anyone to come running after me on my way to the railway yards. While growing up I got to know the city well, I also knew where it was possible to board a goods train. I found an empty goods wagon heading south to Vorokhta, thinking and hoping that Anna had enough sense to get back home under her own steam.

CHAPTER 16

VOROKHTA

Vorokhta was quiet for that time of year, the commotion coming principally from the fast- flowing River Prut, and the bending fir trees. I spent the rest of the day looking, until I could look no further, so I decided that I would walk to Yaremche, though later there was still the train from Lviv to arrive, I could still earn a little if I was lucky. I didn't have to wait long for the train, whereupon I saw two ladies alighting with suitcases, there were no taxis or porters, only the unfortunate street dwellers looking for work. I was standing by a fence, when I was approached by a portly man who asked me if a new where a certain guest house was located. I didn't, but said I did, thinking I could ask somebody along the way. I picked his two heavy suitcases. I was lucky that I headed along the right road, when I asked for directions. I had to stop a couple of times to rest, finally finding the large guest house at the foot of a hill.

I entered the guest house with the two cases, where the owner was expecting the stout man. The owner asked me if I was interested in working for him, saying there was little work at the moment but I could paint the rooms, then when the season started proper I could go down to the station a couple of times a day and carry suitcases for the guests. I agreed straight away and spent my first night in the guest house.

I worked in the guest house until Easter just for my food and lodgings, later on the Jewish owner paid me for every time I carried suitcases for the guests. During the summer months he would pay me reasonably well, yet I would still manage to earn a little extra on the side with tips. The owner would wake me every morning, I was expected to make and take coffee to some of the guests. I had to be at the train station before noon every day, as there was a constant turnaround of guests.

In a short time I was well established in my work, the owner liked me very much, confirming that it was his lucky day when he offered me the job. The food was very good, I had a clean room, although in the peak season I had to give it up and sleep in the workshop.

One summer's day two ladies arrived from Warsaw, both of whom were supposed to be good cooks. I brought them both to the guest house, and one of them started work in the kitchen, though it soon turned out that this lady wasn't a cook. Despite the guest house being short-staffed, she was allowed to stay. The other lady didn't have as much luck and she became a burden on me and her friend. She didn't have any money to eat or to lodge. So, without anyone knowing, she was smuggled into the workshop, where she slept. Every evening, her friend and I would bring her food, in the mornings she would make her way through the gardens, walk along the river bank, then spend the rest of the day sunbathing.

A couple of weeks later, the lady who worked in the kitchen began to steal food from the larder, and I would then take it to the workshop. One day the owner caught me, and because of that woman I lost my job. Although he was very angry, he still paid me.

After walking around the town, I heard about work on a hill called Kuk. The Poles were building a large guest house. I quickly found a job there. The snag however, was that I had to sleep in a dirty, flea- infested shed, the other problem being that the site was five kilometres from the nearest shop. I only worked there for two weeks before I found a better job in Zaba. (now called Verkhovyna). In Vorokhta I made a friend and we both walked on to Zaba. We left in the morning and walked all the way through a wood, only passing one village by the name of Kryvorivna. We didn't come across any shops, and when we grew very hungry we resorted to picking berries amongst the tall pine trees. Around noon we arrived in Zaba, stopped an old Hutsul and asked him how to get to a hill called Pip Ivan, where an astronomy centre was being built.

The old Hutsul pointed us in the direction of the hill, advising us not to attempt to reach it until the next morning. On the old Hutsul's advice we descended into the centre of the village, where we came across a Jewish shop. We bought half a loaf of stale bread and a container of sour milk. The shop owner advised us to buy food for the journey, as we wouldn't find anything on the way and the work is very hard.

We walked through the beautiful countryside until we reached a swift flowing river nearby, called Cheremosh, where we stopped to eat our food. Replenished and rested, we washed in the river, and then fell asleep on the river bank.

That night we slept under cover in the doorway of a shop. In the morning we bought a whole loaf and a piece of pork fat, then started walking in the direction of Pip Ivan Hill. On the road we stopped twice and swam in the river Cheremosh.

Around noon we found a Polish camp of engineers, who were queuing outside the food kitchen for soup. We were given a generous portion of pea soup, rested and continued our journey. Once the river separated our paths, the going got heavier and harder as each step became steeper and steeper.

Pip Ivan is quite a tall peak, the third highest of the Chornohora range, and all the north side is covered in permanent black ice. As we walked towards the summit we could feel the cooler air, up until then we carried our jackets and shoes, but now we had to put them on. The path took us to the top of the hill, where we were met such a heavy snowfall compared to what we had subjected to in January and February, and this was July!

When we left in the morning we were wearing summer clothes, yet here it was winter, workers in hats, gloves and thick winter coats. When I saw all this, it put me off work, but we still went in search of the manager The manager, a Pole, offered us a job immediately, promising us good wages, at the same time advising us to go down to the village and buy winter clothing, what we were wearing was just not suitable.

Whilst deciding, we mingled amongst the workers, making inquiries about any available work. The pay for assisting the stonemasons was between five and six Zloty per day, breaking up the stone into powder, for a cubic metre, the pay was ten Zloty. For fetching water by cart from the lower slopes, the pay was six Zloty. The downside was that bread cost four times more than in the village below, even a glass of drinking water cost five cents. Sleeping arrangements were in a flea-ridden hut, so although the pay was good, we could see why there was a constant shortage of workers.

The building under construction was very close to the Czech border, most of the workforce were Polish, the labouring work was mostly carried out by the local Hutsuls, fetching cement, lime, food and a hundred-year old spruce, all done with the help of horses. There was also a nearby pond containing water used only for manufacturing, whereas drinking water was over a kilometre away downhill. Most of the food consumed was dried, and no cooking was done because of the cost of water. Hardly anything grew here, no berries or fruit, only small barren bushes.

We spent over an hour talking to whoever we could, before returning down the hill. We had to descend quickly to arrive before nightfall and find ourselves accommodation.

On the return journey the following morning, we walked near the Polish camp of engineers, but this time we avoided it in case we were recognised, because the day before not only did we have soup, but we also helped ourselves to two pairs of military boots and two pairs of hard-wearing trousers. While we were swimming in the river, the engineers were doing physical training, leaving their clothes by some nearby bushes. We kept the boots and sold the trousers to the Jewish shopkeeper. It's embarrassing writing about such deeds, but those times were hard for me, and I hope that God will not punish me too hard for my sins.

The following day, we ended up sleeping outside the Jew's shop, with just a few Zloty in our pockets, and this was where I parted with my travelling companion. I stayed in Zaba, he returned to Vorokhta. I still wanted to see more of the area. The old Jew would cheer me up, saying that I would soon find work, only when exactly he didn't know. I hung around for a couple of days, swimming, admiring the beautiful surroundings, and meeting up with a good Hutsul. He was returning from Kut and stopped by at the Jew's for a drink of alcohol. He explained that there was plenty of work, mainly in winter and summer, only the 'foreigners' were very slow at work and that's why they couldn't hold down a job.

After a couple of drinks, my new friend took out his flute and played me a tune; it was almost nightfall, when he left me to go home.

I spent another couple of days in the town, where there was plenty to see, I even saw a traditional Hutsul wedding, with the bride and groom rode to the church on horseback. I also saw a funeral, where a priest would follow the hearse on horseback, this was all very interesting, so I was in no hurry to return to Vorokhta.

I can't remember exactly how many days I spent in Zaba, just loitering without purpose, when one fine day I was approached by a Hutsul on a street, who asked if I was interested in a job nearby. He explained that a craftsman had just arrived from Lviv, and he needed an assistant. We walked to the unfinished building, which I could see still needed the walls rendering. This looked to me as a good find, I estimated there could be six months work here. I wouldn't have to worry about the winter and the craftsman was happy with me too. The building was planned to be a Hutsul museum. I had walked past it many times, never seeing any activity there. It was always quiet, and it was close to the Jew were I slept.

Now I had a job, a wage every two weeks, a roof over my head since I didn't have to sleep at the Jew's anymore, I now had my own room at no cost to myself. I perked myself up a little there. It was close to the river where I used the water to make my soups, where I would go for a swim, where I would even wash my shirts, and it was only across the road.

That summer I had just turned twenty and the following year I would have to do my 'National Service' but nobody at home knew my address, so nobody could notify me. If I didn't volunteer, then the police would start to look for me. I gathered someone might well have told them that I was in the mountains.

One day while at work, such an event actually occurred. A policeman was walking by, noticed me, approached and asked me for my documents. As I didn't have the necessary paperwork, he arrested me, but allowed me to wash myself and gather my things. The craftsman didn't have enough money to pay me in full, so he promised he would bring the remainder to the police station later.

That night I spent in a police cell. The following morning I was driven to Vorokhta with two other men, in a horse-drawn wagon. The policeman sat in the rear holding a rifle, I sat at the front with the 'driver'.

The road to Vorokhta took us through the countryside. Although the road was wide, we had to proceed slowly to avoid all the puddles from the previous rains. There was no conversation with the policeman or the 'driver'. We had reached a point where we were travelling through a dense wood and I noticed the policeman was gripping his rifle firmly, in case I jumped into the wood. I knew the road very well, I had measured it with my legs.

As we approached Vorokhta, I thought we might be travelling to the train station, instead we headed to the police station, where I spent the night. The following morning, I travelled by train to Stanislaviw with a different policeman. There I spent three days and nights, before I stood in front of a commission. I wasn't bored waiting, I'd been locked up in a cell with another man, and on the third day, yet another man arrived, making it three.

I was called first, then checked from top to bottom, spending most of the time looking at my eyes, I thought they might reject me, finding something wrong, but they labelled me under category 'A'. I was later told that I could leave and return to my work, but that I had to register at a police station every month in the town where I worked.

When everything was finished, the first call I made was to a restaurant where I had a good lunch. In the sack I was carrying I had a clean set of clothes, so I changed and went into the city.

CHAPTER 17
BACK HOME IN THE VILLAGE

In the city everything looked exciting, I was feeling happy because I had money in my pocket, I was a free man again, for how long I didn't know, so I just spent the rest of the day walking around the streets until nightfall, when I decided to treat myself to the Warsaw Cinema.

Later that night, I had made up my mind to return to my village, so I made my way to the train station, but when I arrived, I found that I had missed the last one. Once again I set off on foot, eventually arriving in the early hours of the morning.

The potato season was in full swing, so my mother was very happy to have a helper and to have me start work on a large homestead, nine sacks were for the master and the tenth for herself. It was hard work for a woman, and even though I made life easier for her, it was for a short while only, and she had enough on her plate without worrying about me. My mother had two children from her second husband, one of whom took the cow to pasture, while her husband spent all his time as usual with the horses on the homestead, never helping his wife. My mother had very little land of her own, and to compensate she had to work other people's land.

Whenever I returned to my village in the autumn, everyone would be happy to see me. I used to help the villagers a lot, but as winter approached there was no work and I could see I was in their way, so I would leave before Christmas to find work.

I was ready to leave that year, but I met a local girl called Malanka. I met her while gathering potatoes, she also helped her mother. We started going out in the evenings, to dances, even to neighbouring villages, Volosiv, Tysmenchany and Velesnytsya, and because of her, I didn't want to leave the village.

My stepfather had a brother called Peter who was illiterate, even though his father was a school janitor, but having a natural musical ear he played the violin very well. I would only have to sing him a new song once, no sooner did he hear a new tune than Peter would play the music instantly. Because of our relationship we got on very well. I called on him most evenings, he played and I sang. Peter talked me into buying a bass, he'd found one in a neighbouring village and the owner wanted to sell it. We approached the man and paid him five Zloty. It needed cleaning because it'd been kept amongst his chickens, it didn't have a bow or strings, but Peter made the bow himself, and I went into the city and bought all the strings. That evening we had our first practice, Peter playing his violin, at the same time hitting a drum with one foot, while I was making a sound on the bass and singing along.

Now I had a hobby, which kept me occupied every evening and happy too. By Christmas we were seasoned musicians, so we travelled to Volosiv and played at a Polish dance. I played and sang to every dance, and everyone was satisfied with us. I had a fairly large repertoire of songs and enjoyed performing to people, if I played badly, nobody took any notice. In the beginning, one or two people would laugh at me, but I took no notice, I was happy as long as I had a couple of Zloty in my pocket, and a purpose in life.

In the village, people began to show me respect and wanted to find me a bride, to whom I could latch onto. Otherwise, for a man like myself, without a house of his own, no way could he marry in a village, it wasn't the done thing in those days.

Malanka Pitvora didn't have a house of her own either. She understood the situation well, so there was no sense in us embarking on a serious relationship. That was in a manner of speaking 'easier said than done'. She was the first girl in the village who didn't try to 'boss me around', we would go everywhere together despite her stepfather prohibiting her from seeing me. I never stepped a foot in their house, I would walk her as far as the garden fence, beyond that would have meant tempting fate since he had warned me he would shoot me if he saw me anywhere near their house. We had to find a house were we could meet during the day. Malanka had an aunt close to my mother's house where we could meet, sing and joke, but we wouldn't talk about the future.

At the time I used to go to see Malanka I was labelled as the 'man looking for a bride'. My brother Vasyl, who was seven years younger than me, used to take the cow to pasture whilst still at school.

In the village, I knew plenty of boys and girls who I used to go to school with, but when I returned we would never meet socially. There was a vast difference between us, they were all very high up the social ladder, whereas to them I was at the very bottom.

In those days, village life had its own customs, usually stupid in my view. Typically, you would see a 'poor girl' standing in the corner of a dance floor and nobody would dance with her, the 'rich boys' would only dance with the 'rich girls'.

There was another custom that was conferred on the village 'elder', namely an unwritten law that he could prevent any girl he wished from dancing. This would invariably take place in public, the 'elder' would stop the musicians playing, make an announcement, name the girl, say she wasn't allowed to dance, then see if any man has the guts to challenge his decision. I once witnessed such a farcical comedy when an 'elder' forcefully pulled away from the dancing floor a girl he had ordered not to dance. These 'elders' changed quite often, even though they were never elected. It was basically a matter of whoever was the 'strongest' in the village and had a good back up of muscle usually won everything, but if he lost his 'crown' it would take him a long time to be forgiven. There were incidents, in which a person could lose his life or become physically disabled over a silly deed.

That winter I spent in the village, where the 'elder' was a certain Vasyl Maksymiv whose tenure, I later found out, was cut short, for he was quickly overcome by Petro Koval. Vasyl spent three weeks recovering in a barn.

In the village, there were also good customs or deeds called 'toloky' and 'lupeyki'. The word 'toloky' derives from the digging of potatoes, and 'lupeyki' meaning skin, in this case from corn. I was once given the opportunity to attend such a 'toloky', which involved people going to the owner of the homestead where they worked, usually early evening. The participants would dig potatoes for two or three hours for nothing. The owner would then invite everyone to his house for supper, after which music was played and people would dance until midnight.

The night I took part, I only brought a hoe, other people brought baskets too, and as I didn't have one I joined a young girl by the name of Hanya who had a large basket. Together we worked in tandem, filling her basket with potatoes, and then I would carry them onto a waiting cart. This we did until dusk.

In the owner's house I carried on my partnership with Hanya, we went for something to eat, and when the music started she tried to talk me into dancing. I said apologetically that I didn't know how to dance, but that didn't dissuade her, we later walked home together and she invited me to her house for lessons. Little did she know that had she gone to the library, she would have seen me dance. I later found out she was illiterate, for people like Hanya there was no room in a library, only perhaps to stand in a corner because nobody would ask her to dance.... another village custom.

Hanya was young, pretty and a pleasant girl, but when the library was being built in the village, the roofer took advantage of her and she later had his baby. This left Hanya a village outcast, everyone avoided her. I felt sorry and sympathetic to her plight because I was poor and many people avoided me too. From that day on I started to visit her, and in so doing I would now have two lovers in the village

I would see Malanka in the evenings, at various village venues, but I would never enter her house, I would stand by her well, keeping an eye on her front door, in case her stepfather, a mean- looking gamekeeper, showed up carrying a rifle on his shoulder. When I left Malanka, I would creep through the gardens unnoticed, so I wouldn't be seen by the neighbours or my mother. However, whenever there was a bright moon, I didn't have the courage to call, because her house stood out alone, without a fence or a tree, so on those nights I kept away in case I was seen. Otherwise, the following day the whole village would be talking relentlessly about the so-called 'scandalous behaviour'.

My village of Kaminne was known quite well throughout the district, namely for its library. I was present one night when a 'miracle' occurred. In the village was a large cemetery, surrounded by large pine trees. From a distance it looked as if it was covered by a large wreath. At the time the new library was being built, all the pine trees by the cemetery disappeared, then re-appeared on the site of the library. I am not talking about twenty or thirty trees, more like a hundred or so, and who cut them down, who transported them, whoever knew kept quiet. The police spent many weeks interviewing the whole village without finding the culprits. Later, the wood was used to build the library, yet the police still did not give up investigating. Even after the library was complete, the police would look for an excuse to close it for two or three months, or prevent an event from taking place.

The village isn't that big, yet it has two churches, a very Old Catholic one, with a crooked cross, which some people claimed was built in Hetman Mazepa's times. The other was a modern Evangelical one, apparently built because Bishop Chomyszyn transferred a very popular priest from the village, and in his place brought a mediocre one. Parishioners protested, but this didn't help, it came to the point whereby the village didn't have a priest because the Bishop wouldn't allow another priest from a different parish to serve mass. At one time the church was closed, and if someone died, the villagers would bury their dead without a priest.

During that time an evangelical missionary appeared, convincing people to leave Catholicism and join his flock. It was no wonder that some people believed in him and left the Catholic Church. In a short space of time, the village had two churches, all down to the persistent missionaries of the Evangelical Church who went around all the villages, and even many Greek-Catholic priests were converted. All it took was good leaders, and the masses would follow. Facts spoke for themselves, namely that a little village like mine, in such a short space of time, could send five parishioners to study in German schools, even two of my cousins went to such schools, but unfortunately their schooling came to an abrupt end when the Second World War broke out. This breakup was all down to the stubbornness of the Bishop, for not listening to his flock.

Autumn and winter passed, during the day I was with Peter practicing for our musical duo, in the evenings I was in the company of Malanka officially, then later with Hanya unofficially. When I visited Hanya, she would never have a light on, as there were no curtains in her home, we would sit in the dark so no prying eyes could see us. We would sit there for hours, talking and singing, which she liked, and in between she persisted in teaching me to dance.

One day my mother sent me to Hanya's house to collect a bundle of wood she had borrowed earlier, since without wood my mother couldn't cook supper. But once ensconced at Hanya's, I was in no hurry to go back home. In the meantime though, my mother was very much in a hurry and she couldn't wait any longer, so she made her way to Hanya's house. On reaching the house, she was shocked to see us both dancing in the middle of the room. When my mother saw this, she burst out in a barrage of obscenities aimed at Hanya, there was such a loud commotion that all the neighbours came running out to see what was happening. It is difficult for me to explain that moment, the closest explanation that I can give is that I wanted the earth to open up and swallow me. I had to do the 'walk of shame' in broad daylight, in front of all the inquisitive neighbours. Once I got home, there was no place for me to hide; my mother wouldn't stop calling Hanya every obscene word she knew under the sun. I couldn't stay in the house any longer, not in such an atmosphere, so I started to pack my belongings before the whole village learnt of my 'dancing lessons' and I left home.

CHAPTER 18
ON THE ROAD AGAIN

I decided to try my luck back at the sawill where I once worked in Nadvirna, but everything had changed. I found out from my uncle, who still worked there, that the company had lost a contract they had with Germany, the new management, was all in Polish hands. I was admitted into the office were everyone was polite towards me, maybe it was because of my uncle. They offered me a job working on a circular saw, but before the job could be confirmed, I had to sign up to a union and adhere to all their rules. They thought that an idiot stood in front of them and that I could be easily coerced. My uncle was standing next to me at the time, but didn't say a word to me for not signing the agreement. I didn't get the job.

To return to my village was an option, but I didn't have the inclination to go back into the hills, nor did I have the desire as there wouldn't be any work, so I decided to go to Stanislaviw and look for work there, at least I would be closer to Malanka. I didn't want to go into a bakery, I was a little frightened, perhaps even embarrassed, because people might have known me. I walked around the city until late at night in search of work, to no avail though, so I walked to the train station, found a bench, sat down as if I was waiting for a train, and spent the night there.

In the morning I walked to Tranitara Square for something to eat. I still had a little money, and, fortunately, I bumped into an old school friend who told me he worked on a building site. With his influence, I started a new job carrying bricks and lime up a ladder. The work was hard and dangerous, but I was pleased I had landed a job at such a critical time. We both lived at his mother's house in the village of Vovchynets. His mother treated me very well, like a son of her own. She often gave me advice where to buy, where not to, so I could save a little money. Whenever she washed her son's clothes, she would also wash mine.

After two weeks, I decided to write a letter to Malanka. Alas, she couldn't read, so the letter was read by a neighbour and inevitably the whole village soon knew. After a month I called in at a police station, as I'd been instructed to do so by the previous commission. At the police station I was told that I had a letter waiting for me in my home village, calling me up to join the army. That evening I went back to my village to collect my 'call up papers'. Word was already out in the village, because two more men of my year received the same.

I worked for another three weeks, returning to the village the day before my scheduled conscription date. I left my double bass with Peter, Malanka in tears, then caught a train to Poznan in Poland, soon forgetting Malanka and love.

CHAPTER 19
POZNAN (POLAND)

In Poznan I had to go before another commission and was assigned to heavy artillery unit. I was supplied with a uniform, boots, a small rifle, a bed and a large sack, to be filled with straw. Our barrack leader showed all the new recruits his white patch on his sleeve. The barrack housed twenty- one recruits, nineteen of whom were Polish and two Ukrainian, myself and Popenko were in the first barrack. Our barrack leader slept with us and, as luck would have it, he was the one who gave us the most grief, drumming into us how to make our beds and fold our uniforms. Our unit also contained 'regular corporals' who had their own quarters. These corporals knew nothing of life outside the army, all they knew was how to push around the new recruits, often ransacking our beds while we were out training. Before lunch our first task would be to remake our beds, and if any of the corporals didn't like somebody in particular, they would ransack the bed again.

I suffered in the beginning, until I got used to the army life. Admittedly, I had to sweat it out continuously to reach their standard, I didn't want to be considered a slob so I obeyed all the commands. Three weeks later I passed my compulsory training, and I even learnt the 'Poznan marching song' which we practised every Sunday with one of the corporals. I had a good voice and a keen desire to learn. I was quite tall, whenever we marched I was in the lead and would also be the one to start the drill. The first song we learnt was an old marching song called 'Poznan our love, so beautifully painted'.

We sang many more, most of which I have now forgotten, because I never had the occasion to sing them again. I was conscripted into the army in the month of March, and by June I was assigned to the fifty eighth infantry unit, which belonged to the fourteenth division. I had to swear allegiance to the Polish Government; I did this with 'my fingers crossed'. The Polish Army discipline was very strict, I even called it insane to myself when I saw the corporals needlessly picking on the new recruits, only they had the satisfaction of seeing young boys rolling through the mud, or having to wake up to 'false alarms' during the night. We would have our feet inspected, we had to wash them up to our knees every day, using just five basins shared by the whole company. Even so, I wasn't considered one of the 'slobs' though many a time I had my nose rubbed in the sand too.

We Ukrainians often met up with an older recruit from the fifty seventh unit who shared our kitchen in the yard. Once or twice we would start to sing Ukrainian songs. When there was talk about war breaking out, and then later the Ukrainian underground movement materialised in the Carpathian Mountains, our songs became more subdued, but to be fair we were encouraged to do so by the Polish officer.

Towards the end of June our company was given orders to march towards the German border to dig trenches. That day was very hot, we were all dressed in our full kit, the mobile kitchen pulled by two horses at the rear. It was an hour before nightfall when we arrived at a large homestead. We set up camp, the kitchen positioned in the yard, and the soldiers slept in barns and stables. I had just finished dusting myself down when I was called to stand sentry at the gate. I was relieved at ten, that's when I ate my supper, after which I found myself a comfortable place on straw in a barn. I wondered to myself why I was the first to be called on sentry duty, until I was awakened at two in the morning, to stand guard again, this time I cursed everybody and everything.

The following morning I awoke still tired, and another hot day ahead of me. After breakfast our whole company was sent into a field to harvest wheat and oats. Thinking I was a villager, the captain gave me a large scythe. I had never held one in my life, which the captain soon discovered for himself, so he took the scythe off me and gave it to somebody else, then sent me for a wheelbarrow and spade. In the wheat field stood red posts marking the area where we had to dig the trenches.

At lunch time we were sent in fours to the homestead, each one of us having to carry something besides his rifle. Lunch lasted an hour, then back to work in the fields until nightfall. On our way back to the homestead, the last two fours had to take the wheelbarrows.

On Sundays we didn't work, but at harvest time Sunday work was done voluntarily, for which the owner paid two and a half Zloty per day, the money I used to buy myself snacks. The army paid us eighty- five cents per ten days, enough to cover only toothpaste and boot cleaner, though if I wanted to write a letter, I didn't have enough money for postage. The soldiers who came from wealthy families had money and food parcels sent to them, but I didn't have that kind of luck, so I worked Sundays.

We dug the anti-tank trenches, for a full nine weeks without break, the nasty corporals and platoon leaders constantly got on our nerves. At the homestead there was no place to bathe and no river nearby.

We had waited a long time for war and it was difficult to imagine it coming, our rifles hadn't been cleaned for ages, some were already rusty. During the first two weeks nobody paid any attention, everyone was busy in the fields, but always had to take their own rifle with them, placing them in a box close to where they worked, occasionally brushing them by hand.

One Sunday there was an inspection of rifles, on that particular day I wasn't working. Instead, I had to clean my rifle before going into the fields. When we returned that evening, we had to take them to a warehouse where they were exchanged for new ones.

Every Sunday afternoon one of the senior officers gave a two- hour talk. They would speak about the German nation, how poor their country was, that they had to eat cats, dogs and crows, that Hitler spent money on tanks and armour while the nation lived in poverty.

At work we were forever being hustled in our work, being told that Hitler would be upon us the very next day. We had to dig deep trenches and lay barbed wire, and then everything had to be camouflaged, so the enemy wouldn't see us. Where we worked was prohibited to the public.

One early morning, we had just started work when a colonel on a motorcycle drove in from Poznan and brought the captain new orders. That day we had our lunch at eleven, we all thought that war was about to start, but everything around us was quiet. After lunch, we all got dressed in our full kit, all the wagons were packed and we marched back to our camp in Poznan. The march back was at a quicker pace, everyone thought it was because the Germans would soon be upon us, we didn't even sing a single song, we all thought the war had already started.

We arrived back at camp in the evening, where we found soldiers and civilians toeing and froing in a hurry. We were given supper but were not allowed in our barracks. These were occupied by reservists, so that night we slept in warehouses.

The following day we were given new uniforms, rifles and a portion of emergency rations. At this point, everyone now realised the seriousness of the situation that war could break out at any moment.

After lunch our company received new orders, a roll call in full uniform, and then we marched out of town to a place nicknamed 'ramparts'. The city of Poznan was built by the Germans, who had surrounded the city with ramparts. Our company was designated 'rampart seven'. In these ramparts the Polish Army kept ammunition and military memorabilia, and every rampart was numbered. Our company was responsible for heavy weaponry, rampart seven being in a strategic position to counter enemy fire. The machine gun we had was so heavy it took seven men to carry. I was the gunner and had a good aim, and if it hadn't been for the war, I would've been due for a 'gunner's badge'.

In our platoon were four machine guns, all of which fitted into one rampart. We rested the remainder of the day, the kitchen wasn't far, and now we received better food. We slept in the ramparts on camp beds, and then waited day after day, for the war to commence.

I was young, I didn't understand the significance of war, I thought the war would bring radical changes to my life, and so did many others. It was the first of September 1939 that long- awaited day. I recall that beautiful warm day very well, eating a pea mash from my mess tin. From that day on the world changed. It started at lunch time, just when our major, accompanied by his captain, was inspecting the machine guns while I was lying by my gun, eating my lunch. I didn't notice them walking overhead, I was meant to be guarding the gun. I quickly jumped to my feet, buttoned up my jacket, stood to attention and said 'Reporting gunnery number seven, everything checked and correct'. At that very moment, as I was standing to attention a loud boom could be heard in the distance. The captain asked me for a pair of binoculars, which I kept in my bunker by my rucksack. I ran down hurriedly to the bunker, returned with the binoculars, but at that very instant there was a loud explosion of a bomb, which threw me back down. I knew there and then that war had broken out. Rampart eight had been hit, leaving three dead and four seriously wounded. The major and captain were thrown off their feet, their only injury being covered in soil.

That day the German Air Force completely destroyed Poznan Airport and the power station. By the time I reached a higher point to survey the damage, there was no sign of aeroplanes, I saw the city on fire and people in a collective panic, running towards the woods.

That day I also witnessed a brave Polish pilot who shot down two German planes, then purposely flew into a third, both exploding on the ground. That was also the first and last Polish aeroplane I ever saw during the war. There was supposed to be a division of tanks in Poznan, but I never saw a single tank.

The Germans continued to bomb the city, but we didn't use our guns. That evening we buried the dead soldiers in the city cemetery. Afterwards, our company marched through the city, people threw flowers at us, presented us with chocolates and cigarettes, while some of the brave ones came up to us and kissed us.

CHAPTER 20
SAVING WARSAW

That night we left the city of Poznan and marched to defend the city of Warsaw. Since the Fourteenth Division was famous for its feats in First World War, we were chosen.

I couldn't understand why we had to leave Poznan in such a panic, until an officer told us what a great privilege the company had been bestowed on the company, and for that we should be grateful.

At the beginning of the War I was a gunner, but when we left for Warsaw the captain took me under his wing, and I was to communicate between him and the men. I accepted my new function with fright, but an order is an order, and I had no say in the matter. Every night we would march along side roads, as the main roads were blocked with carts and abandoned artillery. We often had to walk in single file through woods, a couple of times crossing small rivers, and once or twice the water was up to our waists. Every night we would march without stopping, unless one of our large guns got stuck in the mud, as a result of which they were difficult to pull. Those who could, would take a rest, some even tried to sleep.

Every daybreak we would set camp near a village. We hadn't seen a kitchen for eighteen days, the last being back in Poznan.

It was every soldier's duty to fend for himself, which would mean calling at homesteads, houses, raiding gardens and orchards. Since my promotion, I would accompany my captain to the officer's quarters, usually at a wealthy household. Food wasn't my problem, yet rest was. I was sent from one company to another with messages that we were going to defend Warsaw.

Another lucky reason for belonging to the artillery was that we didn't have to carry our rucksacks, as the rest of the infantry did. Ours were put on the small two wheeled truck carrying the heavy artillery, which in turn was pulled by a horse. All we held were our rifles and bayonet, not like the rest who carried all their packs. In his pack, each soldier carried a spare shirt, a blanket, a coat and all his own bits and pieces. After a time, many soldiers suffered with strap marks on their shoulders and blisters on their feet.

I walked every night, whilst my captain rode on a horse. Whenever the major and captain were hungry, I would be sent to people's houses, it wouldn't suit officers to beg for food. The Germans never gave us peace, they probably slept during the night, then they would catch us up the following day within an hour, in their motorised trucks and motor cycles. We never saw any German infantry; we only heard the roar of their large trucks and tank engines. Our biggest fear were the German aeroplanes, we couldn't see them from afar, as they used to fly low, firing their machine guns, decimating our ranks daily. I carried my own rifle all the time, and I often wondered whether it be better if I just lost it, as I never used it once during the War.

Everything we were taught before the War didn't help us at all, for two months we were drilled how to attack the enemy, from what distance, how to throw grenades at a tank. All these lessons were useless from the first day; the German Army was far superior. We had to march nightly, not like soldiers, but like prisoners of war, tired, hungry, without a kitchen and sleep. Amongst us were also the injured, those that could walk did so; the badly wounded were left behind in the villages.

All the roads leading into Warsaw were blocked. We often had to wait over half an hour to march two or three hundred metres before we stopped again. When we had these unscheduled stops most of the soldiers fell to the ground and slept. Once we started to move on, the officers would re-mount and catch us up, until the next time a few minutes later, we would again stop, drop on grass or in the mud, to rest or sleep, yet if any soldier strayed from the company, an officer wouldn't hesitate to shoot him like a dog.

We marched from Poznan to Modlin, the entire length of the way blocked with army personnel, and this was how the great Polish Army looked. In the chaos I even lost my Captain, when and where I didn't know. Our company was afterwards led by a Colonel from the reserves, he too rode on a horse, always keeping a pistol at the ready, and always shouting orders, hurrying us along. He too wouldn't give me any peace, often sending me with messages to the Major. In his quarters, as he slept I would stand near him on guard. My rucksack, containing my emergency ration, disappeared off the truck along the journey, To make matters worse, one day I tore my trousers on a branch as we trudged through a wood. In my rucksack I had a clean shirt, never having a chance to change it.

I met my Captain again, near the Vistula River, this time not on horseback, but on a military horse- drawn cart, and next to him sat his lady. He turned out to be very useful to me on this hard road. He told me about his sergeant, who had a large stack of food. The woods near Modlin were full of soldiers, it wasn't easy to find the platoon Sergeant. It took me a while to seek him out amongst all the military wagons, and as soon as he saw me, he expressed joy too, giving me a pair of trousers and a large portion of food, including bread, biscuits and dried coffee.

I managed to detach myself from my Lieutenant so that I could search the wood for a familiar face and ask for advice, because some of the fanatical officers were walking around, pistols in hand, forcing soldiers to swim across the River Vistula, where the Germans had destroyed the nearby bridge the previous day. The river was deep and wide, to swim across it with a rifle and rucksack required a very good swimmer and a hero. Yet the lieutenants didn't waste time choosing, they sent everyone they could across, to defend Warsaw.

I just about managed to escape from the fanatics, I entered the deep wood, threw off my gas mask in some bushes, as it only got in my way, then I was amazed to see an older Ukrainian from my company, who told me that he too escaped from the river because his officers had given instructions to build a raft to reach the other side.

In the woods, there were also many officers, some were with their wives and families, there were a few engineers and they were fully aware of the permanent danger. The Germans had herded us up to the edge of the riverbank, blowing up the bridge, penning us like animals. There was no other option but to wait for the Germans to come and take us to POW (Prisoner of War) camps. My new friend and I decided otherwise, we could see danger fast approaching us. In the woods we came across many wounded and even corpses, yet nobody made any attempt to dispose of them, it was simply every man for himself. Some of the soldiers thought of how to cross the river and escape from the Germans and avoid capture, we saw a few isolated incidents of soldiers, fully laden, trying to swim across the river.

It wasn't easy to escape from the wood, since there were flat, open fields on the other side, so we walked around in the wood until nightfall, giving others the appearance we were looking for something. We made our way to a barn where on entering, found it to be full of wounded soldiers, some of whom were lying on the floor, others were in carts, whereas we were miraculously still able- bodied, so we climbed into the hayloft and fell asleep. I can't remember how long we had slept and when I awoke, all I could hear were German voices shouting in the yard, not understanding a word. We quickly climbed down from the hayloft, and then saw all the Polish soldiers placing their rifles in a pile. From then on our world soon changed.

CHAPTER 21
CAPTIVITY

The Germans herded us like sheep from all directions into a large open field. They quickly surrounded a section of it with barbed wire, and this is where we stayed, under the open sky. I don't know how many of us were there, but I soon realised there was about an acre of beetroots growing next to an empty stable. In three days and nights all the beetroots were eaten and the stable was dismantled, everybody wanted a piece of wood so they could sleep on it. We didn't receive a scrap of food, our captors only brought us two or three barrels of drinking water every day. There were no toilets, we all simply went to the edge of the barbed wire fence where the German guards on patrol had to inhale the foul stench.

I had left my coat and other items back on the cart. On the second night it started to rain, we all got soaked from head to toe, and the ground soon turned into a quagmire. The little luck I did have saw to it that I still had in my possession a piece of bread and dried coffee which, as long as it lasted, would save me.

Civilians came up to the wire fence, looking for their loved ones and relatives. From them we heard snippets of news, why Poland had lost the War, largely because Britain and France had betrayed them. We were also told that we would be released, as soon as the war was over and, understandably, we waited with great anticipation for that day.

On the fourth day, after the Germans had taught us how to eat beetroots and sleep under an open sky, I saw a commotion by the gate, those in the front were ordered to stand in rows of four, I happened to fall into the first column, whereas my partner didn't like to walk through mud, he would much rather stand still and find someone to talk to. I was luckier, however, for having fallen into that column, because the Germans transported us to another camp.

Not far from the camp was a railway goods yard. The Germans distributed one loaf per four people, and were told to climb into the waiting wagons, one hundred prisoners per wagon, standing room only.

Luckily our journey wasn't too long; we arrived at the town of Ostrowo just before nightfall. As we were marched through the town, people approached us from both sides of the street, offering us bread and milk. I was the last to clamber into the wagon and, on leaving, I was at the front, one of the first to be handed bread, fruit, cigarettes and milk, all of great sustenance to me at the beginning.

In Ostrowo, the Germans accommodated us in large military sheds, sectioned off into rooms inside. In the rooms, all we found was a bare floor, so that's where we slept. We were given a daily ration consisting of a bowl of watery soup, coffee and a quarter of a loaf. As in the previous camp, civilians would stand by the gate, looking for their relatives. There were occasions when someone recognised their mother, wife or sister, but the Germans wouldn't allow anybody inside, or any prisoners outside, though giving food was allowed.

My room was close to a road, and from it I had a good view of the road. One day I had a brainwave. My plan was to write a letter saying I was a Polish Officer from Poznan, using my commander's address, adding that I was alive and well, but very hungry. In the letter I pleaded with whoever happened to find it to please forward it to my family. I wrote the letter with a small stone I found in the yard. I wrapped the letter around a stone, and then threw it through my window onto the road, just as a lady was passing with her child. I noticed the child pick up the letter and hand it onto his mother. In the camp we were referred to by number, not by name, so in the letter I added my number. It wasn't long before the sentry called my number, to report to the office.

The good lady Samaritan left me two loaves of bread, a packet of cigarettes, and a good piece of smoked fat. Now my problem was how to bring this food parcel into a room of thirty hungry souls, with only four Ukrainians inside. Once in my room, I broke one loaf into four, even though I didn't like one of the Ukrainians, but I kept the second loaf and the piece of fat under my head. That night, I broke off the loaf piece by piece and quietly ate the whole lot myself.

Once we left Ostrowo I received three such food parcels. God bless the good Polish lady who helped me tremendously. There were mornings when I would get out of bed, stand on my feet, feeling as if I was on the point of blacking out, so I would have to balance myself carefully, until my eyes began to focus.

Six weeks later we left Ostrowo and our new home was to be in Germany, a town called Neubrandenburg, Stalag No. 2A. The barracks hadn't been built yet, so we had to sleep in tents. We were all registered, had our heads shaven, all our clothes disinfected. Everyone had a number stitched onto his shirt, mine was 19318.

Jews also served in the Polish Army, in our Stalag they were constantly persecuted by the German guards. Out of all the inmates, they suffered the most, the Germans had no pity on them. At first there were many Jews who were easily recognisable, and there was no shortage of German thugs who knew how to kill innocent Jews. All the Jews in the camp were given the hardest jobs, building barracks, roads and toilets barefoot, using bits of cloth to wrap around their feet after all their shoes and boots were confiscated.

The food in the camp was terrible, potatoes were thrown into a large cooking vat, straight from the fields, unwashed and unpeeled, joined by a couple of cabbages and we would then have to eat this soiled soup. The Jews would be always last in line for food. By the time they reached their turn, all that was left of the soup was soil, so they would have to pick out the potatoes and cabbages with their hands.

Luckily, I didn't spend much time in the Stalag, some of us were sent to work on farms. In the Stalag there were many Ukrainians, and this gave me the opportunity to get to know more people. We tended to stick together, even when it came to being selected for work details, thus ending up going to Rostock together.

In our group headed for Rostock were a hundred prisoners, nine of whom were Ukrainians. We were marched along one road where we came across a group of young 'Hitler Youth' who spat at us as we walked past. We were taken to a large temporary holding area and were split into groups of, ten, fifteen and twenty. Once we were formed into groups, we were assigned to waiting homestead owners, each of whom was given instructions to provide us with supper. Upon selection we were given food, the only item on the menu being potato soup that had been prepared in large milk urns, and then dished out in large bowls from which we ate, three at a time sharing one bowl. We were a large group, a hundred of us, I don't know if the Germans overestimated the quantity, but we got three helpings.

One small problem within our group was that nobody spoke German, I knew a few words from my bakery days, then later I picked up a few more in Ostrow, but what I knew was hardly of any use. Fortunately, there was one craftsman who spoke very good Polish and he would translate everything for us.

The first night we slept in a large warehouse, and when we awoke we washed ourselves in the same bowls as the previous night's supper. We were given a little black coffee and a piece of bread, after which we split up into our groups and went to our allocated homestead. We nine Ukrainians had one Pole with us, the unfortunate soul, who probably didn't have any friends of his own, so he latched onto us.

It was still dark when we walked with our charge to the homestead, about four kilometres away. On the way there we only spoke in Ukrainian amongst ourselves, though our Polish friend hardly understood us. He walked behind us all, with his head down, locating apples on the grounds that had fallen off nearby trees but had not been seen or gathered, so we did instead. Luckily, our charge, who had been wounded in the war, allowed us to take as many as we could carry. It was late autumn by now, with ground frost visible some mornings, and when we reached our destination, a field full of beetroot, some of their leaves were white with frost.

There were already a few local workers waiting for us with their tools. We Ukrainians had never worked on beetroot in our lives. Our charge, however, had in the past but couldn't now, as he wasn't able to move one arm properly, while on the other arm he kept his rifle on permanent alert. Fortunately, having done the work before, the Pole showed us all what to do. Our charge gave us two rows each to work, so we began slowly to get into a rhythm. Although we were tired and hungry, at least now we had something to look forward to, our apples of course, though we ate the odd beetroot.

Around eleven that morning, the owner of the homestead approached us on his horse. He asked if anybody spoke German, to which our charge pointed to me, since I had tried to speak with him earlier. The owner had a few words with our charge, and then called me over, which I understood and followed. At the homestead, the owner led me to an open kitchen where potatoes were being boiled for pigs, while in another large pan our lunch was being cooked by a young girl. He asked me to taste the soup and say if it was too thin or too thick, I understood hardly anything, so I just replied 'good' in German. He then took me into a room, at the side of the laundry room; this is where we were to eat lunch. In the centre of the room was an already lit wood burner. I swept the room, collected plates, spoons and two large loaves from the kitchen, by which time our charge had brought our boys back for lunch. Our dining room only had a table and no chairs, and the owner told me to bring one of the other men to collect the soup. No sooner had we brought two buckets of soup into the room than the owner passed me a ladle and told me to serve everybody while he in the meantime cut the bread into thin slices. I gave everybody a full bowl, knowing that there would still be plenty left in the pan. We all ate standing, the owner looking at us and commenting 'smek gud' (good taste). The hot soup with the bread went down well, everybody had three bowlfuls.

After lunch, everyone except me went back to the beetroots, the owner kept me back in the dining room. The owner said many things to me, but I understood very little, just throwing in the odd 'yes'. Soon after, a man who worked at the homestead as a coachman walked into the room. I was to help him build 'our beds'. I later found out that the dining room was also to be our bedroom. We worked until nightfall, but didn't finish, the coachman collected our group in a carriage and took us back to where we'd slept the previous night, and this was to be our last night here.

The following morning, on the way to the homestead, we collected the remainder of the fallen apples. I worked again in the beetroot field, but after a short while the coachman arrived and took me back to finish the beds. By lunch we had finished building them, and after lunch we fitted barbed wire over our windows.

That night we didn't return to Rostock, but slept in our new room at the homestead, five on top, and five below. In 'our room' we had the wood burner going, on which we could dry our clothes and fruit. We also had two large cooking bowls we could cook food in. And so it was that every night after supper we would peel potatoes for ourselves.

We were quite happy with our new surroundings. We had more than enough potatoes to eat. In the second week I asked the young girl who cooked our soup to make it thicker. My new responsibility was to cook potatoes for the pigs, I would feed them twice daily and also clean up after them. There were about forty pigs in all, and as to the number of piglets, I lost count, as some were newborn, others were dying, and these ended up in the compost pile and buried. I was actually the 'swine master's' assistant, but I was also called the swine master.

My colleagues worked in the beetroot fields until Christmas. Our boss would always lock our room after supper, but never came back during the night to check. In the evenings we would cook for ourselves, wash our clothes, we had very little free time to speak of. There were occasions when we managed to steal a chicken or duck, as our house was next to a large chicken hut, and to break a chicken's neck was no problem. It was a pity that we didn't have a pan to cook it in, we had to use our eating bowls. As salt was in short supply, I would tell my swine master that I needed it for the soup we made in the evening, which he believed. You and I know full well chicken just doesn't taste the same without salt.

Our roommate, the Pole, had an embarrassing problem, something he probably picked up during the war, he used to wet himself in his sleep. The first night nobody knew, and nobody 'latched on' but when the air hot air from the stove caught it mid-air, our eyes felt the sting. The Pole owned up to his problem, so I explained to our boss that we needed to open our room windows. This came as a blessing in disguise, whenever in the future we cooked any 'special meals' we would just open the windows, and nobody was any wiser.

Whenever I worked with the pigs, there would often be an unfortunate death, which was subsequently dumped onto the compost pile and later buried. I told the boys that the next time a pig died, I would place it covered in a special spot, then later that evening we would recover it. Every evening, when gathering potatoes to prepare for the following day, two us would take a large basket and return with a large pig, unseen or unnoticed. Some of us would washing, others would be collecting wood, and I used to collect bread from the kitchen that was then shared equally amongst ourselves.

Around eight in the evening our boss would lock us in, returning at six thirty to wake us, leaving us alone all night. We didn't pick on the Pole for his unfortunate problem, he had enough to do daily, changing the straw in his bed, which was probably why he didn't have any close friends and so befriended us.

Every Sunday, while each of my roommates could have a lie in, I had to feed the pigs myself until lunchtime. My friends spent the day washing, sewing, even making their own gloves for the forthcoming winter. I enjoyed working with the pigs, it was close to the kitchen where I could always scrounge a nibble from the cooks, for I would always lend a hand and bring in wood and coal for their stoves.

Every week I would pick up a few more words in German, which helped me a great deal, firstly because I worked in the stable and didn't have to freeze outside, thus I didn't need gloves, and secondly, being close to the kitchen I never went hungry and would always manage to take a little extra for the boys.

Working in the beetroot fields was hard work, though the boys didn't complain, the owner and our immediate boss were satisfied. Once the beetroot season finished, the land was prepared for potatoes.

As winter began to set in, the boys were given different jobs, mostly undercover, grinding and threshing. These jobs would bring them closer to the kitchen, where three young girls worked. The only drawback was that nobody could converse with them, so I was often called to act as an interpreter.

In our group there were three married men who did most of the talking in the evening's, the remainder of the group were still wet behind the ears, even though we all served together in the army.

Each of us was different, with a different character, but we each thought we were better individually than the rest, every evening one of us would talk about his own life and experiences. Amongst us was 'brave' Vasyl, who once got himself into trouble in the kitchen. He knew two or three words of German and tried his luck with one of the girls by grabbing her skirt; the girl quickly turned round and thumped him in his face. There were three of us in the kitchen at the time, we saw everything and later got a few laughs out of this incident. Our boss didn't see what happened. Luckily, the girl didn't tell him, because everybody knew that prisoners weren't even allowed to talk to the Germans, let alone fraternise with them. There were well-known cases when a prisoner was shot without trial, so strict were the rules.

I had many opportunities to join in with their banter, they would nearly always ask me something, but unfortunately I didn't understand their 'dirty' words. My only concern was that the soup was thick enough, and that I could get my hands on a piece of bread, sometimes even a pinch of salt, because we used to cook every night and there was always a shortage of salt.

All the Germans at the homestead knew that we were Polish POWs, but nobody knew we were Ukrainian. Our 'employers' were all happy with our work, I was even told so. At the time I didn't have the vocabulary to explain who we were, I often had to use my hands to make myself understood.

I don't know if any other POWs had such good luck as we did in our homestead. On Christmas Eve we were told to finish work one hour earlier, whereupon we all washed and prepared ourselves for supper. I went down to the kitchen with George and our boss for our food. When we reached the kitchen, the owner and the girls had prepared us a small gift. On returning to our room, we saw that each gift had our POW number, the owner personally handed each gift to the appropriate recipient. My task was to thank the owner, at the same time explaining, that it wasn't our Christmas, as we were not Polish but Ukrainian, the only Polish person amongst us Mr. Incontinence.

That Christmas evening, we had a truly Christmas Supper, and afterwards our boss came to our room with the girls, and sang us Christmas Carols. Our presents were simple and humble, each one of us received two nuts, two apples, a few biscuits and a couple of sweets.

Shortly after Christmas we had a bit of a setback in the stable. One of the pigs had a leg stuck between two boards, and when it tried to pull itself out broke one of its legs. We tried to pull the pig out ourselves but couldn't, so in the end the swine master chopped the leg off with an axe, then killed it to stop it from squealing. Nobody took an interest in having a 'head count' for the pigs, there so many of them, so we buried the dead pig in the manure heap, then afterwards told George who devised a plan on how to bring the dead pig to our room unnoticed. That evening, when we collected the potatoes, usually in a large basket, we took half into the kitchen, and the remainder we kept for ourselves. First of all, we took the pig to the chicken coop, and when we were convinced that our boss was out of sight, we brought the pig into our room and placed it near the fire. No sooner had our boss had looked our room than George started to cut into the pig. The snag with dead pigs is that they are full of intestines etc., and nowhere to dispose of them since we only had three bowls and some of the group wouldn't allow George to carry on, frightened that if we were caught, we could face prison. George finally convinced all the doubters that he would do a clean job, but everyone would have to be careful not to overeat, we certainly didn't need any problems during the night, especially as there was only one toilet for us ten.

In the end, there were three protestors who didn't want anything to do with it, but once the pig was cooked, and they were offered freshly cooked meat, their protests were quickly forgotten. It was after midnight when we finished our banquet, everyone was grateful to George, not only had he prepared and cooked everything, he also came up with the idea of hiding all the good meat under the floor. To get rid of the smell, we placed wet socks on the warm oven so that by morning the steam was biting into our eyes, yet the smell had disappeared. At the time we also used to make a pea soup in the evenings, to which we would add meat; this would further disguise the smell. We removed all the pigs' intestines from our room, leaving no trace of our banquet.

We still kept a little of the pig, for our Ukrainian Christmas, nearly two weeks later. Our German captors didn't know anything about our Christmas. We began to prepare certain courses a few days before. On the day itself we celebrated our Christmas as best we could, finishing the day by singing traditional Ukrainian Christmas Carols.

A couple of days later our boss brought us forms that each one of us had to fill in, entering our date and place of birth, nationality etc. I managed to understand everything on the form, albeit with great difficulty. Our boss rewrote everything and then sent it to the Stalag. A couple of days later, we received notification that the following morning we would be taken back to the Stalag, then from there back home.

The following morning we left the homestead with our Polish 'houseguest' and were taken by horse cart to Rostock train station, where another guard was assigned to us and escorted us back to Neubrandenburg, from where we walked to the Stalag.

On our way to the Stalag, we all felt happy that we would soon be free and returning home. There were no protests that the Russians were now our rulers, everybody was so excited to get back home as soon as possible.

On arrival at the Stalag, we saw many changes, for instance wooden barracks now stood where once our tents had once stood. We were marched to the new part of the camp, separated from the old with barbed wire. There were many barracks, some of which didn't contain beds, we noticed other people walking around, but mostly towards barracks, as it was snowing. Inside the barracks were many Ukrainians and Belorussians, who too were looking forward to returning home. When we arrived it was already after lunch, so that day we received nothing to eat, no lunch, no supper.

The next morning nobody woke us, everyone was up early, as there was no heating in the barrack, nor were there any blankets, everybody slept in their clothes. The lucky ones who had coats could cover themselves, but the guards would tell these prisoners to leave their coats behind, that they wouldn't need them because they were going home.

After lunch we would walk from barrack to barrack, looking for someone we might know from our own villages. All of a sudden we heard a whistle, and within two or three minutes the guards were surrounded by two hundred men. I couldn't hear what was being said from my position, all I heard was that soon lunch would be served. The guards went through all the barracks, telling everybody to stand against the wall and wait for lunch.

We waited in the freezing cold for two hours, until we saw a truck approaching with large urns of soup. Those of us who had remembered to bring our plates received soup, those who had forgotten had to wait until the end, but by then there was nothing left. The guards also hurried the people with food to the other side of the camp, so that nobody could return for a second helping.

After lunch we were promised bread, but to receive it we had to write down all our numbers so they would know how many people were there. Nobody had anything to write with and no list was handed over, so we went without supper once again.

There was a constant influx of new prisoners, almost every hour. Our original group was now six, three of the others had found friends from their own village.

At about nine the following day, a prison guard entered our barrack, counted two hundred of us, then led us to the main camp to be washed and disinfected.

Just before lunch, a guard entered our barrack and asked if anyone spoke German. Some of us had been in captivity close to six months, many knew the odd word, but nobody had the courage to speak up. My friends pushed me nearer and nearer to the front, enticing me to volunteer. Without warning George raised his hand and pointing at me. The guard quickly asked me something. I was so frightened that I didn't hear a word he said, just replied 'Jawohl' (yes in German), then the guard told me to accompany him, which I of course understood. I followed him into a warehouse, from where we took three large sweeping brushes to sweep the barrack. The guard left me at the gate, then returned shortly, with a few sheets of writing paper and a couple of light bulbs, as our barrack was without lights. On our way back to the barrack, the guard told me to write the name and number of everyone who was in this room.

My friends quickly helped me, and by evening, we had all 216 'residents' names and numbers. At supper that evening, our barrack received 216 pieces of bread, one loaf to four inmates. In the end I had three and a half loaves left; a few people who had registered in our barrack had also done so in another. There were two people in the next barrack who had not registered, so I gave them half a loaf, leaving three loaves for our group of six.

Bread in captivity is a very expensive commodity. I didn't have the moral strength to be honest enough to return the three loaves to the guard, even though a few people had seen us hide the bread in our beds. There were two hundred beds in our barrack, there were groups who would make a 'divide' separating themselves from everyone else. In our barrack, we had six small light bulbs and two wood stoves in the middle.

It's common knowledge in captivity that the two biggest killers are lack of food and lack of heat, so every inmate would seek the warmest place for himself. Our prison guard instructed me to take the first bed by the door, leaving the second space for my secretary. In the front 'cage' were four beds, which I reserved for myself and three friends, the other two friends had to find space elsewhere. Now I needed a secretary, as I was now the person in charge of the barrack. For my secretary I chose a Belorussian, I'd noticed his neat handwriting when making the barrack registration.

We Ukrainians and Belorussians had the privilege to return home, in exchange for German POWs, an agreement Hitler had reached with Stalin, which was why we two nationalities were grouped together. In the main camp stood seven such barracks, each housing two hundred people, with fewer Belorussians than us, and they tended to stay within their own kind. In my barrack, out of 202 inmates 36 were Belorussians, and amongst them was one intelligent person who spoke better German than me. He didn't volunteer but just lived and slept close to his group of friends, carrying out his secretarial duties.

I had an allowance of ten marks, which I shared with the secretary. My closest friends also had 'functions', one would dish out food, a second friend was the first aid orderly, a function allowing him to escort the sick to the 'hospital', another was the postman whose task was to collect all the barrack letters from the post office, while the last friend took care of both wood burners, his responsibility was to bring coal and clean the burners. All my friends had cushy indoor jobs; they didn't have to work outside in the cold.

The Germans didn't give anyone food for nothing, it had to be earned. After a couple of days, we were transported to the airport to clean the runways of snow; some of us cleared the streets in the town too. Every morning the guards would have a roll call, then inform us of the day's work programme. The unlucky ones with no indoor function, especially those sent to the airport, worked all day clearing snow. Their lunch consisted in a litre of watery soup, and they were expected to work the whole day in freezing conditions. Those assigned to the town had it a little easier, as it wasn't so open and cold, there was always a way to find a little shelter, find something in the street such as the odd copper or a 'fag end' which could later be exchanged for a piece of bread or potato. There were some who would exchange their last crumb of bread for a cigarette, and usually they never lived to see 'freedom'.

Two weeks later a special commission arrived with news about our repatriation. My barrack was number 202 which was the first one to be called. That day, every 'resident' was excused from work, the guard told me to write down the numbers of the first fifteen people to be interviewed. They were marched through the gate into the main camp, where there was a specially designated barrack, containing a waiting area and three other rooms.

The commission comprised three men, two German officers and a Ukrainian, called Vorona. The commission was very thorough. Thus, if one of the Germans had any suspicions, they would send them to Vorona, who didn't allow anyone through. Among the Ukrainians, which came to light later, were many Poles who had lived in Halyczyna (a region of Western Ukraine under Polish rule then), spoke good Ukrainian and also wanted to return home, but the Germans didn't allow Poles to leave, only Ukrainians and Belorussians.

Vorona, if I'm not mistaken was from Tomach, and no Pole could trick him or convince him otherwise. It wasn't enough to say that you were born in such and such a place, Vorona would bombard them with questions like when was Ukrainian Christmas and Easter fell, to recall Saints' feast days, how to make the sign of the cross, recite the Lord's Prayer and other prayers, so it was difficult for a Pole to become a 'Ukrainian'. The 'failed' Poles would leave the commission in tears, and would later be sent back to work on the homesteads.

The commission would 'pass' approximately twenty people per day, they were in no hurry, they were waiting for the Russians to send all the Germans who lived in their territories. Spring had arrived and the commission was still at work, there were rumours that a large number of Germans had returned from Russia, but the Germans were still not convinced, nor did they trust us, so we just waited anxiously.

There were over two thousand Ukrainians at the Stalag, and we were all ready to return home, tired of the cold and hunger, everybody dreamt that they would be released as soon as possible, to finally return home.

At the Stalag we were allowed to write a postcard home, every two months, just to say that we were alive and well, give our camp numbers and nothing else. There were a few lucky ones who even received parcels. If someone received a parcel, his number would be called out at the evening 'roll call'. He would be excused from the following day's work and would instead, be taken by a guard and a 'postman' to the post office, where only he in person was allowed to collect a parcel.

There were very few such lucky men, but when such an occasion happened, it was accepted as a treasure. When parcels usually arrived from Ukraine, each one was wrapped in material and the address was written in blue ink. The parcel would usually contain biscuits, salami, tobacco, dried fruit and smoked fat. Whoever received such a parcel, would suddenly discover he had many so-called 'friends' from the same village, often in the beds next to his, everybody looking and hoping that a morsel might come their way, but not everybody could be pleased, there were two hundred people in a barrack, so everyone had to understand. Hunger has very big eyes, and an even bigger stomach, especially to a young person in captivity. A young person dreams day and night of where he can find something to eat, for it is difficult to sleep on an empty stomach.

Every evening, one of my functions was to distribute the bread, one loaf per four men, being very careful that one quarter was not bigger than another. I also served watered soup at lunch time, everybody demanding a ladle from the bottom of the pan where it was thicker. In as much as I would've liked to, I just couldn't do this, I always tried to be honest. Even so, it was difficult, I too was one of the hungry ones. I helped my friends by sheltering them from the freezing jobs outside, by giving them easy indoor jobs, but I couldn't give them extra bread or soup, I didn't have anything to give, I couldn't give what I didn't have.

When someone received a parcel from home, he would usually bring it to the barrack, where there were very few people since most were out on 'work detail'. The fortunate recipient would normally offer me a 'gift' but these occasions were very rare.

Weeks went by until one day a bulletin was posted that we were to travel to Mecklenburgische Forrest, about fifty kilometres away, for temporary work, as each day there was a greater influx of new prisoners, and room in the camp was running out. The new work detail was accepted with enthusiasm, as everyone knew a man wouldn't go hungry working on a homestead. From the letters we received from home, we knew on what date our Ukrainian Easter fell, hoping to spend that time with our loved ones. In the meantime, we had to endure Latin Easter in the camp, hungry as ever.

Towards the end of May I was told by a guard that our transportation home was not ready, so we were given work near the Stalag, to ensure that we were not far when the departure date came.

Every day trucks would arrive from various homesteads, collecting twenty to thirty men, accompanied by three or four guards. After a few days, it was my turn. Six of us attached ourselves to a group, and we were driven to Neustrelitz, a town where we were to be auctioned. When we arrived, the homestead owners were already waiting, we felt like slaves being sold off to Turks. Each homestead owner approached us, asking for workers he needed, somebody to work with horses, others to look after pigs and cows, and so on.

Our group of six was split into two, I was taken by a miller because I was a baker, George went as a gardener, and Vasyl was ordered to work with horses, whilst the other three went elsewhere. It's difficult for me to paint a detailed and vivid picture of how we were selected. Each homestead owner was looking for strong men to work and yet, although we were young, we were starved, each bearing a sunken face and looking emaciated. Every homestead owner walked around with a list, writing down the number he wanted, helped by our prison guards. I naturally wanted to be included in the same group as my friends, but it was easier said than done because these homesteads were small, and their owners only took two or three men.

I was in demand with the homestead owners because I could speak a little German, so I was used as an interpreter, helping them choose the right person. The German homesteaders engaged in many arguments, fighting over a certain man for his trade. Today, looking back, it was difficult to differentiate the Turks from the Germans. In the books I had read about Turks, it was written that they paid for their prisoners, whereas the Germans took us for nothing.

Although the miller pulled me aside, the guard wouldn't release me until the last, and all my friends kept close together. In the confusion, a young German officer approached our guard and told him he required ten men to work in a flour mill and a sawmill. This gave me the opportunity to collect all my friends and keep us all together in one group. I was retained until the very end when all the business was finished. All my friends, the homestead owner and his miller waited for me. Our group was the last to leave, with one overseer on a village horse- drawn cart.

Within an hour we arrived at the sawmill, and the boys' faces dropped from the very first minute, we soon became aware of how the Germans treated people. We were given a room on the river bank where horses were kept. We all protested, including our guard that we wouldn't sleep on a concrete floor, the floor was soaking wet, three bundles of wet hay were strewn in an attempt to hide it, and the windows were covered with wooded shutters. We refused to enter the room in protest. Shorty afterwards, the owner appeared and launched into an argument with the guard, who in turn warned the owner that if better accommodation wasn't found for us, he was prepared to take us back to the Stalag on foot. The young sawmill owner exploded, a couple of times threatening the guard with his hand. Luckily, the owner's sister intervened and made us a soup using white flour, but when it was served, weevils could be seen floating freely on the surface. I used to see them frequently in the bakery since they tended to breed in old flour. There were two tables prepared for us outside, but when the soup was served and we noticed the weevils, we stopped eating and I pointed them out to the guard. Convinced of what they were, the guard approached the owner and showed him, the latter gloomily dropping his head in embarrassment without saying a word. The tables had promptly turned, the guard this time raised his voice, threatening the owner that if better accommodation was not given to us, he would take us back to the Stalag, and no more workers would be offered to him.

The owner finally had to surrender to our demands and allocated us two better rooms, without any barred windows, and naturally we showed no objection to this new arrangement, even when we had to cover the windows with barbed wire.

The new accommodation turned out to be better than we expected. Under our room was a small cellar, which had an opening used as a chute for potatoes. To reach the cellar, access was only gained from our room through a trapdoor. We quickly covered the trapdoor before being called for our 'second' supper, this time the soup was with potato, and quite thick.

We only had one guard watching over us at the sawmill, only Vasyl who worked with the horses was allowed to collect thick pines from the wood and deliver them to the sawmill. My function at the saw mill was to keep the furnace going, using all the cuttings and scraps of wood, and ensure that the furnace was at its correct working temperature. Although the work was easy, there was no opportunity to find any extra food.

By the sawmill was a rarely used water- driven mill. We were split into two groups, four of us worked inside, whilst the remainder toiled outside, so this meant the guard couldn't keep an eye on all of us. Convinced that none of his prisoners had any interest in attempting to escape, he would occasionally sit and doze close to the furnace to keep warm, placing his rifle onto the ground next to him.

During the first week, one member of our group became ill and had to be taken to a doctor. The guard couldn't escort him and the owner said he didn't have time, so one of the locals took him. It turned out that our friend had an operation on his appendix, and was in hospital for two weeks.

On his return, he told us many stories, news which we were unaware of, about the Polish woman in the next bed who worked at a homestead with twenty other women, in the neighbouring village. Once discharged from hospital, he travelled back in the company of the Polish woman and saw for himself where she was dropped off first. This incident gave us an idea on how best to use the trapdoor into the cellar, especially as we had already seen the surrounding area by night.

That first night, two of our 'bravest' left our room to seek the neighbouring homestead. The remaining eight, sat up all night in fear, waiting for their return. The 'heroes' returned almost at dawn, tired and wet up to their waists from the morning dew without, sadly for them, finding the other homestead. The following night three of us tried, including one from the previous night, so that we wouldn't go in the same direction. This time we soon found the village and the homestead; it was already late, we couldn't leave earlier because we would have been seen. We approached a lit window and, as we stood next to it, we could hear Polish being spoken, men shouting at each other while playing cards. We didn't have the courage to go inside, instead we crept towards a bush opposite a door, thinking that one of them sooner or later have to come out. All we could hear was ace, king, queen, or one, two, etc. Unexpectedly, a Polish girl stepped outside, and began calling a cat, we all froze as the girl yelled out of fright 'Jesus and Mary'. We were ready to bolt, but then another Polish girl walked out of the building and, after a moment of hesitation, they both recognised our Polish uniforms and figured we were escaped prisoners. We were instantly invited inside, but we were too frightened to enter in case somebody turned us in.

Our first visit was short, we didn't want to push our luck, so we quickly returned again as on the previous night, wet up to our waists and forced to use the fields to avoid the roads. It was one in the morning when we returned, the other boys stayed up waiting for us, but when they saw our wet trousers they burst out laughing, saying that we had got wet for nothing. It wasn't until we showed them half a loaf that they believed us. Before we left the girls we asked them to keep our visit to themselves, promising we would visit them every second day, and also begged them for bread because we were very hungry and had to work very hard.

Until we met the Polish girls we were always famished, unable to find any extra source of food; we certainly couldn't eat wood or sawdust. Naturally, we told them how eternally grateful we were, and in return they were very sympathetic towards us. We couldn't leave our rooms until after eleven, when it was dark and safer, and three of us would take it in turn to visit.

The Polish girls all worked in the fields, only a small wood separated us, and all the time we visited them we never came back empty- handed. They knew beforehand when we would come, I would always whistle at lunchtime, this was our signal, that a visit was imminent.

Our arrangement lasted until after the harvest, we had beans and peas and were able to cook them on our stove, our guard didn't mind. On Sundays we were allowed to swim in the river and even sunbathe afterwards, life became more bearable for us, the greatest difference was that we didn't starve.

Unfortunately, all good things come to an end. One Saturday, three homesteaders came to visit, one of them was the first miller I was supposed to have worked for. I later found out that our present homestead owner was a 'big fish' in the 'party' so he could do much as he pleased, without much opposition. Our place was taken by ten French prisoners and two guards. Our group was split into four. I chose George and Vasyl, as we three had become close friends, so we set off with our new 'boss' to his homestead. We had a room without any covering over the window while the owner slept in the adjoining room and would lock our door every night.

Conditions were very good, we had plenty to eat; managing two breakfasts, one in our room, the second in the kitchen, and even an afternoon snack. I had never worked in a flour mill, though as an assistant I wasn't bad. George's family owned their own homestead back home, so the new boss was very pleased with him. Never having lifted a finger back home, except watch his mother do the milking, Vasyl struggled and, in order to stay with me and George, he clearly had to adapt quickly. Our new boss also owned a few fields and would occasionally send us to work them. Our guard only came twice a week to check on us, so security was quite lax, even on a Sunday we sometimes helped the German farm workers, for which we were paid in German Marks, and with this money we could go to any shop and buy whatever we liked. The local village people got to know us, the owner would also allow us on a Sunday to use his little boat along the river.

One Sunday in the late summer, George and I sat on a bridge, trying to catch fish. Riding towards us on bicycles were two Polish girls we had met in the homestead. When I left the previous homestead I had written to the girls, informing them of our new address, and that's how they found us. We were not allowed to talk to girls, though this did not dissuade us. We all went back to our homestead where I told the owner that one of the girls was my sister. The owner invited us all into the kitchen, and we were quickly given a tasty snack, after which we invited them into our room. However, our boss stopped us, saying that we were prisoners and he was responsible for us. We spoke to the girls outside for a couple of hours until they left, we never saw them again.

That autumn we were assigned a different guard, who proposed that we sign papers and become 'civilian workers' because there was little hope of us returning home, and if we agreed, we would also to have to wear the letter 'P' . The three of us categorically refused his proposition, and remained prisoners of war. On hearing our remark, our boss was also disappointed, he too would have preferred us to sign and become free workers.

Overall, our boss was very satisfied with all three of us, we too were happy with the fact that we had plenty to eat, bread and butter every day, we drank milk, occasionally stealing and drinking the odd chicken egg. When our field work had finished and there was no work in the flour mill, I would help George to cut wood in the saw mill or help Vasyl in the stables.

One evening the guard rode along on his bicycle and called us all over to see the owner. He informed us that he had received new instructions that he would be taking us back to the Stalag the next morning.

I immediately realised that this was because we had refused to wear the letter 'P'. To return back to the Stalag in winter was certainly not something to look forward to.

In the Stalag we met many fellow prisoners who had arrived earlier, but nobody knew the reason, especially as to return home had now become an impossible dream. To make our arrival even worse, there was already a sprinkling of snow on the ground. We were assigned to a different barrack where we were given lunch, and fortunately we were able to bring food from the homestead in our rucksacks. I recognised many familiar faces in the barrack where the 'leader' was Ukrainian and well respected by the inmates. He had escaped from a homestead during the summer, and when recaptured he was put into 'solitary confinement'. Although his German was poor, he kept strict discipline in the barrack. I learnt a lesson from this and understood what qualities in a man the Germans looked for.

In the barrack my friends started to tease me, saying that we were off to work the next day, we would find it too cold to sleep at night and that our 'barrack leader' would take us into his room. I didn't take to heart what was said about our old guard, but George had bumped into him, recognising him instantly, then came looking for me. On seeing me, he shook my hand firmly as if we were 'old buddies' and took me to his barrack that same night.

George and Vasyl spent the night in the assigned barrack before joining me the following day. My old guard had spent all his time in the Stalag, he'd been badly wounded during the war, and he was very pleased to see me again. At that time he didn't have a 'barrack leader' as prisoners were just starting to return, but he remembered me well, he had even inquired about me, knowing full well I was due to return. Once again, unexpectedly, he became useful to me, although it didn't please everybody. Old friends soon recognised me, even the three from our original 'ten' they all greeted me amicably and were happy to be together again.

The following morning, George and Vasyl joined me and again went back to their old functions in barrack 202, though our barrack was now number 25. Almost every hour there was a fresh influx of prisoners, usually Ukrainians and

Belorussians, our guard had told me that we were to be released from camps and become free workers in Germany, going back home wasn't even a dream.

Freedom for a prisoner is a great happy feeling. When we first heard the news, people jumped with joy, soon the hardship of being a prisoner would come to an end. Even though going home was no longer an option, imprisonment, with the roll calls, the appeals, the cold and hunger that had lasted eighteen months, had nevertheless taken its toll on everyone, it had all gone for too long. Now everybody was walking from barrack to barrack, searching for friends, but the Germans were in no hurry to release us. Life again returned to how it was, sending us to work, mostly clearing snow, as we'd had a heavy snowfall after Christmas, every day workers were taken to Neubrandenburg to clear the streets.

One evening , soon after the Ukrainian Christmas, the usual evening foot patrol instructed to inspect the barracks was walking outside our barrack, when one of them noticed a prisoner urinating outside and not in the toilet. No sooner had he seen them than the prisoner ran off. The guards shot into our barrack, yelling and demanding who the culprit was, nobody owned up.

In the Stalag, whenever an officer entered a barrack, whoever first noticed had to shout 'Attention' whereupon all the prisoners would jump off their beds and stand to attention. As the 'barrack leader', I had to quickly run to the officer, present him with the barrack number, the number of prisoners and to say, 'All present and correct'. This particular officer turned on me, shouting aggressively what kind of discipline was present, when he had only just seen a prisoner urinating by the barrack. Unfortunately, I didn't understand him properly, and instead of shouting 'Attention' when the officer walked into the barrack, I asked the prisoners who the culprit was. Because of the misunderstanding, the officer called everybody out into the snow, ordered them to stand at attention, made them march and then lie into the snow. In the meantime, I felt and stood there like an idiot, watching my fellow inmates rolling in the snow, all because I didn't understand what the officer had said.

A few days later I noticed a guard escorting an old friend from home town, Kaminne, called Dmytro Slywczuk. We recognised each other instantly and hugged one another like two lost brothers. An officer happened to notice this and quickly ordered everyone back to their barracks. Dmytro was assigned to another, but the following day I managed to bring him into mine, where I gave him a function as a food helper just so that he didn't have to clear snow. I treated him as my closest friend, and we remained so until the spring.

During my second stint at the Stalag I noticed life had changed for the better compared to the first time. When the French prisoners arrived, the food became better, there was no soil in the soup, and even a little fat could be seen floating on the surface. The French were treated as prisoners under a multinational agreement, something that didn't apply to the Polish Army. Inevitably, the Germans treated us like animals. Nonetheless, everybody in the camp benefited from the arrival of the Red Cross. This was the first time in my life that I'd seen Ukrainians receive more privileges than the Poles. The French prisoners received many food parcels through the Red Cross, containing nuts, biscuits, marmalade, cigarettes, butter and dried milk, and all these goods were distributed by the French themselves, not the Germans. Every Sunday after lunch, the French would visit the barracks, firstly handing out to their own, then came our turn, I would take eight men from my barrack with blankets and share out the food among the inmates. After me, other Ukrainian 'barrack leaders' would queue, at the very end would be the turn of the Poles, who only had three barracks and very often, by the time it came to their turn, there would be precious little left. Why we had such privileges from the French I could never understand, even until this day.

In our Stalag, prisoners who held leadership roles like me were not allowed beyond the perimeter of the camp, which was why in our camp many Poles worked in various positions as sub-officers, but our captors didn't feed anyone for nothing, so they were given work in the kitchens, warehouses, and the post office. In short, these were the easy jobs, but there were also the hard jobs such as digging graves for the dead in the cemetery, which was made more difficult in the winter months. There was also the unenviable job of emptying all the camp toilets, which meant that the prisoners had to carry all the toilet waste in containers on their backs and then empty them along the perimeter fence. The Poles kept the unsuitable and the unqualified inmates for these tasks to one side.

During my second winter at the Stalag, there were two barracks full of these prisoners who had the easy jobs, everyone had some sort of function, some of the jobs were good, in other words the ones that came with 'perks', while others were not as desirable. In the winter months we were usually sent to the airport or to the town to clear snow. We were told the previous day how many prisoners were required from each barrack, which I would organise. Nobody liked to work during the winters months, but there was no other alternative because we had to fulfil our orders.

One evening a guard ordered me to have ten men ready for the following day for 'post commando'. Although I had never heard of such an order, I had ten prisoners ready the following morning. When someone leaves the camp, they are usually given lunch at work, returning to the camp for supper. That evening, one of the prisoners who had returned from the 'post commando' called me aside, handed me a large chocolate and asked if he could be sent to the same work detail tomorrow. After 'roll call' another prisoner who had been on the same work detail gave me something, then asked the same question. At that time, I couldn't work out what the attraction was, until a guard told me that Polish sub-officers had been in charge of this work detail, but many of them stole and were caught by an inspection at the gate, resulting in their dismissal from work. With this information, I forewarned my workers, not to fall into the same trap as the Poles.

As Polish POWs, we were allowed to write one postcard every two months, a very short one at that, saying we were well and well fed. All the post was sent to the main post office in town, where the sorting was done by the Polish contingent, but when they were caught their work was taken over by Ukrainians. The work was done by ten men who would leave in an open truck escorted by two guards. From the town back to the camp was about four kilometres uphill. The guards would sit in the back with ten of our men, then they would pick on four or five parcels, break them up and share them with our prisoners, they did exactly the same with the Poles. The chosen parcels were from France, Belgium and Holland, usually small but highly rewarding. Most of the guards were aware of the scam, and so they would patrol the main gate themselves, allowing the truck entry without inspection, obviously knowing full well they would later be rewarded.

Prisoners from my barrack did this work for two months, every day I would be offered a gift, which in all honesty I didn't refuse. Let people judge me as they wish, those who have never been prisoners or ever gone hungry, let them try and refuse such precious gifts. The lesson to be taught is that parcels should be securely packed, the best packaging being wrapped in material. Ukrainian parcels were never tampered with, not only because of the packaging but also for its contents. Parcels arriving from France and Belgium contained chocolate, cigarettes, biscuits. The Ukrainian ones contained biscuits, warm underwear, gloves, etc. A small parcel was easier to break into and its contents hidden in pockets.

My close friend George wasn't happy what I shared with him, but I had another four friends too. He pleaded with me to be sent to the post office, although his function in the barrack was a 'first-aid orderly'. When George finally went, he shared everything with me only. I gave my friendly guard many things, he had a family in the town, so everything I gave him came in handy. After two months I had accumulated many such gifts, so shortly before we were informed of our imminent release, I went into town with my guard to buy a suitcase, as there wouldn't be enough room in the rucksack I arrived with.

Imprisonment and captivity are unbelievable moments in one's life, when most people think only of themselves. I survived, I was lucky, maybe I fell on good fortune, or will God punish me for my actions?

Today, I regret not having the strength to refuse the gifts I was given. I blame the German guards, it was they who taught firstly the Poles, then we Ukrainians, how to steal. There were many sons and husbands waiting for a parcel, and for many it never arrived, that parcel would disappear en route, nobody knew why, nobody would question why, or even look for it, for it was a time of war, it was a time of hunger, shame and blame.

Stalag 2-A Neubrandenburg Mecklenberg 53-13 was near the town of Neubrandenberg, I don't know how many people were registered there, I had no idea. I remember my number being 19318. Towards the end of our captive days, I do remember seeing the number 80,000 plus.

In the month of March 1941 the Germans started releasing us into civilian life, allowing us the rights of a free worker, this was the privilege given to us by the Germans. I was also pleased that the stealing would come to an end, and that it would give me some peace of mind.

In the next couple of months, the Stalag was to become more of an employment exchange, there would be invitations to join workforces in towns and cities, working in all types of industry, and in villages, offering work in farms and homesteads.

By April, a large number of prisoners had left, there were incidents whereby tradesmen like tailors and shoemakers were required, they had the right to apply wherever they liked. Those prisoners who didn't have a trade could apply to work at a farm or factory, though it was important to stay with their friends.

Dmytro, George and I also waited for a good opportunity to find work, so that we could stay together. I became a very close friend with George, we lived through good and bad moments in the previous eighteen months. I also cared for Dmytro because he was from my home village. We didn't have long to wait, we read an advert that a bakery was looking for two bakers in Wismar. I read the advert on Tuesday, and on Thursday, transport was laid on for Wismar. I was looking forward to find work in my own trade, but my dilemma now was what to do with Dmytro and George. When the time came to make a decision, I decided to take Dmytro under my wing as he spoke little German, whereas George was more resilient and would be able to look after himself. Dmytro agreed to come with me, even though he had never seen the inside of a bakery. I filled the necessary forms for both of us, and left the rest to God's will.

I spent two nights with Dmytro, trying to talk him through the various procedures in a bakery, how to mix dough, how to scale, sieve flour and everything else, I knew his German was poor but, fingers crossed, maybe he could trick his new master. I explained my intentions to our guard, and he was to send George to Wismar at the earliest opportunity, as soon as a job arose.

I had accumulated a suitcase of commodities over the last two months, there were thirty two of us leaving that day, and we still had to go through security, but my guard carried my suitcase through earlier. On that day the 15th of April 1941, I became a free man.

CHAPTER 22
FREEDOM - WISMAR

Dmytro and I travelled to Wismar, by train with just the one guard, who on that occasion was without his rifle; there were thirty two of us travelling. George stayed behind in the Stalag for another week. When we arrived, our new employers were already waiting. Our guard stayed to help us find the right people, I helped with the translations, for by that time my German was good. Unfortunately, Dmytro was given a job in a small bakery, where the owner and two bakers helped him; I was given a job in a larger bakery.

My new boss, who was young, showed me into a nice room above the bakery, which I had to share with another baker. I started work at four in the morning, but my problem was that my boss wanted to see what I could do, and told me to mix dough by machine. I had never seen an electrically operated mixing machine in my life, so I stood by the machine, clueless and explained my problem. The boss then told one of the other bakers to place some flour into a large bowl, and I was to mix the dough by hand. This was no problem for me, and when I had finished, the owner knew immediately that I was a baker.

However, Dmytro had a bigger problem, he didn't really have a profession, he could repair a shoe or boot, and he played well on the cymbals, but the only time he'd seen dough being mixed by his mother at home, probably without him paying much attention. His first morning, started much the same as mine, his boss asked him to mix dough. Fortunately, the mix didn't turn out too bad because he followed my instructions. His luck ran out at the next stage, he was unable to progress further. At around six that morning, Dmytro's boss rang mine, asking how I'd got on, what they exactly spoke about I don't know, but soon after breakfast Dmytro arrived at my bakery with his boss. Dmytro started to curse me, claiming that I'd made him look like an idiot, and that his boss knew very well that he'd never seen the inside of a bakery. His boss started to yell at me too, demanding why I'd said Dmytro was a baker, when in actual fact he wasn't. I managed to convince him that I'd never worked with Dmytro, that he'd been hired in a large bakery as an assistant and that everything here was strange. I went onto say that I'd had the same problem that morning, never having before seen an electric mixer. I managed to pacify the old master baker, they both left, and returned to their bakery.

As it turned out, Dmytro became a baker in Wismar, for which he later thanked me, and until the end of the war he never went hungry again. In the meantime, as we'd arranged the previous week, George joined me in Wismar a week later, he was taken on as a gardener in a neighbouring village and became a happy man there. Life was better than in the city, we were constantly woken by nightly alarms there, and a couple of times American planes bombed the local factory where aeroplanes and heavy artillery were being constructed and assembled.

The city of Wismar was also a port, everywhere you looked it was full of soldiers, whose job it was to defend the city. The city was also surrounded with large air balloons, and many a night Dmytro and I didn't sleep, we hid in a cellar, and on the occasions we went to the village and got caught in the middle of an alarm, we had to wait until the all clear was given.

We had every Sunday off and could go wherever we liked, we were free and unlike the Poles and those folk who wore the letters 'OST' meaning east, we didn't have to obey any curfew.

On one such Sunday, we were walking along the pavement towards a cinema we suddenly heard clear Ukrainian voices coming towards us, two well dressed men in leather jackets, strolling and holding their bicycles, they looked like German farmers. I quickly approached one of them, and we started a conversation, they'd worked on a homestead in a nearby village, and they came from France. We stood talking for a few minutes, when I asked them if they would join us for a beer, they refused because it was unsafe to leave their bicycles unattended. We soon parted after they had given us their addresses, saying that there were more Ukrainians where they worked, so we arranged to meet them the following Sunday.

That week we planned how best to reach their homestead, going by train would mean a half hour walk, so we decided to ask our bosses whether we could borrow their delivery bicycles. My boss agreed, but Dmytro's German wasn't good enough to ask his boss, so I asked him on his behalf. His boss wasn't very keen, but eventually allowed, when I explained that we had met other Ukrainians, and where we were going. On a Sunday evening, like Dmytro one of my duties was to prepare ferment for the following morning. One of my colleagues agreed to stand in for me, and Dmytro's boss, stood in for him.

When Sunday finally came, we left the city after lunch, and headed towards Rostock. It was the beginning of May, the weather was warm and pleasant, and without getting lost we found the homestead. We asked a worker where we could find the people from France, to which we were directed. Our hosts were already waiting there, six couples, without children, except one older couple had an eighteen year old daughter called Anna. We were overwhelmed to hear Ukrainian spoken, not just by the men but from their wives too. That day was like a 'feast day', hearing our mother tongue, a pleasant atmosphere and great hosts. They had prepared a table full of food and drinks, and this was still during the war. After lunch and a few drinks, one of the men started to sing, I didn't need inviting, so I joined in, and after more wine I was in my element.

One of the men pleaded not to sing too loud for there were Poles and Latvians living there, but the women didn't take any notice, encouraging me to sing because I knew many songs. Although he'd played the cymbals back home, Dmytro didn't have a singing voice, he just talked all the time.

All a while I excused myself and stepped outside, where I met Anna, who hadn't come to the gathering because her parents didn't allow her. Anna invited me to her house, then broke down in tears, regretting her parents' decision not to allow her join in. It was summer, everyone had their windows open, she could hear all the singing and laughter, and felt she was missing out. When I excused myself, she heard me leave the room, that's when she confronted me outside. I spent an hour in Anna's company, then again as I was leaving, she invited me into her house, that's how I got to know Anna Nahirna. Anna's father didn't get on very well with his neighbours, socialising very little with them, maybe it was because they were much younger, and to me he appeared a humble and quiet person, although I heard a few unpleasant stories about him, when he was still living in France, then moved to Germany during the war.

On the other hand, Anna lived well with her neighbours, probably because she was more of their age group. However, Anna had to respect her father's wishes, although she lived well with everybody, more so, when she heard Dmytro's and my voices, happy in conversation and song. No sooner had I walked through the door of Anna's house, than she introduced me to her mother as the man with the lovely voice. 'Very welcome, please sit down' said her mother. 'Maybe you could sing us a beautiful song?' I apologised for barging in on them unexpectedly, and told them that I was visiting their neighbours with my friend.

That evening, Dmytro and I ate at Anna's, I could see Dmytro felt uncomfortable, his conversation with Anna's mother wouldn't gel. When Anna's father entered the house, Dmytro put on a serious face, and felt more comfortable in his presence, although I sensed something was - wrong.

On the way back Dmytro opened up and told me that he couldn't keep his eyes off Anna. I didn't realise before, Dmytro was a little older than me, fair and taller, whereas I felt like a dog with a bone, I didn't want share Anna with anyone, after all I saw her first. We both kept silent for the remainder of the journey, it seemed Anna had broken two hearts that day.

The following Sunday, Dmytro's boss wouldn't allow him the use of the bicycle, and I didn't feel comfortable going alone or walking that far, so we decided to travel by train. Anna met us at the train station, which kept off suspicious eyes on the walk to her house. After a couple of weeks, I had enough money to buy my own bicycle, and didn't have to wait for a Sunday.

In the city we were constantly on the alert, for British and American bombers knew about the aeroplane factory, and cities like Hamburg, Lubeck, Rostock and Wismar, were under constant threat. During the summer months, alarms occurred almost every night, civilians were sent to underground cellars and bunkers. There were times when I had just closed my eyes, and I could hear the sound of the alarms, while George was lucky living in a quiet village away from the city.

In the autumn, the Americans had apparently developed a routine, they would bombard four cities simultaneously, at the same time every night. The nights were long, sitting in a dark bunker, and if I was travelling on my way back from Anna's, I'd often get caught out by an alarm and would have to do without my breakfast.

I normally started work at four in the morning, but there were occasions when the nightly alarms didn't cease until six in the morning, and if I was still travelling, I would have to wait outside the city limits, as the police wouldn't allow civilians into the city until the all clear was given.

I spent many summer evenings with Anna, standing in her corridor, under the watchful eye of her mother. Her parents never allowed her outside in the evenings, either alone or even with someone else, she obeyed them and never showed any hostility towards them.

One Sunday morning I was woken by Dmytro. 'Get up! Get up! War! Hitler has tricked Stalin'. We were both so pleased that we both went to visit George in his village. Dmytro wasn't jealous now that there was a new war, Anna had become irrelevant. We always got on well with George, working as a gardener he never went hungry, whenever we saw him he would always offer us vegetables and chickens.

Two or three weeks later we decided to go to the cinema one Sunday, they always showed newsreels and gave information about the war, soon we would witness a dramatic change.

In the autumn arrived the first shipment of girls and young women from Western Ukraine. They were brought by a goods train, sixty women to a wagon. They had travelled for a week, they were all tired, unwashed and without food or water. On arrival, they were swiftly selected by rich women to work as domestic help. I was often called to act as an interpreter; it was an unexpected meeting, even a tearful one, because I was their 'brother'.

On the whole, only a small percentage of them worked in homes, the majority were sent to factories, surrounded by barbed wire. I received many visitors at work, many of the girls couldn't cope, they were teenagers from small villages, some of them had never seen a city, I helped them as best as I could, giving them good advice.

In the beginning, there were many frightened girls who slept in barracks, they were fed in their own canteens, never allowed into the city, and worked twelve hours a day. Although they were from Ukraine, they should have been entitled to the same rights as people like me, but unfortunately for them these rules were never applied. Those who worked in private homes in the city were under a curfew, the factory workers were not allowed to leave their compounds. I don't know the reason, but all the workers coming into our city were women, not until about a year later did I see a few men appear from some of the POW camps.

My good friend Dmytro had an abundance of Ukrainian girls, and yet he started launching unwarranted accusations aimed at me, I couldn't figure out why, I hadn't done him any harm. In the city, he had two girlfriends on the go, never giving either of them a moments peace, though he still carried 'a torch' for Anna.

Most of the girls came from poor villages, in the clothes they travelled in, I would see some of them on a Sunday, washing their only dresses, they were too embarrassed to show their faces in public.

Today, Anna lives in Canada, she is in her second marriage.

Yevdokia went to live in England, where she became a widow very early.

Nastya, moved to France, where she became an active Ukrainian member.

Ruzya, Dmytro's wife had an accident and walks with a limp.

When the Germans invaded Ukraine, they didn't just bring our young girls, but also as much produce as they could.

On the 3rd of January, 1942 I received permission to visit my mother in Ukraine. My boss arranged everything, tickets, travel documents and a whole itinerary. At first he was totally against it, he wouldn't even listen. It was all thanks to his old mother, he on the other hand saw himself as a 'party man' always playing the 'important man'.

CHAPTER 23
HOME FOR CHRISTMAS

I left Wismar on the 3rd of January 1942 and travelled to Berlin by train. At two in the morning the following day, I travelled to Krakow, where it was knee deep in snow. From Krakow I travelled to Lviv, where the weather was even worse. I spent the whole night at the station, where I had a supper and breakfast. My ticket only took me to Stanislaviw, and I needed to go on to Tysmenychany, the nearest station to Kaminne. Luckily, I met a familiar face at the station, somebody from my home village. In Stanyslaviw, it would normally take two or three hours, waiting in a queue for a ticket, especially before Christmas, people travelling with large cases and baskets. My friend escorted me to a ticket office manned by a German soldier. I told the soldier that I was my friend's brother-in-law, and within five minutes I had a ticket. Now all we had to do was to find space in the carriage, this too I left to my 'brother-in-law'.

We got off at the fourth stop, it was freezing cold, the snow crunched underfoot, luckily the moon shone, so we soon arrived at my mother's house. We knocked on the door, which was answered by my mother; my friend asked if we could spend the night. My mother, not recognising me, told my friend, that she had a large family, thus no room. I couldn't keep quiet any longer, my mother still in shock said, 'Oh God! I thought you were a strange man, but it's my long lost child! Children, Peter, Dmytro, it's our Ivan' I was greeted by my whole family.

My mother greeted me, tears streaming down her face; 'I thought you were dead, people said you were killed in the War, but I prayed to God that this was not true, and that He would help, and when you stood in the doorway, I didn't recognise you, because you were covered'. I went over to greet my younger brothers, and even my travelling friend stood in tears next to the family. I saw strangers in the house too, which I later found out, was a new stepfather, and a new stepsister, my mother's previous husband had died. It also surfaced that my brother Vasyl had married my girlfriend Malanka.

News soon spread from the other passengers off the train on which I'd travelled home, and it didn't take long before Vasyl appeared with his wife Malanka, I later spent the night at their house.

I'd sent letters home from the prison camp, and again when I was released, but obviously they never reached their destination, since I'd never received a reply.

On Christmas Eve, the whole family sat around one table, my new stepfather as head of the household began the proceedings with prayer, then we all joined in singing Christmas Carols.

At my brother's I slept alone on their bed, they slept together on the oven (in those days, ovens were also used to heat the room, besides cooking). One early morning, there was a knock on the window, it was young men who belonged to the 'underground movement' my brother recognised them and let them in. They came in with their new rifles, obviously heard about me, and started asking me questions about life in Germany, if I spoke the language, about life in Germany, and about my future intentions. I later found out from my brother, that they were regular visitors, they were younger than me and I didn't know any of them.

During my week's holiday, I discovered many snippets, some good, others not so good. I never had the opportunity to talk to Malanka as we once used to. I met many interesting people in the village, I had gained in status, I was no longer just a shepherd. I talked about the underground movement, what involvement my brother had with them, and I also enquired, why my brother had married Malanka.

Time didn't stand still in the village. I had to make a decision, either do what my brother suggested, or quickly return to Germany, I chose the latter. I said goodbye to my mother, my brothers and friends in the village. Vasyl and Malanka travelled with me to Stanislaviw, were I said goodbye to my brother, and to tearful Malanka, as to a sister-in-law, not to a lover.

CHAPTER 24
BACK IN GERMANY

I entered my room in Germany, to find a letter from George, saying that our friend Dmytro was a phoney. No sooner had I left to visit my family than he'd gone to visit Anna. I couldn't understand why, he had two girlfriends in the city. I never said a word to Dmytro about the letter, just made arrangements with him that I would pick him up on Sunday on the way to Anna's. Dmytro, the day before, feigned a headache, and said he'd seen Anna's father, who said Anna wasn't well. I ignored everything Dmytro said; I was also visiting other families.

When I met Anna she was very cold towards me, and immediately threw questions at me, repeating the same questions two or three times. Her attitude angered me, so I just walked out. I made my way to one of her neighbour's houses, where I was greeted warmly, everyone knew where I had been, and they all wanted to hear my stories of home and Ukraine. Back home in the village, I'd made a new contact, from whom I received the address of the 'Ukrainian Committee in Krakow' which gave me more respect and authority.

I ignored Anna the rest of the winter, there were plenty of girls in the city; I ignored Dmytro too, for a week or two.

One of Anna's neighbours, received news about his brother, who was in Berlin, so one Sunday I accompanied him. In Berlin there were many Ukrainians, every Sunday they held a mass, and I met many new people. Not everybody in Berlin had work, among them were many escapees, our Committee had many problems with them, as there was a shortage of food and accommodation. Anna's neighbour Vasyl, had a brother called Oleh, I'd only met six months previously, and because of him, I spent two hard years in a concentration camp.

I often visited Berlin during the summer; I sold 'ration coupons' to Oleh , so he could exchange them for bread, I'd accumulated hundreds in exchange for German Marks. I'd learned from another German how to acquire coupons. In the bakery where I worked, the German baker who packed bread in the shop was soon taken into the army, his place was taken by a Frenchman, who'd been wounded in the war, but he couldn't speak German, so I had access to the coupons. All the workers in the bakery were old men, I was the youngest, and the toughest job was by the ovens. In those days, ovens were fired by wood, so it was a hard job, too hard for the old German bakers.

Towards the end of 1942, we began to bake bread for prisoners; we added sawdust and dried beetroots to the mix. To mix a bread dough using flour is easy, but to add sawdust, makes the dough less pliable and harder to mould into shape. The beetroot we used, had all its sugar extracted, the Germans used it to feed their cattle and pigs. The end product was a hard baked loaf, dark in colour, unbelievable in flavour. The bread for the German market was made early in the morning, bread for the prisoners was baked afterwards.

My boss benefited tremendously from this, he began to use more sawdust, leaving him more bread to sell without coupons. After a couple of weeks, with more practice, we began to master the new recipe, leaving us a little extra time to rest.

In the bakery, I had my own routine, every day I had a different function. Every Thursday, I had a designated hour when I'd remove all the scraps and rubbish, out onto the pavement. In those days we didn't have a bath in the bakery, nor did we have flushing toilets. There were three young ladies working in the bakery, but they didn't carry out buckets of sludge. By the bakery, we also kept two pigs, the boss needed an idiot to feed and clean after them. It fell on me to carry out these jobs early in the morning, so that our young ladies could sleep peacefully. If the buckets weren't carried out on time, the smell would become worse, and in the summer unbearable. That's why we started early in the morning, everyone knew his job, the pig's stable was cleaned out on Saturdays.

One afternoon, I was walking along with Dmytro, talking to each other in a low voice, when all of a sudden we heard a Ukrainian voice from a beautiful young girl, wearing a short sleeved dress, standing overhead on a restaurant balcony. She asked us to wait a couple of minutes, and when she came down stairs, I was the one who instigated the first moves again. Her name was Nadia, and she was from our capital Kyiv. Her language to us sounded strange, we were not used to her dialect, on top of that, she used many words which we'd never heard. And because she was from Eastern Ukraine, she had to wear the label 'OST'. We stood and talked outside the restaurant for about half an hour, and then she invited us inside for a drink.

Nadia told us that she'd worked at the restaurant for a month, she even heard stories about me; she knew I had a French girlfriend in the village, this she'd learned from her friend. I took an instant liking to her, she had plenty of free time, and I now hardly saw Anna thanks to Dmytro, my trusted friend.

I got hold of many postcards from Prague. They had embroidery patterns, and in my spare time I began to write a little poetry for my own pleasure, and slowly the thought of Anna disappeared.

For some reason Dmytro had stopped seeing Anna, apparently because she was seeing a Latvian. Dmytro carried on seeing his two girlfriends in the city, the road to the village had began to be covered in moss.

The road to Anna was far, it took a whole hour on a bicycle, but to Nadia it was just around the corner. I spent a lot of time with Nadia around the city, we would even ride out to see George in the village. Nadia knew of my relationship with Anna, she would joke and tease me that I still loved Anna. Nadia was a little older than Anna, taller and fair, she was better educated and sweeter too.

One day I had an accident in the bakery, while firing the oven a splinter of wood entered my hand, and because of this I was unable to work for a whole week. That Sunday, Nadia and I made arrangements to visit her friend in Schwerin. We didn't risk travelling by bicycle, so we went by train. The journey went by eventless, but on the way back we came stumbled into a control detail. Nadia was fearless, so she went first but was stopped at a gate by a policeman. I latched on to an old German lady who was travelling with us, talking to her in German to avoid suspicion. I got through without a problem, but the police detained Nadia, I couldn't leave her alone, and I couldn't convince the policeman otherwise, so we were taken to the police station.

We were kept all night at the police station, there were no grounds to arrest us, but I received a good telling off from my boss, who had to bail us both out. My boss was a big 'party member' and well respected in the city. Nadia was reprimanded for not wearing her 'OST' label and we were both fined. Although we were both Ukrainian, the German Authorities looked upon us differently, I was from the West and she was from the East (OST).

I often had heated discussions with my boss about this incident and others. As a big party member, he was ready to rule Ukraine. He once brought in a large map of Ukraine, spread it out on a large table, and for two long hours grilled me about where the biggest and richest villages where. Jokingly, he would promise me that he would take both Nadia and me when Germany steps into Ukraine and materialises its plan.

We were to be his workers, he would even build us a house, the Germans would be the ruling race, they loved the richness of Ukraine. He disclosed other similar plans, whereby the rich fertile land would grow the best wheat in the world.

I used to go to the cinema twice a week, on the days they changed the newsreel. Every day the 'front lines' changed; the radio stations would broadcast hourly bulletins. The front never stayed still, it would take many casualties. The time had come for my boss to put on his new uniform of the tiger.

My boss found me different lodgings for his own peace of mind, just in case Nadia would venture into my room. At the bakery lived four young ladies, the boss's daughter and three single girls. Even when I was at my new lodgings, my boss would ask the landlady when I went to see Anna, and when I saw Nadia.

My new lodgings were only a five minute walk to the bakery, but in case I slept in, I would set two alarm clocks. I wasn't responsible for the running of the bakery, the Germans wouldn't appoint a 'foreigner' in a responsible position, these positions were always held by one of their own.

I started to send bread coupons to Oleh by post, to cycle there took up too much time as I was always required to act as an interpreter for somebody in distress, leaving me only two or three hours sleep at night. One such case was for Vasyl, he wanted to change jobs, so I had to make extensive enquiries, which wasn't easy for foreigners, moreso in wartime. These extra jobs I could only do after work in the afternoons, which cut into my sleeping hours. I was required for silly menial favours, such as finding a spare part for a bicycle, one of our boys was beaten up by a German worker, another escaped from a homestead because he didn't like his boss.

Vasyl managed to get himself a new job as a fishmonger's assistant in the city, he now felt a little closer to his friends, no longer isolated as he'd been back in the village.

In 1943 a few Ukrainian boys, me included, started a 'war' with a few Latvians. It all began when a few of 'our' Ukrainian girls started dating the Latvians, and we stupid young men didn't like this, so to stop this we started a fight in a local park, all because of 'our' girls. I carried a large heavy gate key, George carried a stick he'd made from the branch of a olive tree, Vasyl Boyko carried a metal bar and Dmytro didn't carry anything.

When the four of us walked through the park, the Latvians would turn pale and would always bypass us. One day, however, a gang of Latvians set upon Dmytro, who was walking through the park alone, once they caught up with him they gave him a good beating. A few days later we ambushed the Latvians in the same park and gave them a taste of their own medicine.

Four days later, a soldier from the Gestapo came into the bakery and arrested me. He asked me if I required an interpreter, to which I declined, I understood all his questions, though that didn't stop him giving me a good hiding. The Gestapo soldier took me from the bakery, still dressed in my uniform, he then marched me along the city streets, until we reached a police station. At the station, my friend Vasyl Boyko was already there, and shortly afterwards we were driven to a holding camp, the name of which I don't remember. The first two days we received very little to eat, on the third day we were only given one cup of coffee.

Two weeks after this ordeal we were taken to a railway station, where we put onto a train from Hamburg, on its way to Berlin, but we alighted at Oranienburg, thirty five kilometres north of Berlin, the home of the famous concentration camp Sachsenhausen.

CHAPTER 25
SACHSENHAUSEN

Sachsenhausen was 'hell on earth' the opposite of paradise. From here there was no going back, at the entrance, over the gate was a sign, later used in Auschwitz, which read 'Arbeit Macht Frei' meaning 'Work makes you free'

On our arrival, we were put into 'quarantine' for three weeks, where we were taught all the rules of the camp, what we had to do and what we must not do. We were assigned to Barrack No. 21 which was run by a one armed Pole. In all my life till then I had never met such a sadistic killer, he would without question or reason beat your back with a stick, he never spoke, only shouted, everything in German, I didn't know where he found such cursing words.

I was categorised as a political prisoner, we were given a red label, which was in the shape of a triangle, and a number. Ukrainians were not recognised as a nation, so we either had to wear the letter 'P' for Polish or 'R' for Russia, the Hungarians wore the letter 'U'. At that time, I had enough of Poles, and didn't want to wear 'P' so I chose 'R'. Once a Russian approached me and started talking in Russian, but I couldn't speak any Russian.

I was arrested in October 1943, it was November, on our first night in the barrack in Sachsenhausen I slept on the top bunk and Vasyl Boyko slept on the bottom. To keep warmer, Vasyl climbed into my bed, but suddenly he heard a commotion, and then quickly jumped down into his own bunk. I must have fallen asleep, or I couldn't hear the barrack leader approaching my bed. In his usual raised voice, he shouted that I was covered in two blankets, the other was Vasyl's, then he took his stick and started to beat me with all the strength that he could muster from one arm. I slept on the floor under my bed until morning, my whole body black and blue, I never shared my bunk again with Vasyl, I only covered myself with one blanket.

At breakfast the barrack leader was serving breakfast and recognised me by my bruises, he then asked me why I was holding my bowl in my hands, so I replied I was thirsty and would like something to drink. That I replied in German shocked him, for such incidents were very rare in prison that a person with the letter 'R' could speak such good German.

The barrack leader came up to me, said he wanted a word, then ordered me to go into his office. My lips were still sore from his beating, I expected another, but he told me that he needed a Russian interpreter. It turned out that all the Russians had to fill in a form, quite simple really, all that was required was their names and date of birth. The unexpected meeting with the Russian, whilst in quarantine, helped me.

I spent three weeks sitting at a table next to a German Officer who shared his potatoes with me, this is what he liked and this was what he ate. The

Russians referred to me as the 'interpreter' but called me 'Vanya' a pet name for Ivan in Russian. Whilst I was interpreting I sat at a different table, and every day I had breakfast and lunch.

During the last days of autumn, while the sun was still warm, I would go outside and sit against a large wall, my body was still sore from the first night's beating. I was told that over the other side of the wall, three Ukrainian leaders, Bandera, Melnyk and Rebet were imprisoned; some of the other prisoners had seen them as they went to the toilets.

In the quarantine, everyone was given a uniform, which consisting of trousers, a jacket, coat, underwear and a hat. Everyone's trousers, jacket and coats had a number sewn onto them, we also had a red label sewn onto our jackets. Every new arrival was given a number, written in black ink and sewn onto a piece of white cotton. The letters 'P' for Pole, 'F' for French, 'R' for Russian, this was sewn onto each pair of trousers and jacket. In the German concentration camps, prisoners were differentiated by colour, we didn't wear any numbers, there were also different colours for thieves and deserters.

The Germans liked to categorise foreigners, in one category a 'political prisoner' was considered one who stole a chicken from his master, and also in the same category was the man who had sex with his daughter or wife. There were also those who escaped from 'hard labour' and those who were caught 'racketeering'. We all wore the 'red triangle'.

Most of the prisoners in our camp were Russian, who constantly tried to escape, and among them were many wounded. In the three weeks I spent in quarantine, I didn't see any new arrivals of Jews, although to one side there were three large barracks of children, ranging from five to ten years old, two hundred in each, it looked like a 'nursery'. I would sometimes see them through the barbed wire. These children were orphans, their parents had been burnt in the crematorium, this was Hitler's programme, that's how he destroyed the Jews, barbaric and shameless.

I had the opportunity to leave the compound through the gates, I often had to go to the offices, where I saw the 'crematorium programme'. The Jews would be brought in large wagons, they all had to strip and place their clothes on a pile, the women were separated from the men, and then sent to the ovens, and not to the bathrooms. All their discarded clothes were soon collected by barrack leaders, and were then distributed to the workers in the main camp. Shoes, boots and handbags, were sorted by designated workers who later passed through electronic scanning equipment, if anyone was caught, they were never seen again. However, there were 'rewards' if anyone found gold hidden in the heel of a shoe, his reward would be a bowl of porridge.

There were other 'work details' one of which entailed the testing of new military boots that had been delivered direct from the factory. Prisoners would march up and down, along rugged and sharp roads, what better way for the factory to test its goods.

One day I bumped into a Ukrainian, who wore the letter 'U' on his chest. I later asked our barrack guard, why I saw a Ukrainian, with the letter 'U' if they were now worn by Hungarians. He explained that Ukrainians in the camp are old people and in the beginning they gave Ukrainians 'U' but when the camp filled with more Hungarians, they adopted the letter for themselves.

In the 'quarantine' I made all the letters, and I could do one for myself anytime, and so I did, but hid it in my pocket, waiting for the time, when I would leave the 'quarantine'.

Once Vasyl and I finished our stint in the 'quarantine', Vasyl was sent to Stuttgart to work in his own profession as a locksmith. I was sent to a building site in Frankfurt. In the 'quarantine' we lived through many nightmares, the worst for me was that unfortunate first night. I was pleased for Vasyl having secured a job in his own profession, but unfortunately for me there were no vacancies as a baker. To get a job in a kitchen or bakery, was virtually impossible without the right connections, and on this occasion my searching and pleading led me into a dead end, as I didn't make it through the 'selection'.

It was towards the end on 1943, I couldn't remember the exact date, when I was selected in to a group which was to build a factory producing chemical gas. At the camp I was assigned to the second barrack, which at that time was still empty.

The building site was not far from the barrack, only a five minute walk through the wood. The camp was wrapped by a barbed wire fence, and on every tower stood a guard with a rifle.

On the building site worked many free men, everyone wore a white ribbon on their sleeve, and all the workers consisted of men in their sixties, only Otto the engineer was a youngster. Everything on the site was done by hand, there were only two machines, one a cement mixer, the other a large crane, which was used for earth moving.

All the civilian workers were craftsmen; none of them ever held a spade, only the prisoners were hurried along with the use of a whip. I was given a heavy spade by my overseer who was a large bellied German civilian craftsman.

Outside, the autumn was damp, my first job was quite heavy, my only encouragement was the pine wood alongside us. For the first three weeks I worked with purpose, I believed the slogan 'Work makes you free'. However, the strength in my body soon drained, and my spade was no longer full. The civilian craftsman liked me, but nobody noticed, and I wasn't allowed to speak to any of them, but when I was angry, I plucked up courage.

At that time I was still very young, too young to die, and I was still quite immature. Today, when I think and write about this, I am so ashamed to mention what I did.

Work became harder by the hour, escape was out of the question, and there was nothing left to live for, only sweet dreams and thoughts. I had neither the will nor the strength to wait for either the end of the war or a miracle, so I thought I would join the 'SS'. One day after lunch, during work, I approached the civilian craftsman, even though I wasn't allowed to speak to him, and to approach somebody from the 'SS' was out of the question. That evening before parade, I lost two teeth; I even thought I would lose my sight. The craftsman gave me such a beating, in front of the prisoners, and called me all sorts of obscenities, that I could hardly breathe, or stand upright, I just lay on the ground. I couldn't make it back to the barracks on my own two feet, a couple of Belorussians helped me into the barrack. The following morning, I collapsed near the gate since I didn't have the strength to stand. I didn't go to work that day, I was taken to the camp hospital, where even the hospital workers added their own pain to the 'SS Man'.

I spent four days in the camp hospital, even there the workers would steal bread from the sick, leaving them little to eat.

On my release from hospital, I was sent to the 'earth moving detail' which was in the wood. My overseer was a Czech, who beat me every minute, hence my first night's supper didn't go down too well.

When I left the 'quarantine' I sewed the letter 'U' on my trousers and jacket, thus encouraging the Czech to shout, 'You traitor from Ukraine' . He beat me so much that I thought I would die.

In our work detail there were twenty five people. We had to cut pine, birch and thick beeches, carry the logs on our backs and put them aside, then with spades we had to make a clearing. To carry a tree log needed twenty four people; I was always forced as a 'Ukrainian volunteer' to stand at the 'thick end'. To lift such a log was painful, it was hard to carry it on your shoulder, it wasn't easy to release it either, if it wasn't suspended correctly, it could catch or hit your leg.

After two gruelling months, the Czech had almost finished me off. He tore the letter 'U' off my jacket. I could hardly walk to work, I just dragged my feet, I was now so thin that I was called the 'skeleton'.

People in my condition, 'skeletons' were usually sent back to the camps, the factory only paid for able bodied workers. To add to my misfortune, we had just experienced a heavy snowfall. There were ten 'skeletons' incapable of work, so in order to hide us ten from view, we were sent away from the camp, to spread soil over gardens belonging to a nearby training school for the Fire Brigade. The soil we had to spread was delivered in the autumn, now the soil was so frozen, that sparks flew when we hit it with pickaxes, and we 'skeletons' just didn't have the strength to break it.

We were about to leave and return to camp, as it was impossible for us to break up the soil. Nearby stood a lone German, who observed us for a while, and after a few minutes came up to the group, and asked if anyone could speak German. There were ten of us, but no volunteers. Although I understood him I was tired of living; I stood alone propped against a wall to screen myself from the icy wind. Someone in the group waved his hand towards me, and the German approached me, politely asked me if I could help him and go with him to the warehouse. I agreed and followed him, we were near the kitchen, when I spied a wooden barrel of beetroot peel, ready for the pigs. I dug my hand into the barrel, using it as a shovel, devouring the peel as quickly as I could. The German stopped in his tracks and stared at me in amazement and disbelief. I saw that there was much more in the barrel, so I took off my hat and filled it, and once inside the warehouse I finished off the contents in a matter of minutes, I even felt lucky, finding amongst the peel a discarded chicken's claw. The German left me alone to eat, then returned with a piece of dried bread, after which he started to talk to me.

My hat was now red from the beetroot peelings, and after a moment or two, the German asked me the reason why I hadn't admitted to him I could speak German. I told him of my misfortune, as swiftly and briefly as I could. To my disbelief, I felt my life had changed from that moment, all thanks to the German who helped me so much.

He told me that the school had two large cellars, full of black soil, and all that was needed were shovels and wheelbarrows. There were ten of us plus two guards. Two worked by the window, the rest trampled the soil with their feet. As soon as two of us were in the cellar, work started briskly, the first two quickly took off their gloves, giving encouragement to the rest. Before lunch all the spades and shovels were in motion, even the two guards didn't stand around idly. We used two wheelbarrows to move the soil; the guards too, were getting warm helping us.

Lunch was organised by the German in a warm room, in the meantime, the guards were busy gathering wood for the stove. That evening before we left, the German gave one of the guards a letter, and then we trudged through the snow back to the camp. On the way back, I could feel my hat freezing from the cold, but kept the reason why literally under my hat.

It was a four kilometre walk through a wood, we had to be back before nightfall, nobody had felt any inclination to escape though.

After work there was always 'roll call', handing out of letters, a piece of bread and supper, and this all had to be done very quickly, 'Schnell! Schnell!' because the lights would soon be switched off in the yard.

That evening at roll call, the Commandant read out my number and told me to report to the office, where I was given a new hat, a black armband, a new number and the letter 'U' on my chest. There was also a message, which read I was to take over a new command, as of the next day. I also had to make myself presentable that same evening. In my room within the barrack lived three Belorussians, all three were former partisans. They had a razor, a sharpening stone, even a pair of scissors to cut hair.

My new promotion was a blow to the barrack leader, he even changed his mind after a while, when I found out about his affair.

At the new job, I quickly fattened up the 'skeletons' I arranged with the German that he would bring us all the scraps from the kitchen, and all of us, soon retrieved some strength. Every lunch time we were given a thick soup, sometimes the German would even bring us bread, crusts and off cuts in abundance.

There were three Latvian girls working in the kitchen, supervised by local elderly ladies. Now there was nothing thrown away into the barrels, instead it all went into our stomachs. After a time, we all began to put on weight, but the commandant insisted that I change my men one by one. I didn't have the courage to argue, as he was highly regarded in the camp. He once sent me a young Frenchman, it was spring by this time, we were all working in the fields, the young boy had eaten some soup, he stepped to one side, and what I then saw I had never seen in my whole life. Out of the Frenchman's mouth came all his intestines. All of us stood in astonishment, even the two guards, we were all helpless, nobody had a clue how to help, when suddenly the boy, using both hands, started to push into his mouth what had just come out. The boy was sent to the main hospital, and what happened later I never discovered.

Not long after this incident, the main Camp Commander was replaced. My barrack leader, the Czech, was sent to the kitchen. A well built Pole was put in charge of the four- hundred strong workforce.

My work also came to an end in the Fire Brigade School; everything that had to be done was finished. I sincerely thanked the kind German, I didn't embrace him, I would have been too embarrassed. The following day I was given a new 'work detail'.

I took over a work detail on the building site, 'A1' Now I had thirty men under my command, and two civilian craftsmen, who both liked me, as I never stood around doing nothing, and wherever there was work I was willing to give a hand. My command worked on the cement, some workers mixed, others fetched and carried. Never a bad word was said about me nor did I physically beat people to work, I would only shout, and that was enough.

On one occasion I stood in for a machinist who needed the toilet. Two minutes later approached our sadistic one- armed Pole just as a wagon overturned, he immediately started ranting at me, claiming I wasn't doing my job properly. He told me to remove my black armband because I had no idea about the job. This happened just before lunch, and the two German craftsmen could do nothing about it, they wouldn't even utter a word to this sadistic creature.

Lunch was brought to us to the barrack; I always served the men soup. The Pole would not leave my side, to ensure that I wouldn't have any authority over anyone. I stood in the queue with the rest of the men, and when I received my portion I stepped outside with another man. The Pole came up to me swinging his arm, then without reason threw himself onto me like an animal. Nobody came to my assistance, he managed to kick me a couple of times, my left eye was badly swollen, and the bottom of my back was bruised.

I don't know if he had lunch that day, because he spent all his time in our barrack, until we returned back to work. He took off my black hat, and gave me a spade and a wheelbarrow, then told me to collect shale for the machine. Half an hour later, Otto the German engineer arrived with an assistant, I didn't hear or see what happened, but the Pole got his marching orders, and was taken off the site by Otto's assistant. I was then made the 'foreman' and everyone said it was because of me.

On the building site I had many friends, some dug holes, others were mixers who did nothing else, but the men knew I was fair, and for this I was widely respected.

In the middle of summer, I was put in charge of one hundred and twenty men, my secretary was a young Ukrainian priest called Ostap Pshenycznyj from the Karpaty region. He wasn't physically able to carry out much manual work, but he was intelligent, educated and quite political, but too frail to work. He couldn't handle a spade either with his right or left arm, I often had to defend him and so I kept him by my side for over six months.

I couldn't do everything myself, I had many people at my disposal, I had to move myself from group to group, to keep myself busy, and the project too.

That summer I received a parcel from Nadia, it contained biscuits, tobacco and dried peas. The peas came in useful, I would make myself soup in the evenings.

Because I wore the letter 'R' I wasn't allowed to write any letters, so I had to find a sympathetic person amongst the tradesmen, there were some good men.

My trusted and dear friend Dmytro, didn't have the courage to write to me, although one thing in his favour was that he gave Anna my address. Now I had two girls sending me food parcels, I knew they knew each other, but they kept a distance between themselves. Now my number was often called out at roll call, to collect a parcel or letter. Nadia often wrote, and on two occasions sent me a photograph of ourselves. One letter I received I wanted to read in private, so walking along, my lips began to move, and began to quietly sing a song. We all knew that everything had to pass strict controls, before a letter or parcel was passed onto us, but whoever received such a prize, had a reminder of what life used to be like, and could dream that those times would return.

As I entered my barrack still singing, a guard stood there holding his dog, and said, 'I can hear the joy in your voice, you have a good bass, your voice carries far, and doesn't allow anybody to sleep'. He then reprimanded me again saying, 'Where did you learn such dirty words, and where did you find the courage, to write a letter to the commandant'? I hadn't written any letter, I could swear that, there must have been some misunderstanding, there was only the kind German, to whom I spilled my grievances. The priest was a witness to our conversation since he was sweeping the barrack floor at the time. The guard stood there, holding onto his large dog by his chain, he also carried a large pistol by his side. This guard was Ukrainian, I could tell by his dialect that he was from the Karpaty Region, but I always thought he was German whenever the guards came on inspection control.

In the camp grounds, we had a punishment block which housed all the camp misfits and thieves, in truth it wasn't always the case, but often misdemeanours happened.

Otto, our engineer, began to push our workers harder, we had heard rumours of volatile times for the Germans. Whenever a wagon of sand arrived, sometimes two or three, even after hours, the work had to be carried out to the end by the unlucky ones. These jobs were carried out on Saturday afternoons, even Sundays, all the wagons had to be empty by Monday.

Amongst four hundred men there was always an element of crime, somebody would steal bread from his 'neighbour' some found the courage to escape from work, there were the 'skivers' while others tried to build their own radios.

During the week, each barrack leader had to write down the number of every 'wrongdoer' and by Saturday the list would be ready.

Every working day, guards would stand in their towers observing the building site too, which was wrapped by a fence of barbed wire. In the mornings, when we arrived the guards were already watching from their towers. In the evenings, before our return to the barracks, there would be a head count. If in the event somebody escaped from the work detail, the guards would be punished with night and day guard duty. We remaining workers didn't escape lightly either, we too had to stand, sometimes all evening and night, without any sleep, while the guards searched.

There was a happy ending for one prisoner, a fair haired, good- looking gipsy, though his accomplice was caught during the night. There were many attempts of escape, but more often than not the outcome was dire. Once I saw an attempted escapee shot by a German guard.

Life carried on until November, but the following month saw a radical change. The technical brigade was liquidated, and the 'skeletons' were not exchanged. In the beginning at Sachsenhausen, every Thursday we would see a new influx of prisoners, but then a new order came, that the camp was to be disbanded. That meant, if somebody didn't feel physically able to work on the building site, they could apply for 'voluntary exit' whereas the able, like me, had for the time being to remain working.

Throughout the whole of 1944 we assembled machines and motors, and when the 'front' was upon us, we had to load them onto wagons. By January only half of the original internees remained, then soon afterwards most of the remainder had gone, until there were only fifty of us left. As to the camp personnel, only the Commandant and nine guards were left.

We waited at the building site for a steam train, two special empty wagons. Now there was a race with the Russians, every stop the Germans made resulted in loosing precious time. The Germans had laid mines on the River Oder, which the Russians discovered, and during the night we heard distant artillery fire, but the onslaught didn't begin until March. When it came, we didn't sleep a wink that night, I don't remember the exact date. The train was loaded and ready to depart, we heard the guns getting closer and closer, one such shell hit the building site, soon after we quickly departed, the actual train wasn't severely damaged, and as it pulled away I thanked God.

An hour later we arrived in Berlin, at Sachsenhausen, where we found many changes. First of all, two or even three people had to share a bed, the food was bad, all we had was the juice from swede. The little food that I did manage to hide I kept in my pocket, and then went out to look for old friends. As I searched, people approached me and asked for scraps, it was difficult to get accustomed to this kind of life.

I went from barrack to barrack, everywhere people huddled in small groups, causing a commotion; some were saying that the Americans would be on their way that year, German cities were now being bombed in daytime.

A goods vehicle entered the camp, a guard called out for twenty volunteers. I don't know why, maybe because I was young, I volunteered and became one of the twenty. A guard wrote down everyone's number, and now I belonged to the hard workers, who were afraid of no job.

We arrived in the centre of Berlin; where we were met by two guards, who took us to a nearby large building and then taken to its cellar. The cellar was pitch black, the guards had to use their flashlights, and then we noticed so much water that you could row a boat.

The water was up to our knees, we had to take off our trousers and shoes, we were given shovels, and then ordered to collect all the debris, such as yellow fruits, pieces of wood, boxes, chairs and small tables. There was one crafty soul amongst us who had been on a similar work detail; he had prepared his shoes and trousers, tying them beforehand.

The cellar was quite wide and the water quite deep, but not deep enough to cover the unexploded bomb we were looking for. Our first task was to divide into groups, some of us brought sand downstairs, others took buckets of water upstairs. The work was heavy and dangerous, but I wasn't afraid, I only thought of how to get through to the next minute. The water was cold, but inside I was pleased, mainly for not being hungry, and also for being alive, in one piece and working.

We quickly made a barricade, using the wood and other suitable items we fished out of the water. We were given as much as we wanted to eat, the guards didn't prevent us from eating, they were no better than us, but they wouldn't allow us to take any food back to camp.

Twenty of us carried water for four days, it took five of us two whole days to dig out the bomb. Looking back at that life- threatening situation, it's easy to write about now, but so hard to understand why we were content at the time, all we had was the knowledge of temporary knowledge of freedom, even though it was short-lived.

When we recovered the bomb, we placed it on its side, the two guards hid themselves behind a wall while the bomb disposal unit disarmed it.

The following week I went on a different work detail, I noticed a group of people by the gate, and amongst them a familiar face, so I joined the group for the brickworks, but when we arrived we found that it used to be a brickworks, but had now become a munitions factory. I helped to load the grenades onto a barge, which was berthed by the factory on a river or canal. The grenades were without firing pins, so there was no great danger, though the work in general was tough.

Two shifts operated in the factory, so the beds were always warm. In April, one fine day just before lunch, I was on the night shift so I was asleep, when a heavy bomb fell on the factory. American fighter planes swooped down, hailing us with bullets, and with all the phosphorous on site, four wooden barracks, the kitchen and food store were at once ablaze. People panicked, some tried to run into the woods for cover, but their exit was blocked by an iron fence. Those prisoners who at the time were working were the first at the gate, and even though the fence was electrified, they managed to penetrate it. Soon there was a massive exodus of terrified people heading towards the wood.

Unfortunately, in the woods was riddled with German soldiers pointing rifles at us, none of them uttered a word to us, many prisoners saw the situation as a means of escape, I hit upon an alternative route, away from the mass hysteria, ran to the side of the approaching army, using the trees as cover, I soon spied a clearing which I aimed for.

I saw a civilian, approached him hurriedly and begged him for some water. The German said, 'Yes, yes, come here, don't worry, nobody is going to hit you'. It turned out that I wasn't the only one with a bright idea, believing it would be easy to escape from this hell. Hitler was no fool, he had his dogs everywhere, all on his side. I drank the water and then asked for a piece of bread, to which he retorted, 'You go and join your group, and when you get back to your camp, you will have your supper'.

The wood was full of German soldiers, on the other side was a newly built village, buzzing with traffic, ready and waiting. All the latecomers were herded towards two waiting trucks by civilian helpers, and our supper was served in Sachsenhausen.

The camp had taken on many more prisoners, arriving relentlessly day and night, in the meantime the sound of heavy bombardment was deafening, nobody knew what the following day would bring.

At roll call the next morning, I was assigned to one of two groups to go back to the grenade factory. The previous day, four barracks were burned down, we had to remove all the bodies. We were there for three days, we had to search the whole compound, place all the charred bodies onto trucks, then the guards transported them to the crematorium.

During the last few critical days of captivity, I bumped into my old friend Vasyl Boyko, he was pointed out to me by a former Belarussian partisan who was in quarantine with us. Vasyl was loitering by the kitchen, looking for scraps and peelings, he was now classed as a 'skeleton' hardly managing to move his feet when he walked. How could I help this poor soul? I gave him a few raw potatoes, knowing that at least he could cook them in his barrack. I made an arrangement with him, that he would cook the potatoes, then later we would share them.

On the second evening, he wasn't in the barrack, after two hours did he turn up, saying that somebody had stolen his potatoes as he was cooking them. I didn't make any more arrangements with him, because I realised he hadn't been honest with me.

A new atmosphere descended on the camp, the whole camp was to be evacuated. New rumours spread in our midst, people were speculating that the German guards would clothe the prisoners in German uniforms. There were always such rumours floating around, but there was a difference about the Germans', they sensed that their days were coming to an end.

To find the truth for myself, I walked into a barrack of Germans, where there would always be an idiot who'd spill the beans. I soon learned all the latest gossip from them, they didn't hide anything from me.

The following day, all the prisoners were issued German uniforms, apparently all the German guards agreed to this, there was no other alternative. Every prisoner, now in his uniform, received a helmet, rifle and boots.

In order to evacuate the whole camp, the Germans had to organise a form of defence, so they mixed the prisoners in with their own SS columns. The first columns consisted of French and Scandinavians, each prisoner received bread and tinned soup for his journey.

It took two days of relentless toil, day and night, without any interval, to evacuate everyone, one hundred after another hundred after a further hundred, and so on. We were told to leave last because we were from Eastern Europe, the first wave of prisoners each received half a loaf, and when it came to our turn, we were left with nothing, no bread or soup.

On the twenty second of April we left camp, we saw Russian planes circling overhead, they were apparently meant to be our saviours, but they even stole the date for their own history books.

We marched in group formation all the time on foot, using minor roads, all we ate was grass and water and our feet soon began to blister. We slept under the open sky in open fields, the German guards ate bread and meat while we were forced to eat grass that we boiled in our mess cans. If one of us found something on the road, it could be cooked that evening. Sometimes, we would come across fleeing Germans on carts, who gave us some of their food.

As throughout the whole war, the strong and physically able survived, they could organise themselves, search and find, beg, borrow and steal, the weak and the ill were always the hungriest.

I can't remember how many people were in our group, or even guess, or who was the strongest, but I do remember that the Slovaks were the first to die.

When our group left Sachsenhausen, everyone took their own personal possessions, namely food, as this was the most expensive commodity. Most people carried coats and blankets in rucksacks, but I noticed from the very first night, that there was an element of Russians who carried nothing, but during the night raid the weakest 'skeletons'. They would steal food from under their heads as they slept, they were not even scared of the German guards.

To safeguard myself from these bandits, I and two friends had codes and passwords, something one of us picked up in the camp, and to this day I am sure that saved my life. The three of us always slept together, hardly ever feeling the cold because we had blankets. Life in those days was measured in pennies, and it paid to have friends, even in hell, and this later proved itself to be true, particular when people began to die along the journey.

In the camp I had many friends, most of whom were from Belarussia, I even had one from Russia, just in case. We lived in one room; they only knew two or three German words, so I was useful to them. There were those who worked for me in my command, and liked me as their own mother. I never did anyone harm; they all saw this and understood. I never hit anyone, for we all wanted to see the end of the war.

Living cheek by jowl in one room with a person for a year, you really do get to know them, sometimes they wouldn't give me a moment's peace, but on every work detail, I gained their respect and they trusted me. If you had friends in a camp, you had respect, those who had good friends, had good backing.

In the beginning of 1945, the three of us were separated for a short while, that was the time when the Russians, positioned on the other side of the River Oder, began to build up their strength. After six weeks we met up again; this time under different circumstances, for the Russians now had their own leader. The Russians in the camp began to organise themselves, they needed me as their interpreter, we had to prepare ourselves for a meeting, with the Russian Army. Thank God for my good fortune that it didn't materialise, the Germans had sent us on our journey before the Russians arrived, but they were catching us up, slowly but surely.

The Russians in our group didn't give up in spirit, they waited, knowing that sooner or later they would be repatriated with their own.

Two or three times, our group came in contact with the Red Cross, which lifted our spirits; the parcels were loaded onto the guard's wagon. The first parcel was divided into three, the second into five, and that was when the confusion started, the strong took advantage of the weak, leaving them with little.

Once, as we passed a village, the owners of a small homestead gave us some unpeeled potatoes, this is how the Germans fed us throughout our adventure. Is it surprising that amongst men, there are pigs? We were herded and hurried along our journey like cattle, the guards, with their rifles alongside, setting us a good pace, because they carried nothing on their backs.

The guards had their own wagon, which carried all their belongings. The wagon had four rubber tyres and was pulled by starving prisoners. During the first couple of days, the wagon moved slowly, as at that time it was fully laden. Towards the end of the week, the weaker ones would collapse and drop out by the wayside, and I saw the guards shooting the weakest. The strongest walked at the front, they too would pull the wagon in turns, but the unfortunate who didn't have the strength to walk, were shot dead one by one when they could no longer walk.

My friend Vasyl was one of those who died on the roadside, I couldn't help him at all, and the guards kept me constantly by the wagon, from where I had no means of escape.

For twelve hard and never-ending days we marched, costing many their young lives, those who didn't survive the great hunger, the Germans left their bodies to rot. Those who dropped to the ground from hunger and exhaustion and unable to carry on were shot by the Germans, their bodies scattered everywhere here and there in the ditches, that's how the German regime looked and behaved.

Every night we slept under the open sky, every morning we would wake to those who didn't make it through the night, all we ate was grass, no bread was to be had from any source whatsoever, and that's why so many of us died.

We left Berlin on the twenty second of April 1945, I heard that we would be marching to a port. On the third of May we reached Schwerin, luckily we didn't land on a 'worse devil'.

I was at the front pulling the wagon that morning when I distinctly heard a German officer on the other side, calling out a command for the column to run into the woods. I heard and understood every word that the Americans had taken over Schwerin. Within minutes the wagon was bare, the guards had emptied it from all sides, then I saw the guards were running into the bushes and quickly taking off their military uniforms.

There were still a few packages and food on the wagon, even fried chicken. Suddenly, there emerged a brave Pole, who climbed into the wagon and who wanted to share the food with us all. Two minutes later our brave Pole fell to the ground and stopped breathing. The wagon was surrounded by a thousand men; they were hungry and acted like wild animals. Fortunately, I managed to escape from the wagon with only bruises.

I unexpectedly fell upon my two friends and, with all my strength, persuaded them to leave the group, I didn't trust the Germans, I wasn't convinced that we had seen our last bodies. They listened, and we then went deeper into the woods, from where we could hear nearby gunfire, so we kneeled and waited for a minute. We thought it best to rid ourselves of any incriminating souvenirs and went on. We soon came across a road and walked along it, where to, we had no idea, until we came across a house at the edge of the wood. We entered the yard, standing there was an old German, next to him a French prisoner, then inside, another who was injured.

Inside the house, we told the Germans, that the war had ended, but they didn't believe us. The old man's wife gave us a glass of milk each, and the Frenchman, a bucket of raw potatoes. At the back of the house, in the German's garden, we began to boil the potatoes. Whilst we were waiting for the potatoes, the Frenchman came to our aid, by advising us what to do next. It took a while for the potatoes to boil in our bucket, even though there was plenty of dried wood. Before our eyes the scenery was changing, the terrible German had now stood back. From our fire, through a gap in the trees, we could see a nearby road, we also saw a German soldier walking at the front of his unit, with a raised white flag. All of this happened, in the afternoon, on the third of May 1945.

That evening, by the wood, we ate a mountain of sumptuous tasting potatoes, so much that an hour later I was rolling around, from an unusual pain, from overeating.

The German Army abandoned their ammunition, artillery, food and drink in the woods, not far from Schwerin. The surviving prisoners were now partying, eating and drinking everything the Germans had left behind. I felt uneasy staying in the woods, with all that was happening around us, so we slept in the barn where it was more comfortable and safer, even though there was constant barrage of gunfire, all night long.

I woke up very early the following morning, my two friends were still sleeping. I washed and shaved, to the later surprise of my friends. We were supposed to meet the Russians as heroes, unwashed and unshaven. If we looked presentable, our 'own' would believe that we were true heroes of the German prison camps.

In the woods, we found a German tent, which we used to store our belongings, other prisoners too, asked us to look after their possessions, not thinking that I might want to escape. The Frenchman told me that it was thirty kilometres from Schwerin to Wismar, but my immediate problem, was the contingent of Russian prisoners, as they now all had firearms. I kept a keen eye on the tent, making sure that nobody entered, there were many that would.

When my two friends returned, they allowed me to see to my needs, and looked after the tent. Before they had realised, I must have been half way to Schwerin. When I left, I took an empty sack so as not to give anyone the impression that I was leaving. I left the wood and found a road, where there was chaos; the whole road was blocked, with broken trucks and cannons. There was an opportunity to fill my sack with some food, I found a few loaves and tinned meat. My problem now was that I was too weak and numb to carry such a load, sweat was pouring off me, but I persevered. On the road, I managed to exchange my old mouldy bread for fresh, which lightened my load, and managed to carry the sack to the market.

In the city, I saw German soldiers who had not long surrendered standing around near a square, so I decided to take a rest nearby and observe for a while. I couldn't help but notice two German officers with new bicycles, so I approached one of them and asked if I could have one, they agreed, even giving me a belt for the rear parcel carrier. Now I felt great, the proud owner of a bicycle, and a sack to carry on my back.

I picked up road signs pointing towards Wismar, feeling overjoyed inside, it had been two years since I last cycled. I didn't stop turning those pedals over and over until I reached the outskirts of Wismar, on the way passing many soldiers and civilians. When I finally stopped, I wiped my brow and thanked God, I didn't think that I would ever again see Wismar and its familiar streets.

In Wismar, as in Schwerin, the Americans were now ruling the roost, the air even smelt differently.

CHAPTER 26
BACK IN WISMAR

For the first time in my life I saw Russian soldiers driving around the city. The sight of them frightened me; some of them had already been drinking, so I quickly pedalled towards my old lodgings. I had just pushed my bicycle through the house gates, when from nowhere appeared two American Military Policemen. They started to speak to me in their own language, but frightened and unable to communicate, I released my bicycle and raised both my arms. In the confusion, my old mistress, noticed me and came to my rescue. The American soldiers, realising that I was known to the old lady, turned and left.

My mistress was frightened by my appearance, though no less than I was of the Americans. She spoke about her predicament, her family, the loss of her husband, and was left with two small children. 'It is good to see you alive and in one piece, we can now all live together'. How could I fault all the Germans?

We spoke for about an hour, and then she poured me a bath, told me to remove all my clothes and climb in. She held a stiff scrubbing brush in her hand and scrubbed me from head to toe. She threw away and burned my prisoner's clothing, then hid my sack of food in a cupboard. The clothes I left behind were taken by my old colleagues, so she found me her late husband's clothes.

I put on a hat to cover my short cropped hair, and I now looked more like a normal person; I headed into town to look for my old friend Dmytro. I took a five year old child with me but couldn't walk for too long as he soon tired. I never found Dmytro or his master, even where Dmytro used to work had turned into a bomb site. I didn't find Vasyl either, his mistress said that he'd gone back to his village. I tried carrying the little boy, as I wanted to call at my old bakery, but when I reached the centre, the sight of the military presence frightened me. I had no other alternative, but to return, I'd only taken the child, thinking it would give me the look of a local. I saw much destruction everywhere I turned, most of all the Russians driving around.

In the end, I mustered enough courage and decided to walk onto Bademuderstrasse, to the bakery were I'd once worked. As I approached the building, a cold sweat came over me, my mind went back to the last time I'd set foot there, when the Gestapo arrested me. As I looked through the shop window, everything was bare, all I could see was an old cat taking advantage of the sun. I walked down the corridor cautiously, again feeling the sweat on my brow, until I saw the old bakery master, who was pleased as punch to see me and exclaimed that I'd been sent by God.

After a moment the bakery master noticed that I was not alone, firstly thinking he was my son, then asking his age. The old master was preparing a sour dough, at the same time scrutinising me from all directions. We shared a glass of wine. He then said he couldn't use the machine, as they had been without electricity for three days. I could see he was struggling on his own, so I went outside to collect firewood for the oven. I promised the master, that I would take the child home, and then return to give him a hand.

On our way back, we passed Vasyl's, but didn't want to call in, as I knew that Frau Sammer would be waiting with lunch at home. After eating my lunch as quickly as I could, she came into the room, then said that I should now call her Marie, because we were now living in new times, and the old times had gone, she was now a widow with two small children. She promised me my old room and hoped I would work in bakery, as I was young and strong. I thanked her for lunch and her kind words, then hurried back to the bakery to help the old master with his bread.

In such a short space of time, my life in the liberated world had turned full circle. Firstly and most importantly, I was now a free man and I thanked God that I was physically able and unharmed. Secondly, Frau Sammer and the old bakery master greeted and welcomed me back warm heartedly. I had my old job and lodgings, all that was left for me to do was to find my old friends who'd escaped the city before its surrender.

I walked along the same footpath, passing the same lime trees I did two years earlier, and where I was frogmarched to the police station by the two Gestapo men. I had to pinch myself, thinking, 'Am I dreaming'? Back in the camps, these dreams were so regular that when I awoke, I wanted to cry, for they'd only been dreams, and not reality. Now it was so difficult to believe that it was truly reality. As I approached the bakery, my mind began to play tricks on me again, I couldn't distinguish one from the other, for outside the bakery stood a large military vehicle, and on it were four Russian soldiers. I pretended to ignore them, strode to the door and knocked but nobody answered. I was about to leave, when one of the soldiers approached and asked if this was the right place where he could get some bread. I turned towards him and replied in German, that there was nobody there that everyone had fled to the villages because they were scared that the Americans would bomb the city. I recommended, that he tried the bakery where Dmytro used to work, knowing full well that the bakery was no longer there. The bakery master saw everything from upstairs, he later told me that they had already called twice that morning, but because he was on his own he was too frightened to let them in.

I entered the bakery; the master was overjoyed that I would now mix the bread dough by hand. I washed my hands, rolled up my sleeves and started mixing. Once upon a time, mixing one hundred bread by hand was easy, but that day I developed a hot sweat and had to slow down. I wiped the sweat off my brow, and after that moment I didn't remember anything, everything had turned black and I fell to the ground. I came to when the master was reviving me with cold water and helping me to my feet, he escorted me outside, sat me down on a chair and told me to rest, then he went to finish mixing the dough himself.

In those days, doughs were normally meant to rest for an hour, the time it took for me to come to my senses, after which I was able to help the master, to scale and mould the dough pieces. The master didn't advertise the fact that he was baking bread, but soon people picked up the smell of freshly baked bread, and even though the bread was still in the oven, a considerable amount of people had already formed a line outside the shop. Suddenly, there was a fierce banging on the door, this time the master opened it, only to find three Russian soldiers, who wanted to take the whole batch of bread for their unit. They couldn't speak German, and I didn't let on that I understood them. The master kept turning to me, asking me again if I understood anything, I said no and carried on with my work, ignoring the Russian soldiers. I was also lucky that I wore my bakers' hat, otherwise having short hair, they would have guessed I was an prisoner or soldier.

I took very little notice of them, but sweat was pouring off me from fright, not from the heat or the work, and I overheard them say that they would have to bring along an interpreter.

In the meantime, the master mixed a second dough, as the queue outside was getting longer by the minute, because there had been no fresh bread for three days. Before the soldiers returned, the Germans had bought the first batch of bread, so they had to wait for the second batch that had just been inserted into the oven.

The young Russian interpreter began asking the master what had happened to the first batch of bread, which had already been baking in the oven when the soldiers called the first time. The master replied that his regular customers had quickly bought everything; some customers had left with nothing, that's why he was baking the second batch, to satisfy everybody. The soldiers were not satisfied with the explanation, one of them took out his pistol and started goading the master with it, and then another tried to count the bread in the oven, but failed as there was no electricity, and so no light in the oven.

The Russian soldiers could see for themselves a large queue forming outside, whereupon the interpreter, ordered the master to bake a third batch of bread. The master replied that as we had no flour or salt, we could not work in the dark without electricity.

In the meantime, I quickly cleared up, swept the bakery, took out the rubbish, and quietly and unnoticed, left the bakery, not even informing the master. I never returned to that bakery ever again.

On the way to my lodgings I called at Vasyl's, this time Nastya was home alone, she said they had just spent three days in the village, fearing the Americans would bomb the city, which didn't happen. Nastya was very happy to see me alive; she had come to expect the worse after all the stories she heard about the camps, and how the Germans treated their captives. She spent many hours talking about the hardships she had to endure with Vasyl, and of the many times sirens had driven them out of the city to seek refuge in the village where they used to work.

At that time nobody understood the situation, who had taken control of the city, whether it was the Americans or the Russians. It turned out the British had taken over the city, so most of the people hiding in the villages returned, leaving the Russians in control of the outskirts. During the first three days people could enter each zone freely, the Russians allowed people some movement, but only until six in the evening. Afterwards, they only allowed passage to women and children, not men.

I intended to sleep at my lodgings; I even promised myself that I would, but Nastya wouldn't let me leave, she was now scared to be left alone. They lived in two rooms, which I'd found for them a couple of years before. I had to explain to Nastya that since my freedom I had eaten too much, too quickly, which meant I had to constantly use a toilet, as my organism was not used to the sudden intake of extra food.

Vasyl arrived soaking wet just before dawn, having to avoid Russian patrols and all avoid roads, instead sneaking through peoples' gardens.

Later that morning Vasyl escorted me into the Russian zone, that's where all the Ukrainian people lived in the villages. They were not aware of the situation, so I hastened to warn them to collect all their valuables and to return into the city of Wismar, before the Russians closed the border.

I called in to see Frau Sammer to explain my intentions, then forewarned my compatriots in the village, and finally I collected my bicycle and left.

Vasyl had turned me into a 'Frenchman'. He gave me his black beret and fastened a French badge on my chest. It had become compulsory for each person to carry his or her own national identity, except for the Germans who had to wear a white armband.

On my way to the village, I decided to see the bakery master, and enquire how we'd got on with the unexpected guests. He said that he'd given each Russian soldier two loaves of bread but they protested and demanded more. One of the regular customers heard the commotion and approached the British Military Police, who happened to be nearby, and on their arrival, they quickly dispersed the Russian soldiers.

The bakery master also said that he intended to bake more bread the following day, as he was told that the electricity, would be working, and that a delivery of flour was also expected. He was pleased to hear that I was cycling to the village of Melkenburg, because that was where his mother, his wife and their two children lived. He had very little time himself to visit, as he didn't dare leave the bakery unattended.

The road to Melkenburg was familiar to me, I knew all the pathways, and even where the thick tree roots, grew on top of them, though I had to be very vigilant, as it was easy to fall over.

On approaching the boundaries of the village, I noticed a military checkpoint manned by British soldiers. They politely lifted the barrier without detaining me. A further hundred metres on, I approached a second checkpoint, but this one was unmanned, except for a solitary civilian, with the letter 'P' on his chest, labelling him as Polish. I got off my bicycle and walked round the barrier to the other side, when suddenly I heard a Russian voice shouting 'Stop! Or I shoot'! I stopped but gave the impression I didn't understand. A Russian soldier stood up from the ditch where he was lying, then in a loud voice asked me where I was going. I again stood still, giving the impression that I didn't understand. I turned towards the Pole, and then spoke to him in 'broken' German. He too spoke very little, in both German and Russian, but I soon figured that I was able to proceed, even though I had to ask the soldier first.

I cycled onto the next village, not long after which, I saw a Russian officer approaching me on a bicycle. I stopped, allowing him the right of way, but he stopped too, and then spoke to me in Russian, saying he was carrying out important military work, and that his bicycle was not up to the task, and that I would have to swap my bicycle for his. He then went on to say that after an hour, when he finished his work, he would return my bicycle. Under the circumstances, I felt unable to protest, so without further ado, I handed over my German military bicycle, in exchange for an old 'Russian wreck'.

I waited over an hour, and was too scared to wait any longer, so I continued towards a familiar homestead about three hundred metres away. In the centre of the homestead stood a group of Russian soldiers, gathered around a very large pan, in which they were cooking what looked like a cow. The smell emanating from the cooking was just too much for me, I couldn't restrain myself, so I approached them, and asked in German if I could have a piece of meat. Most of the soldiers were drunk, but one of them took out a large bone covered in meat. I found myself a place away from the soldiers, still hoping that the Russian officer would return my bicycle. I ate all the meat off the bone, then had to find a place to relieve myself. I walked behind a barn, but suddenly froze, when I saw two soldiers forcing themselves onto a German woman. I suddenly forgot about my bicycle, and carried on with my journey.

When I arrived in Melkenburg, I soon found the bakery master's mother and wife. I passed on his news and good wishes, and carried onto the next village, where my old friend George worked as a gardener.

I was cycling through a wood along a familiar path when I saw another Russian soldier approaching me. He had a bicycle, but was pushing it, and not riding it. He was as 'drunk as a lord' but seeing me with a bicycle, he wanted to swap his for mine. His bicycle was in much better condition than mine, only his handlebars were bent, because he'd probably fallen off in a drunken stupor. I was too frightened to argue with him, so we exchanged bicycles and then both left in opposite directions.

After about a kilometre I saw an old man walking around in the yard of his small homestead. He noticed me and shouted in German 'The Russians have taken everything'. I tried to reassure him, saying that I wanted nothing, only a spanner to fix my bicycle, and explaining to him, how I'd come across this damaged bicycle in the first place. The old German then replied that the Russian soldier could have been the same one who had been looking for women, not even half an hour ago. He went onto say that the previous day Russian soldiers had been in the area and raped two German women. For their safety, his wife and daughter-in-law were now hiding in the woods, and that he had to take food to them.

We spoke for a while, as he was very interested in what was happening in Wismar and about the long-term prospects, whether the Russians were to remain.

I was still traumatised by what I had just seen. It was the first time in my life that I'd come into contact with Russian soldiers, and the experience left me stone-cold. Nor had I ever before ventured into the unknown, but in those days I still had little fear. It was then that my friend Vasyl proposed this trip to me. I had given my word to Vasyl that I would visit the remaining Ukrainian families in the 'temporary Russian zone' as the word had spread that it would soon become a 'permanent Russian zone'.

I never imagined seeing what I had, namely the two Russian soldiers raping the German woman in broad daylight, the incidents I'd had with the bicycles, all in such a short space of time. I came to the conclusion that the Russian soldiers were savages, especially after also seeing one from a tank division wrap a watch around his neck, one with an alarm. He would wind the watch, wait for the alarm to sound, then repeat this action, all the time I was there.

I eventually arrived in the yard where George worked as a gardener. Unfortunately, I was told by the owner of the homestead who knew me that George had taken a horse-drawn cart, loaded it with young men and girls and their belongings, then left for Ukraine the previous afternoon.

I left and headed swiftly towards Lisow where Anna, her parents and other friends of mine lived. When I arrived I was told the same story as with George, that all the Ukrainians who worked on the homestead had packed all their belongings and gone home.

To prove to Vasyl that I had been in the village, I found two old postcards still stuck onto a wall in her room, which I had sent to Anna; that was all I could find.

The return journey to my bakery master's family went smoothly, and when I arrived his wife had a parcel and a letter ready for me. I thanked her and quickly cycled back, before the Russians closed their checkpoint.

As I approached the Russian checkpoint, I saw many other people waiting for an opportunity to present itself, which came very quickly. Two wagons with French POWs were on their way home, in Wismar was their collection point. Their wagons stopped at the checkpoint, whereupon all the prisoners alighted. They went up to the Russian soldier and perceiving him as their saviour, tossed him into the air. In the confusion, the civilians like me who were waiting to cross the checkpoint, quickly ran round the barrier.

I gave Vasyl an account of my day, telling him about the exodus of all our friends from the villages, departing back to Ukraine. Vasyl quickly explained to me that all his savings and belongings were with Anna's parents. He took my bicycle, leaving his own with me because it was newer, and left in hot pursuit.

That night I stayed with Nastya, she was scared to be alone, worrying about her husband, and I couldn't sleep either, having to pay frequent visits to the toilet.

The following day I met up with some old acquaintances, who worked in a local laundry. We were not close friends, they were in fact younger than me, but invited me to stay with them in their barrack. They had a good stock of food; they even had a barrel of good old wine, so I spent most of my time eating to satisfy my perennial hunger, then every hour I would have to run to the toilet.

On the third night, whilst we were cooking supper outside, my old friend Dmytro came with his girlfriend. He was well dressed, shaven and looked like a proper gentleman, not like me scruffy and undernourished, waiting hungrily for supper. He admitted how difficult it'd been for him and George to take all my belongings from my old lodgings, when I was arrested by the Gestapo. They hid all my things in the village, but when the time came to leave, all they took were the clothes they were wearing. I believed him, I saw firsthand how the Russians handled people, but what annoyed me most about Dmytro was that he didn't ask me once how I was or if he could help me in any way. No, he quickly took his girlfriend and left.

I spent another couple of days in the barrack. While there, the Russian's were constantly trying to talk us into leaving for 'home' but we kept stalling them by saying that we were trying to get together some food for our journey. In the meantime, we found out that, besides the French, there other nationalities getting together, people who wanted to remain in the 'West' and not to go back home to the USSR.

I went with Dmytro Mychalkiw, (he died in the 1980's in Leicester, England) to make further inquiries, and we were told and convinced that there were many such people who didn't want to return 'home', and we even found out that the British gave food and protection from the Russians.

Before WW2, all the Ukrainians who'd worked in France, had then been captured and sent to Germany had the right to return to France.

This is precisely what my old friend Dmytro did, since his girlfriend had been taken with her parents by the Germans. The same happened to George, who caught up with Anna's parents, but found that all his belongings had disappeared and had been confiscated by the Russians at the border. Anna and her mother hid all their valuable possessions in their village, then bypassed the checkpoint by crossing the border through private gardens, an ingenious means of escape.

When Anna heard that I was back in Wismar she asked Vasyl if I would help them. She wanted me to return across the border to collect their valuables, for which she was prepared to give me half. I passed on a message with Vasyl, saying that, even if all their valuables were of gold, under no circumstances would I cross the 'border'.

One day, Dmytro Mychalkiw and I escorted Vasyl to the French enclosure, from which all the people there were transported back to France. Vasyl owned two new bicycles he intended to take to France with him, but the authorities refused him. Mychalkiw and I were standing by the gate, watching what was going on in the enclosure, when suddenly we noticed that a Frenchman had cycled off on Vasyl's bicycle towards town.

In a short space of time many such 'enclosures' had sprung up, and I found myself in one of them, along with several hundred others. The Russians kept visiting the enclosures, with all their usual propaganda, trying their hardest to convince people to return home. Sadly, there were many who believed them and returned. I had to make new friends, as all my old friends had gone their separate ways.

I never got to see Anna in Wismar, I later found out from Vasyl that she'd returned to France with her mother. Her father was arrested by the Russians at the 'border' a twist of fortune so to speak, since he later managed to escape and rejoin his family in France.

I never saw Nadia again, I heard from her friends that the Germans took her to a prison just before the end of the war. Whatever happened to her later, I never found out.

By the end of the week, all Ukrainians in Wismar lived in enclosures and camps. Later, the British started to move us onto another camp in Hagenow, where there was also a large goods station from which hundreds of Ukrainians, mostly girls, departed for 'home'. To their misfortune, there was nobody of 'higher authority' amongst the Ukrainians who could advise them to see sense, and to convince them not to listen to the Russian lies and their propaganda.

It was in Hagenow, were for the very first time I ever received a parcel from the 'Red Cross' as a former POW.

After a few days, the British were convinced that the remainder of the people had no inclination to return 'home', so they transported us to the site of one of Hitler's former homes in Lubeck, our accommodation was to be the former horse stables.

On our arrival, we found that a Polish administration unit had been set up to run everything. I was registered as a former POW which entitled me to double rations and milk.

I soon gained weight, and jokingly, the people who knew me called me 'fatty'. Our camp was predominantly Polish, it contained few Ukrainians among whom most were too scared to admit to being Ukrainian.

I belonged to a group of six people; we found a corner, on concrete in one of the stables. We all spoke Ukrainian amongst ourselves, and one time we even burst into song. As we began to sing a Ukrainian Folk song, we were joined by other Ukrainians, who we didn't know existed, even though we shared the same stable. We later found out that, within the camp, there were also Ukrainian girls. I wasn't personally interested in girls at that time, only in food, but when Mychalkiw proposed that I join him and go into the girls' barrack with him, I did.

It turned out that in 'Hitler Kaserne' I would meet my future wife Olha, who lived in the same stable, but on a lower level, with families, on my floor it was for men only. That same evening I was introduced to her, she suffered with her tonsils. The poor girl just lay on a made-up bed of gas mask packaging. She shared the room with her cousin, also called Olha, and another two girls who'd escaped from the Russian Zone. They also came from the same camp in Hagenow, I remembered seeing them, but at that time didn't know they were Ukrainian. When I saw such a poor and unfortunate girl, it broke my heart to see her in such a sorry state. She wore the same threadbare dress and torn shoes she'd escaped in, having had to leave the rest of her belongings in a hurry, at the homestead where she last worked. Previously she had worked in a German ammunitions factory for two years.

In the camp, I was on double rations and milk; in addition, I received two parcels from the Red Cross. I sold the cigarettes, coffee and chocolate on the 'black market' and, with the proceeds, I was able to buy Olha a dress and shoes, so that at least she could go into town, because in the shoes she had, it was impossible to walk. To repay me, we made an arrangement, that she would wash and iron my clothes, which gave me more opportunities to see her.

In Lubeck, there was also a Ukrainian camp on Dunnerverk, which I only found out because there was a funeral of a young Ukrainian who died by drinking moonshine or a similar concoction, there were, unfortunately, other such incidents. I don't know why, but at the funeral I proposed we sang a popular burial song 'Vydish Brate Mij' (Do You See, Brother Of Mine)

After the funeral, I was approached by some of the lads from Dunnerverk, who invited me to their barrack, to which I agreed, and one evening I visited them with Olha. That same evening, in front of the barrack, there was some sort of party; many people were dancing merrily to music and I recognised and old friend Ivan Wojtkiw, who worked near Wismar in a homestead, but didn't want to work there, so he volunteered to join the German Army, and I acted as his interpreter. Our friendship helped me a great deal because he got on well with a German who was able to get his hands on many luxurious products, things we could only dream about. From that day Ivan helped me tremendously, and from his help I was able to help others.

Olha began to look better after a while; I helped her as much as I could with food and clothing, I treated her like a sister. One day we went for a stroll to Lubeck, where there was a 'black market' and I was approached by a young Pole from the POW camp, who used to be in my command. He invited us to his barrack, where only Poles lived, most of them POW's. And when we entered the barrack, my friend introduced me to his fellow roommates as his former barrack leader. No sooner had he uttered those words than a group of his friends who were previously on their beds jumped to their feet, ready and eager to give me a sound beating, but my friend quickly intervened, saying that I was a 'golden person' that it was his fellow Poles who were the swines, and this was promptly confirmed by one of his friends who knew the facts. My Polish friend wanted to invite us for a bite and a drink but I refused, saying that I had to go and see an eye doctor. That part of the lie was true, because when the Germans evacuated us from Berlin, a convoy of civilian vehicles which passed us, was attacked by American planes, killing many horses. The POWs who had anything shaped like a knife; me included, tried cutting a piece of horse meat for themselves, but I was hit by a guard with his rifle butt. The following day my left eye was swollen and had closed up, and I couldn't open it for a few days. I later went to see a private eye doctor in Lubeck, and to this day my left eye is weaker then my right.

We spent over two months in the Polish Camp, many people transferred to the Ukrainian but I didn't, because I would have lost my double rations and parcels.

Lubeck and Wismar were under American and British control, but the outskirts and beyond eastwards, was controlled by the Russians. They often came to our camp, purposefully to convince people to return back to the 'homeland'. They passed us with their loudspeakers, announcing that Lubeck would soon be under their control, which later it was, so the area became unsafe.

I got to know from fellow Ukrainians that there was a camp solely for Ukrainians in Heidenau, situated in the opposite direction to the Russians, and we would be safer. I got together ten volunteers and Olha, hired a goods wagon, and then trundled off to Heidenau.

CHAPTER 27
HEIDENAU

When we arrived at the camp in Heidenau, I found that the administration and running of the camp was carried out by Ukrainians, and there was also help from the Serbians, who had their own smaller camp next to ours. All the Serbians were military, and they were even given permission by the British Command to carry rifles and pistols.

When I entered the administration block with my 'party' to register, I recognised an old friend from the Dunnerverk camp, a Miss Mandryk, who I met in Lubeck, in the Polish Camp. Whilst I stayed there, I found out about the Ukrainian Camp, which was on the other side of the town, so I often went there, and got to know many people. One day as I walked towards Dunnerverk, I overheard two pretty Ukrainian girls, and as we passed I said to them that they looked familiar. We started talking, one of them exclaimed that she'd lost her brother Taras, while the other had lost her husband. I tried to cheer them up, and said that I was sure that I'd noticed Taras at the transitional camp, and that she would soon find him. We soon parted, they went into town, and I to camp, but as I was approaching the first few barracks, the heavens opened up with heavy torrential rain, forcing me into the first barrack I came to. As I entered, I came across the family Mandryk, the mother of the two girls I had just met minutes ago. Mrs Mandryk began explaining her tragic passage from the Russians, then on the way she lost her son Taras, and one of her daughter's lost her husband. I tried to pacify Mrs Mandryk, saying that I'd met her son in the camp, and even spoke to him. Mrs Mandryk believed me, and when her daughters returned she told them the story. The daughters then told their mother that this man had first lied to them, and was now trying the same on their poor old mother.

Needless to say, I was confronted by the two Mandryk sisters, who worked in the administration block in the camp. They both recognised me and called their fellow workers round, introducing me as the person who for the first time in their lives had tricked them.

After the little scene, the whole of my party were registered, and I was even asked to be a member of the camp security. In addition, because we knew each other, myself and Olha were invited to the barrack where the sisters lived.

The sister's father was barrack 202's monitor, and when he asked me if I was married, I jokingly replied yes as I didn't want to leave Olha alone, so we were given one room. I later married Olha, and when the sisters found out they said that I'd tricked them again in the administration block, because had their father known, he would never have allowed me to share a room with a woman if we were not married.

I shared a room with my wife Olha, and three other couples. Each couple hung a blanket as a screen, to give themselves a little privacy.

Camp life soon became tedious, I needed to find something to do, the food was bad and not enough, which forced me into looking elsewhere. One day, Olha and I were walking through the village, we weren't supposed to, but because I was in security, I had those privileges, and could come and go as I pleased.

In the village, we walked past a bakery, and without thinking I walked straight inside, asking for the owner. I was told that the owner was asleep and that he would be back in an hour. Olha and I carried on walking, returning after an hour, to find the owner on his feet. I introduced myself to him, and he politely invited me inside. We agreed that I would work for him one day a week, on Fridays, and that he wouldn't pay me in cash, but with bread.

My only problem was how to leave the camp, especially since I belonged to the camp security, which meant that I had to stand guard sometimes. We had guard duty 24 hours a day because we still experienced problems from the Russians, who persistently came with their old lies, trying to convince people to return 'home'.

Once I started work, if it coincided with my security duties, then I easily found somebody to step in for me, especially if they were rewarded with bread.

In the camp, there were other people with similar ideas to mine, who didn't want to sit around jobless, so they found work in neighbouring villages, working on homesteads or in private houses. These enterprising people would exchange food for coffee, cigarettes, chocolates and other items, which the Germans had difficulty in obtaining. That's how the 'black market' started, when the Germans didn't have enough meat and sausages, they even exchanged wheat, which they would take to the bakery, the owner would exchange a kilo of wheat for a kilo of bread. His customers would have to pay for bread using cash, and officially a loaf of bread cost 45 feniks (cents), but a loaf on the black market would sell for 45 marks, and sometimes more.

Our camp in Heidenau was to the south of Hamburg, a large German port and city, from where many Germans came to barter with our 'residents'. Entry into our camp for outsiders was strictly prohibited, but that didn't stop many people exchanging their coffee and cigarettes with the Germans for clothing.

In the camp, we had a bigger problem, thieving. There were people who went on night raids to neighbouring villages, some of them even armed, and they never returned empty handed, and caused endless embarrassment to the camp administrators, the camp as a whole, and the British authorities. Whenever something went missing or stolen, the victims always blamed the camp inhabitants, but however many inspections took place, none of the culprits were ever caught.

The thieves who went on nightly raids would go into stables, killing pigs and young calves, then cutting them up into small pieces, so that they could be smuggled back into camp unnoticed. There were many former workers, who worked on nearby farms and homesteads, who were willing to give out information, where meats, sausages and other useful items were stored.

The camp was situated on the edge of the village, access to it was very easy, and the security was set up to prevent 'uninvited' guests, not to stop people who lived there returning. The night's catch was usually stored under the barracks, sometime buried, or even just covered. If someone had a quarter of a pig, it was too much to be consumed quickly, so these people would exchange it for cigarettes, or coffee, and that's how the black market at the camp blossomed.

Alcohol was also available. It was brewed and traded by the local Germans, who made it from beetroot or potatoes, then exchange it in the camp for luxury goods. One evening, one of the thieves returned by mistake into my barrack, where the camp security was lodged. He stumbled in frightened and soaking wet from the dew, he had been chased by the local villagers, and so had to leave his catch in the wheat field. He explained more or less where he'd left his catch of gammon. That Sunday, I went with my friend Ivan Levyckyj to try and find it, and luckily we did, there must have been at least twenty five kilos of meat in the sack. Our problem now was how to return unnoticed to camp nearby as such a quantity couldn't be left behind. We decided it would be best if we buried it, since it was getting warmer outside, so to leave it to the elements, would harm the meat. We buried the meat in three holes, then returned to camp.

Somebody must have noticed us bury the meat, because on the following night one of the hiding places had been uncovered. The other two hiding places were undiscovered, allowing us both many visits, returning well laden with our buried treasure.

Another incident occurred soon after my assistant Ivan Levyckyj had enough of security life and moved to Hanover for different work. The new assistant assigned to me was called Bilenkyj. One day, unexpectedly, we were visited by the main security officers, assisted by Bilenkyj. My old friend Anton Feshuk, who buried the gammon, found himself in a very awkward situation, because he kept a pistol in the barrack, under his pillow. When he heard the security patrol was in the next barrack, he put his pistol into his pocket, then went into my room, saying to my wife, that it was for me, and put it into a cupboard.

At that time I was working in the bakery, and when I returned for lunch, Olha told me about Anton coming into our room and hiding something in the cupboard. We never had an inspection in our room, not even by the Serbian security, who knew me very well; they often came into the bakery for bread, and had business dealings with my employer.

There were also people who worked in security and stole, then taking advantage of my secluded room, would hide their loot inside. The new assistant Bilenkyj was an obnoxious person, nobody liked him. One day, a few of us decided that if he didn't mend his ways, he wouldn't be able to walk to his fiancé, but would have to be carried. We wrote this onto a piece of paper, and then nailed it onto the notice board next to my room. The following morning Bilenkyj saw the note, then angrily tore it off the board. He didn't know who'd written it, although he had his suspicions. Nevertheless, the note didn't help, in fact it made him worse, so in the end we decided that he needed to be taught a lesson. We chose the person who was to do the honours, and with a water tight alibi.

Our volunteer was Hetman, whose task was to attack Bilenkyj in the changing room whilst he was sitting on a stool. Hetman sneaked behind Bilenkyjk, then hit him two or three times on the head, until he lay unconscious. Somebody walked into the changing room, saw Bilenkyj lying on the floor, and swiftly left again to alert the first aid people. He was quickly taken to the camp doctor, who attended to his wounds and bandaged his head.

The camp security started investigating who would do such a thing. At the beginning, they didn't suspect me, because I had a good alibi, I was playing cards with three security guards in the main recreation room, and I had plenty of witnesses. They first took Nimka, then Hetman and lastly Terpeliuk. They beat all three of them severely, but none of them owned up. The next day they interviewed me, but kept me in one of the Serbian barracks. When the Serbian guards swapped shifts, the replacement guard was known to me from the bakery, and said straight away, that he wouldn't give me up to the guards who were carrying out the interviews, he saw what they did to the three, two of whom were totally innocent. That night, Nimko couldn't take the torture anymore, and so told the guards that it was Hetman who'd beaten up Bilenkyj. After Nimko's confession, I was released with Nimko and Terpeliuk. Hetman was further detained and not released until late that day.

Afterwards, Nimko and Hetman told us of the barbaric torture they had to endure from the guards, the methods they used were unbelievable. At least one good thing changed, we finally got rid of Bilenkyj. His replacement was Hrechuk, who turned out to be a very good person, who got on well with everybody, and also liked to drink.

Sometimes I felt that I was always being picked on, there was always somebody who looked for an excuse. Once, while I was at work, Mandryk, who was the barrack leader, accompanied by two guards from the main office, approached my wife, and told her that she had to vacate the room we occupied in the barrack and to move into the communal room. My wife was pregnant at that time, told them that she wouldn't leave alone, but would wait until I returned from work. In the meantime, one of my colleagues came running to the bakery to tell me that the hierarchy wanted me out of my room and into the communal one. On my return from work, I confronted Mandryk, and told him that nobody had the right to throw me out of my room without the say- so from the Admin. Mandryk showed me notification from the senior guard, Zabotynsky, but I disagreed and went to the Admin myself. I didn't know the people there, but I brought them bread and rolls every week from the bakery. I told them that my wife was pregnant and that I worked in a bakery. I insisted they gave me written notification, reiterating that nobody had the right to evict me from my room. I won my case.

On another occasion, Mandryk asked me if I could accommodate for a brief period a young girl student from Delmenhorst , where there was also a Ukrainian camp called Chepak. I agreed, and the young girl stayed with us for two weeks, until she was found a room in the student halls.

In Heidenau, we had a Ukrainian School, with many pupils, some came from neighbouring camps which didn't have their own schools.

The neighbouring Serbian Camp for some reason had special privileges, which enabled their guards, whether at their own camp or ours, to carry rifles, until one Sunday the Serbs played a friendly football match against the Germans. During the match, one of the Serbs hit a German, the Ukrainian spectators went to the aid of the German, and suddenly there was a mass brawl on the pitch, not the Serbs against the Germans, but the Serbs against the Ukrainians. Because there were only a few Serbs, they threatened the Ukrainians with their rifles. From that day, the British confiscated all their weapons, only allowing their officers to carry pistols.

The Serbs had another privilege, amongst them were many officers, and they obtained bread from the bakery where I worked. Bread could only be bought using coupons, so the Admin would write out certification, how much bread the bakery would exchange for the wheat flour it received. The bakery owner received fresh flour without coupons. The Serbs took a lot of bread, the crafty Serbian officers, would write their own certificates, and that way they received as much bread as they wanted. The Admin became suspicious that there were too many certificates being issued, and I was accused of signing them.

The senior guard Zabotinsky came up to me and took all of my letters, to verify if it was my handwriting on the forged certificates. They kept me on tenterhooks for a while, but couldn't accuse me, and so they never found the real culprit.

At that time a young German apprentice worked with me at the bakery, and once a week he attended a bakery school in Tosdedt. At the school, there were many other apprentices from neighbouring bakeries. My apprentice would exchange cigarettes and chocolate for bread coupons. The other students also stole coupons, I gave them cigarettes and chocolate, and they would give me bread coupons. I never sold the coupons myself, this was done for me by Techeyko, Terpeliuk and Fedorko, I would give them coupons in exchange for money, and use it to buy cigarettes and coffee, from Shumyla and Kalyniw, so all in all life wasn't bad in the camp. I didn't have to queue at the camp kitchen for pea soup, or bread which was made from maize and wheat flour. On the contrary, if you had good bread, you could exchange it for almost anything.

We spent two Easters at the camp, which was a very busy time for me, for nearly every woman in the camp would bring me a Paska (Ukrainian Easter Bread) to bake at the bakery. I would do all my designated work in the morning, which left me all afternoon and well into the evening to bake off the pasky. On both Easters I baked around seven hundred Pasky, large ones, small ones, long ones, and round ones. Each woman would make it into any tin she could lay her hands on; nobody had a proper baking tin, people made the tins themselves out of re-cycled tins from various preserves, which they mostly took from the camp kitchen or warehouse. There were one or two women who had their own proper tins, which they'd brought from 'home' whilst escaping from the German raiding parties, although there were very few of these people who'd brought their own cart, pulled by a horse, with all their belongings.

At the camp, people didn't keep horses for long; they were usually sold to local farmers or exchanged for pigs, fat, and other edible livestock. Nobody sat around in the camp jobless, the British needed strong young men for work. Near Heidenau, the British had a large stock of motor oil, where many Ukrainians worked. In another town, the British felled a forest, and all the wood was transported to England. The workers were taken by goods vehicles daily, to and from work, so almost everyone at the camp had some purpose. When somebody had a job, they wouldn't be forced to do another, though if a person belonged to a choir or drama group, this was classed as a pastime.

In the camp, there were tailors, electricians, women who crocheted, embroidered there were also three choirs and an operatic society. There was also a barrack used as a church for Catholics and Orthodox, shared by both denominations. The Orthodox priests were Muroshnychenko and Hybarzhewsky, and the Catholic Potelyckyj (who I think died in the camp) Fylymon and Pobyhushka, who died in the USA.

The main choir (Svitskyj) functioned in tandem with the drama group, led by a professional conductor called Tamarchenko, who had at his disposal a professional pianist called Siewa by the conductor, I don't remember his real name, it could have been Severyn.

The Camp drama group staged productions like Zaporozhets za Dunayem, Natalka Poltalka, Svatania na Honcharivchi and others. We also had a famous quartet, whose components were Besalov, Dechtiarov, Pasternak and Pushkarenko. They were a fantastic quartet; they were one of the most popular groups.

We also had a good jazz band, which often played at dances, concerts and accompanied other groups for shows etc.

Besides the high school at the camp, there was a nursery and a junior school leading up to the high school, an Open University, post-high school, where various subjects were taught.

There was a choreography class taught by Maryna Milan, a painting department under the guidance of a Mr. Berezowsky.

During the summer months, in the centre of the camp, close to the administrative and cultural barracks, a team of gardeners dressed the area with a variety of colourful flowers.

In the second year, the camp started printing its own newspaper called 'Visti' giving readers news items, and many other topics.

Most of the people in the camp had some sort of work or hobby, except for those who were idle and didn't want to work, but they were very much in the minority. The majority of the camp comprised of young energetic people who didn't like to sit around, always striving for a purpose in life, even though most of them had been hoarded onto wagons from their homeland, by the occupying German army and shipped off forcibly to Nazi Germany to work as their slaves.

The older camp inhabitants were usually those who'd escaped from the clutches of the Red Army, mostly educated people, amongst whom were doctors, university professors, school teachers, tradesmen, all adding a little culture to the camp.

We had youth organisations such as the Scouts and Sum (Ukrainian Youth Association), we had a strong football team, in which played professionals from Halyczyna F.C. and also from a famous team called 'Ukraine' . The football team would often travel to neighbouring Ukrainian camps and to local German teams, and even played against the British who were stationed near our camp.

The guards at our camp also formed a team. I even played for them on a few occasions but was left out unceremoniously, as I'd put on too much weight and couldn't run fast enough. The team soon broke up because all the better players left and joined the more successful teams.

This is how I spent almost two years of my life. We left Lubeck towards the end of August 1945 and lived in Heidenau until the 18th of July 1947. Every day somebody brought news of our fate, picking up snippets from anyone who had a story to tell. Quite often the camp was visited by various commissions, signing up people for work in other countries. I wasn't in a hurry to leave Germany, life in the camp suited me and I was quite happy to stay. One day however, when I returned from work, Olha started nagging me that all my friends had signed up to go to England for work, only we would be left behind like sitting ducks for the Russians to come and take up back to our 'homeland'.

England only admitted strong, young and healthy couples without children, they wouldn't take single men or women, so many 'singles' would 'pair off'' as engaged couples, which the authorities allowed. I belonged to the category of childless couples; we did have a boy who was stillborn in a local hospital. After the birth, I had problems with the German doctor, because I argued with him, as to why Olha was in labour from Monday to Thursday and he couldn't save the child in that time. After that incident, the hospital sent notification to the camp, saying they wouldn't accept pregnant women anymore, and on two occasions the hospital refused to treat two women, after which, Dr.

Onufryk, our own camp doctor, insisted that I return to the hospital, and apologise to the German doctor, which I unwillingly did.

The following year Olha gave birth to a second son in April, but he too died after a week. The German hospital staff left the child outside in the open air, and because there was still a chill, the child quickly developed a fever and died.

During my time in the camp, an old friend, Slywchuk looked me up. He tried to go and live in France, but the medical commission found a small stain on his lungs, therefore refusing him. I welcomed him with open arms, although during the time I was in the POW camp, he didn't send me a single letter, in case he ended up with me. I managed to get a letter through to him using a civilian, but at least he passed on my address to the family Nahyrny and Nadia. Anna Nahyrny managed to send me two parcels. Unfortunately, by the time I received them, its contents had gone mouldy and green. Nadia sent me biscuits, dried peas and tobacco, from unfinished cigarettes, which she collected from the restaurant where she worked. I stopped smoking the first day I entered the POW camp, always exchanging tobacco for bread. The dried peas I used to soak every morning before work, later that evening when I collected my ration of bread, I would boil the peas and add a small piece of bread, which made me a nice bowl of thick soup. Those peas helped me a great deal, unfortunately I never got to see Nadia again, so I didn't have the opportunity to thank her for those priceless parcels.

Slywchuk at the time worked in a bakery, and could have sent me something, having access to most things. He later admitted to me that he was very scared, that's the kind of friend he was.

Another 'friend' called Rak approached me 'out of the blue' saying that he knew me from home, that he knew my mother and stepfather. I was puzzled, because I really didn't know him, but he was very persistent, questioning me about Sachenhausen, because he said that he'd been in a similar camp. He needed confirmation that he'd actually been in Sachenhausen, so I told him everything I knew and had seen, but even with this information he failed to convince his party members. He wanted me to join OUN (Organisation of Ukrainian Nationalists) but instead, I joined SUM (the equivalent youth organisation) I attended all their lectures, and once I was taken into a field during the night, where we were taught military exercises, but because I was an ex soldier, these exercises were not compulsory.

On his second visit, he brought along his friend Matviyiv and they enrolled me into OUN. Matviyiv often called in on me because I had plenty of money, he was always demanding money for 'party funds'. I had plenty of German Marks, so I gave generously because I trusted him. Before I left the camp, Rak and Matviyiv gave me a password, which I would use to pass onto members of the OUN in England, which in actual fact turned out not to be very long.

Eventually we were informed by the authorities to be ready and packed, though we had to wait until the 18th of August 1947. In the camp, I felt so much at home that I even had my own dog called Sultan, and when the time came to leave I decided to leave him with the bakery owner. To take a dog with me into England, would have meant placing it in quarantine for six months, which was also costly and had to be paid in British pounds, which I didn't have. I had lots of German Marks, so many that I handed them out to people for nothing.

Finally, the day arrived for our departure. I took my dog Sultan to the bakery, said goodbye to the owner, who put the dog into his stable, but when I returned to the barrack, Sultan was already there waiting for me, apparently there was an open window in the barn which Sultan used to escape. Reluctantly, I took the dog back a second time, on this occasion he was tied securely. Nevertheless, it was heartbreaking to leave Sultan behind.

Ivan and Olha, Heidenau Germany 1947

CHAPTER 28

HEIDENAU - ENGLAND

On the 18th of August 1947 we boarded open wagons, and were taken to a transit camp at Poggenhagen, near Hanover. We were shown into barracks and were told to wait for transport, which would take us to England. The food in the camp was very good, the weather was good too. The men spent most of their days playing cards, whilst the women sat in the shade talking.

After a week, people started returning to Heidenau, to say goodbye to their friends, for who was to know if they would ever be seen again. My wife Olha went too, where she was told that Sultan had escaped again from the bakery and was sitting outside our barrack window. Olha gave Sultan to a neighbouring lady, but the dog wouldn't eat anything, he'd just sit in one spot. On hearing this news, I felt sorry for the dog and, not knowing our exact day of departure, I made my way by train back to Heidenau. As I entered the camp concourse, Sultan saw me immediately, and came running towards me, then jumped into my arms and started to lick my face. That night I slept on a bed in a barrack with the boys, Sultan meanwhile wouldn't move an inch from my side. The following day I gave Sultan to Loish, then made my way by horse drawn cart to Tosdedt train station.

We'd hardly done a kilometre when I saw something white running through the field, it was Sultan. He quickly caught up, then tried to jump onto the moving wagon but to no avail. I asked the driver to slow down a little, this time Sultan was able to jump onto the wagon, and once again launched into licking my face, as if he was pleading not to leave him again. We rode to Tostedt, from where we caught a train to Hamburg and then onto Hanover. The last train overflowed with passengers that we had to stand between the wagons on the buffers. I couldn't help Sultan, because with one hand I held onto my suitcase and with the other I held onto the wagon, so as not to fall between them, Sultan sat on the buffer and on my foot. Whenever we stopped at a large station, we both alighted onto the platform, to rest my arms and stretch my legs. At every station more people boarded, and when the train departed, I stood in the same position, with Sultan at my feet all the way back to Poggenhagen.

We spent another two months at Poggenhagen, Sultan slept at the foot of our bed, and if he ever needed to go outside to relieve himself, he would jump out of the open window. During the day we took him for a walk, and if we ever needed to go to another town, Sultan would lay on our bed until our return.

At one point, Olha became quite ill, she couldn't eat, even though the food was very good, she gave her portion of food to Sultan. I took Olha a couple of times into Hanover to see a private doctor, we had a camp doctor, but I didn't want to take that risk, in case she wasn't fit to travel, which had already happened to one woman.

Eventually we were told that there was room for us in England, but before the final journey, we would be placed in another transit camp in Munster. Inevitably, we took Sultan with us.

This camp was guarded by Latvians and we had to wait another four weeks for our transport to England. The days went by slowly as there was nothing to do. I knew very little about England, all I knew was it was an industrial country, and at that time its climatic peculiarities didn't interest me. The important decision I had to make was to leave Germany and go 'West', and not 'East' back to the 'homeland'. Sitting idly around the camp all day was boring, fortunately still having Sultan gave us the impetus to walk him.

One day, during one of our walks, and elderly German lady approached us and asked if we wanted to sell her our dog, because she'd lost hers during the war. We knew we couldn't take Sultan to England, so we made an arrangement with the lady that on the day before our departure, we would hand Sultan over, which we did, for which she rewarded us with fresh fruit. From our camp to the lady's house was about three kilometres, and the next morning the day before our departure, one of the guards came to my room to say that Sultan was outside the camp gates. I had little choice but to take Sultan back to the old lady's house, this time telling her to tie him up, as we were leaving the next day. She must have taken my advice, as sadly we didn't see Sultan ever again.

On the 18th of October 1947 we boarded our ferry. We were given a good supper and later shown to a seating area, which had comfortable soft seats. As soon as the ferry departed, all the toilets and washrooms quickly filled with passengers. My Olha was one of them, she vowed later that as long as she lived she would never travel by ferry again.

That night the sea was rough, but we were pleased, that early the following morning, on the 19th of October, we could see the shores of England. We docked at the port of Harwich, and from there we were taken by train to Cambridge, finishing our journey on a double-decker bus, which was a frightening experience, as I had never ridden on one before, so I sat on the lower deck. The bus ride took us to our camp and new home in West Wratting, which was formerly an RAF base during WW2.

At the camp the men and women were assigned to separate barracks, which were bleak and cold, the men could only see their wives in the canteen or their barracks during the day only.

Our camp interpreter was a Ukrainian called Mr. Zdankiwski, he also taught English to anyone interested. At that time, learning the English language hadn't entered my head, I was more concerned on how to scrounge food, to supplement our meagre portions.

One day I talked Pyshniak into travelling into Cambridge, he too didn't know any English. By the camp was a bus stop and in a short time a bus approached us with the word 'Cambridge' on the front. We hopped onto the bus until it reached its destination. We got off the bus and followed a mass of people carrying baskets and bags, assuming they were going to a nearby market, we were suddenly surprised when we realised that the young people were hurrying to their classes at the University.

Ivan Prytulak after his arrival in Cambridgeshire England

Cambridge wasn't a very large city, and once we'd strolled around for a few minutes we came across the market, where we managed to buy some fruit and bread rolls, bread was unavailable in those days without the appropriate ration cards.

Once we had seen enough of the city, we searched for a bus with a 'Cambridge' sign. After stopping many people, I finally made myself understood that we needed a bus to 'West Wratting'. On our return journey we travelled free of charge, somebody must have paid our fare because the conductor didn't take any money from me.

We reached the camp just before nightfall, by which time our wives were concerned for our wellbeing, though presenting them with fresh bread rolls and fruit soon eased their scorn.

The women in the camp stayed for only nine days, before they were transported to Bury in Lancashire. All the men had to remain in the camp due to a housing shortage after the War. We were told that as soon as our wives had found suitable accommodation, we would be reunited. In the meantime, due to the labour shortage in England after the War, we were to work at 'The London Brick Company'.

In the factory we had a former Polish colonel as an interpreter, who spoke English very well. He explained all about the work involved, the various departments, from which we were allowed to choose. I volunteered to work at the furnace. My job was to take the baked bricks and stack them in piles outside, or at some point I had to load the bricks onto railway wagons. It turned out that four of us chose the furnace, each one of us was added to three English workers, making a team of four. The English workers were paid according to their output, we were paid fifteen shillings (the equivalent 75 pence today) per week. This was enough for a postage stamp and even for a couple of beers on Saturday and Sunday.

We worked with the English workers for four weeks, after which I asked the ex- Polish colonel if the Ukrainians could work in their own teams, to which he agreed. I was installed as a foreman, but we had one problem. Every morning we were taken to the factory by bus at 7.30a.m. The English teams allocated one person daily, to come two hours earlier and prepare the furnace. It was seven kilometres from the camp to the factory, a good hour's walk. Buses didn't run so early, so I decided to buy an old bicycle for the equivalent of today's 50pence. It had no brakes, though it was quicker than walking. On the first day I reported to work at 5a.m. the same time as the English workers. By the time my team arrived two and a half hours later, I had everything prepared and we started work immediately. Breakfast was at 9.30a.m. In the past when I belonged to an 'English' team, I was sent to the canteen for four mugs of tea. From the factory to the canteen was quite a walk, so in order to save time I took my bicycle. As luck would have it, from the opposite direction a goods vehicle was backing up to the furnace. The road was narrow and I had no brakes so I couldn't stop, I steered to the side along the rail track, even so there wasn't enough room for me to pass, the truck accidentally caught me, knocking me and my bicycle onto the rail track. My chest took the brunt of the fall as I crumpled in a heap onto the rail track, my leg must have hit a sharp stone as it too was badly cut and so were the palms of my hands.

I was taken unconscious to a hospital in Cambridge where I spent two weeks recovering. That was also the end of my working experience in a brick factory.

In the hospital I was surrounded by English patients, giving me the opportunity to learn the English language which previously hadn't interested me. I was visited by a Ukrainian woman who had worked in the hospital for six weeks, in which time she had picked up a few words, enough to act as my interpreter.

When I was discharged from hospital, I was given a walking stick and sent back to the camp. On my return, I found out through correspondence with Olha, that she and two other ladies Malanka Vytvytka and Sonia Kurin had found suitable accommodation for their husbands in Bury.

Before the three of us travelled north to meet our wives in Bury a couple of days later, I wrote to Olha not to mention my accident to anyone, in case it hindered my chances of getting work.

After spending two traumatising months in Cambridge, I stepped gingerly off the train at Bury station with the support of my trusty walking stick. I brought a small suitcase and a large radio, both of which I couldn't carry, relying on the help on my friends. At the station we were met by our wives, accompanied by a welfare nurse from the factory. When I glimpsed at our wives and the nurse from our train compartment, I quickly threw my walking stick under the bench and proceeded to walk without it.

The road we took was quite slippery after the recent sleet, possibly in my favour, disguising my slight limp. The nurse suggested I accompany her to collect my ration card, whilst the rest of the party carried on to the factory.

By that time, I had quite a few more words in English under my belt than my colleagues, and that's why the nurse had chosen me to escort her to all the various offices, registering me so that I could qualify for ration cards.

Once registered, the nurse and I walked to the factory and found Olha and her party waiting for me in the canteen. After lunch, the nurse showed us around the whole factory, explaining to us what each machine did and what out functions would be.

That evening I felt very lucky to finally be able to walk or rather hobble, to our 'new home' in Bury. As I felt my leg throbbing, I clutched onto Olha, leaning into her body for support, wondering why I'd discarded my walking stick. I could've kicked myself, though that would surely have made matters even worse.

CHAPTER 29
BURY LANCASHIRE

The following morning I woke with a nagging pain and my leg was swollen, but I soldiered on to my new job at the cotton mill. At the factory I was assigned to two English workers, the three of us had to maintain the smooth running of one very long machine, which had two thousand spools running from one end of the room to the other. Occasionally, the cotton thread would snap and had to be quickly repaired whilst the machine was in motion. The work was easy, even though we had to constantly walk up and down, following the flow of the cotton, always in the correct direction.

My foreman was a very good man, he taught me everything I needed to know about the job and also helped me with the English language. In addition, he give me sound advice about local customs and the English way of life, all of which was related as we walked up and down, again and again.

On my third day I was walking too close to the machine, which suddenly caught and trapped my leg, resulting in the machine stopping. I yelled for 'Jack' who, on hearing my cries for help came running to me, once he'd accessed the situation he carried on running to where the key was kept, so he could release the machine's gear. I couldn't take the pain, or wait for Jack to return with the key, so I managed to jerk my leg and wriggle it through its clasp on my leg. The trapped leg was my left and 'good leg'. I was led to the first aid room and met by the nurse who I had already met. She rubbed ointment onto my left leg and bandaged the sore part. I was able to return upstairs unassisted, and was given a sitting job cleaning spools.

On the way home that evening, I held onto Olha's arm tightly, stopping several times for a rest until we entered our room.

The next morning when I woke up, both of my legs were in pain, I went straight to see the factory nurse who on this visit bandaged both of my legs. I was allowed another couple of days cleaning spools, I returned to my job at the long machine, this time more vigilant having learned my lesson.

Before my arrival in Bury, Olha had met a few other Ukrainians, some of whom had even been in the town before her. Once I was settled in my job and lodgings, in my spare time I began to seek out fellow compatriots who lived in the town. One of the people I met was Zahayevych, and together we began to organise a local branch of 'SUB' (Association of Ukrainians in Great Britain); I had already received my membership card in Cambridgeshire. We were twenty four in total, comprising of ten couples and four single men.

Our first 'room' was in an English couple's house, they also rented a room to a couple of single Latvian girls. In those days, most food could only be bought with ration cards, which were kept by our landlords, all our food was cooked for us, using only the cheapest ingredients, luxury goods like butter and bread were never given to us.

The house was also shared with three greyhounds, who lay on the sofa, not giving us room to sit, so after supper Olha and I went upstairs into our cold unheated and unlit room, the landlords even left us without an electric bulb for lighting. I couldn't even shave in my room; I had to make time in the mill during my break.

A couple of months later we found better accommodation thanks to a couple of friends, where Olha was allowed to cook for ourselves and we never went hungry. We were very happy with our new lodgings and stayed there for almost a year. Towards the end of our stay Olha became pregnant, and instead of being overjoyed, we were afraid that when the landlady noticed, she would vacate our room.

I explained my situation to Jack and he suggested that I buy my own house. To buy a house then or even now one needs money, which at that time we had very little of. For doing a full week's work including Saturday I earned £3.90 and Olha earned £3.10. Out of that we paid £1.00 for our lodgings, our food and travelling expenses. When we first arrived from Germany, we wore very poor and threadbare clothes, so we prioritised to buy ourselves decent clothing, a suit each we could wear to church every Sunday in Manchester. And once we paid for our bus fares and subscriptions, I attended English evening classes, so there was very little left. To save a little money I bought a new bicycle, which I used to travel to work and wherever else I needed to go.

One day Jack showed me an advertisement of an old house for sale in the local paper. That evening Jack and I went to see the house, it was old and run-down with a communal yard. The owner wanted £250, which comprised of a £100 deposit and 150 weekly payments of £1. I agreed even though I didn't have the deposit, I had many friends who I thought would help me out, but when I asked them nobody was prepared to give me a loan. In the end I went to see the mill director who agreed to lend us £50 on condition we repaid him £5 per week. We had savings of £50 giving us enough for the deposit. The house was unfurnished, contained three bedrooms, a kitchen, dining room, corridor and a basement.

Once I bought the house I soon found lodgers, the first being Vytvytkyj and Kaniuk. On Jack's advice I bought a second hand bed and wardrobe at an auction for £2.05 a sofa for 5pence chairs for 5pence each, for a total of £6.00 I furnished part of the house, the only large outlay was a gas cooker which cost me £10. I charged my lodgers £1 per week per room and they had to furnish it themselves. I later took in a third couple, giving me a weekly income of £3 and by the time Olha had stopped working, I had paid off my loan of £50 to the mill director.

Around the same time I bought my first house, the Ostapiuks bought their first house too. One by one, all the Ukrainian families unpacked their suitcases and did the same. Within twelve months, every family in Bury had bought their own house.

Most Ukrainians worked in the cotton mills, were the pay wasn't terribly good, yet their thrifty nature enabled them to live to a reasonable standard, and most importantly they were masters of their own homes.

VICTORIA COTTON MILL BURY 1950s
Left to right: Olha Prytulak, Olha Semehen (cousin)

Almost every Sunday there was an exodus from Bury to attend the Ukrainian Greek Catholic Church in Manchester, and then a walk to a club where people could meet up with old acquaintances. I had the opportunity to meet two old friends from the camp in Heidenau, we had even come across to England together, namely Anton Tysiacznyj and George Sharabun. Anton immediately proposed that I organise a branch of OUN (Organisation of Ukrainian Nationalists) in Bury, I'd already been made a member by Rak and Matyiw whilst in Heidenau, I was even given a password to use once I met similar members in England, but I didn't meet such members in Bury. Instead, I was eager to open a branch of SUB.

One Saturday aftrenoon during spring, Zahayevych and I travelled to the larger neighbouring town of Rochdale, where we attended the first ever meeting of SUB. At the meeting we agreed to open our own branch in Bury.

The first such meeting in Bury was held in a mill house where Zahayevych lived, together with Lysykanych, Suprun, Choma and Mazuryk. Shortly after, our group grew with the addition of four unmarried ladies, M. Firman, Z. Tyoch, V. Nasterenko and M. Marchak. We also introduced three members' wives, Mrs Borsch, Mrs Yarosh and Mrs Pyshniak. In the early days of our organisation we had 26 members. The first head was Mr. O. Zahayevych, I was the secretary and the cashier was Mr. M. Korin.

In a short time, more and more Ukrainians came to live in Bury, fellow compatriots had friends who worked on farms and wanted to better their lives by moving into a town. We were getting busier and busier at work, often working overtime to meet demands.

Our main priority was to find 'new people' accommodation, which became easier, for the early settlers had bought their own houses and were glad to take in lodgers, helping them with their overheads.

One of our largest groups of people lived in Walshaw a suburb of Bury, Stetyk, Harbuz, Matiewicz, Bahan and Hawryshko had all crossed from Belgium. We also had members living in the next small town of Ramsbottom, within the first year we had amassed 35 members.

I even devoted some time trying to find members of OUN, but my efforts failed, so I approached Tysiacznyj my immediate superior, saying there were two possible candidates, Skaskiw and Korin. Tysiacznyj agreed to my proposal, now we had three members. The three of worked in the same factory, which gave us the opportunity to spend most of our breaks together discussing party politics. We approached the newly arrived people from

Belgium, and in conversation it surfaced that they were all party members, so from then on our visits to Walshaw became more frequent.

Around that time, one of our single lady members a certain Mariyka, managed to transfer her fiancé Shumka to Bury, he too was already a party member, and so he took over some of my workload. We now had twelve members, I was the local leader, my pseudonym was 'Pryt' with the influx of extra members, and this gave me an incentive to work harder for the community, I was a hard worker and demanded the same effort from my fellow members.

Our first function was to stage an exhibition of 'Ukrainian folklore' including wooden handcrafts and embroidery. The exhibition was a success, the fact that the Mayor of Bury opened it helped us a great deal, as well as the owner of the premises where the event took place.

Zahayevych had a good friend who lived in the neighbouring town of Blackburn, a Mr. Zdankiwski, the same man who acted as our interpreter in West Wratting. Zahayevych quite often travelled to visit his friend, it transpired on one of these trips that Tebrij, a party 'lieutenant' had been informed that Zahayevych was a 'Melnyk-ivych' (Andrij Melnyk a Colonel in the Ukrainian People's Republic Army in the First World War and founder of the Organisation of Ukrainian Nationalists. In the 1940s, a more radical Stefan Bandera became the leader of OUN and his followers were called ' Banderivchi' or Banderites which became the party most Ukrainian immigrants subscribed to in the UK) and that he should therefore be removed from his post as the head of the Bury branch of SUB, the Association of Ukrainians in Great Britain, and replaced by a member of OUN.

This heinous and unenviable task fell onto my shoulders, I had to look for a convincing excuse to remove Zahayevych from his post. The party hierarchy proposed Skaskiw as the new head, so an extra ordinary meeting was soon organised. Zahayevych was known to his fellow Ukrainians as ' Mr. Engineer' at the meeting I came out and said that it wasn't true he was an 'engineer' but a mere tinker. There was uproar of laughter in the room, while Zahayevych wasn't allowed to say anything in his defence. After the commotion subsided, Skaskiw was voted the new head and I remained as secretary.

Throughout this time the Ukrainian community grew in Bury, so much that we were in desperate need of a hall where we could conduct our meetings and get-togethers. In the meantime, all the meetings of OUN had to be held in my house, even though I had lodgers who were not party members.

We managed to hire a church hall belonging to St. Marries Catholic Church for all community gatherings, for other meetings we acquired a room at the local

YMCA (Young Men's Christian Association), this meant us all becoming members, but at least we had premises to conduct our weekly meetings. We started our own football team, I was the club secretary and my wife had the task of washing all the players' football kits. We played in a local amateur league for four years, I often had to pay for new football boots, bus fares, we always had a shortage of players and money, I had to reach out to neighbouring towns to make up the numbers, I used Karman from Rochdale, Shablinsky from Manchester, Basiuk from Oldham, and we even had a Hungarian and an Italian in our team.

We managed to organise many pastimes such as a choir which was conducted by Musyka, a drama group led by Shumka, then later by Koliarchuk from Rochdale, and finally with Kwasnyj. I was a keen member of both, I also took on the role as the choir's administrator. When our drama group staged Bilasa-Danylyshyna, I played the role of the priest. All in all, the Ukrainian community in Bury was very active.

Every year we staged Saint Nicholas's Day, were we gave out presents to the adults, the married and the single. In 1948 the community celebrated the birth of its first addition to the second generation, Bohdan Lysykanych who in later years became a Ukrainian Catholic priest. Soon after children were born into the families of Borsch, Kaniuk and Ostapiuk, whose son Eugene later became a professor of psychology. My son Jaroslaw was born on the 15th of November 1949. And that same year the Ukrainian community experienced its first death, a single lady named Mazuryk.

Ivan, Jaroslaw and Olha, Bury Lancashire 1950

The Ukrainian community was growing all the time, with a constant flow of new arrivals, all of which encouraged SUB to seriously think of buying its own premises, as children would soon need their own nursery. There was also pressure from the choir and drama members to own their own building. Until then we always relied on the YMCA and the church hall for our meetings, but there were occasions of 'double booking' invariably our 'English' landlords had the last word. On one such occasion, the parish priest allowed us to use the church vestry for our OUN meetings, which were held behind closed doors. Luckily there were only a few of us, the priest was English couldn't understand our conversation, although living in the adjoining room he couldn't help but hear us. The vestry was adequate for our 'party' meetings, but too small for larger general gatherings.

My own house sometimes doubled up as a vocal point for choir practices and 'party' meetings, especially when new members were being sworn in by Tysiacznyj. My house was even once used for the blessing of Holy Water by a Ukrainian priest during the feast of 'Jordan' on 19th January.

Before the community bought their own premises, my house was used for many functions, one main event was the Whitsuntide Walk, when we joined the English and Irish Roman Catholics in the town centre, my house being very close, it was used for men and women to change into their Ukrainian National costumes. Local people in the town clapped as we paraded along the streets into the square, where we were met by the town Mayor and other dignitaries. There were other 'foreign' immigrant nationalities living in the town, but if my memory serves me well, none ever took part in the parade.

In 1953 the Ukrainian community in Bury bought its first building on Rochdale Road for the sum of £1,200. At that time the head of SUB in England was Dr. O. Fundak.

The more people moved into the town, the bigger the nightmare for me. For instance, although I was the local OUN leader, there were men who had become party members back in Ukraine, and wouldn't join ranks with us, people like Lewycki, Zin, Bartkiw, Yawniw and Demczuk. It should be said that they were very sympathetic towards us, came to our meetings, but wouldn't partake in an active position.

Similarly, there were OUN members like Skaskiw and Bereza who lived in Bury but registered in the Manchester branch. There was also a third category of members, a certain Chvil-Soter, a committee member who didn't feel obliged to attend any 'party' meetings. He lived in the Bury Ukrainian Club, as a few other single men did, but purposely played chess in a different part of the building during our meetings.

All these unnecessary idiosyncrasies paralysed my community work, to my mind these so called members were dirt under my shoe. I constantly complained about them to their regional leaders, I couldn't understand or condone their attitude. The regional leader at that time was Drabat, a childhood friend of Zin, Bartkiw and Haydukevych. Every time Drabat attended a regional meeting in Manchester, he would always spend the night in Bury.

I loved my community and 'party' work and carried everything out to my best ability. I had a function in every committee. I read Ukrainian papers and periodicals such as 'Dniprovoyi Cvyli' and the 'Ukrainian Samostyjnyk'. In the evenings I would visit people in their homes and promote these readings. I read as much as I could, to prepare myself for meetings with new knowledge and current affairs. On the advice of the 'party' I enrolled on an extramural Ukrainian grammar course taught by professor V. Yaniw. In the beginning there were twenty of us, but every week two or three people dropped out, and by the end there were three of us left, Harhaj, Voychykowski and myself. Some people found the course to be too demanding, others were embarrassed when they saw more corrections in red than their own handwritten text in black ink.

At that time I was grateful to the 'party' for teaching me self discipline, a desire to learn and read books, something that didn't interest me in Germany, where playing cards was my only pastime. The more I read various books and newspapers, the more I grew to realise that our 'party' hierarchy wrote one thing yet carried out another.

I enjoyed the 'party' discipline, always being punctual and the first to arrive, carrying out all my duties fairly and without a fuss. Naturally, I expected the same from my fellow members.

By 1952 there were 32 'party' members in Bury, everyone including myself having only spent three or four years in school. There was always plenty of work and plenty of trouble, especially when it came to discipline, the 'party' members who were registered in Manchester didn't help matters, we had a member called Haydukyvytch who lived in nearby Heywood a good friend of Drabat's, he felt that attending local meetings wasn't compulsory, perhaps even a little below him.

I had the opportunity to meet Drabat many times in Bury, when he spent the night at Skaskiw's house. I pleaded with him many times to have a word with some of the members who wouldn't take an active part in community work. Alas, my pleading fell on deaf ears. Drabat would only say that each member has his own function to perform and was responsible for his own work. I was reminded that my role as a local leader was not to be interested in what other members did, only to carry out my own work diligently.

That same year somebody from Bradford who used to live in the same village as Shumka, wrote a letter to the 'party' Head Office saying that back home in Ukraine, Shumka had worked for the Bolsheviks, grassing on his friends and passing on sensitive information.

I had to write to Head Office is response to the accusation, but to me Shumka was the best of the bunch, a very helpful person who knew far more and did more than any other member.

Shumka was summoned twice to a regional hearing. In his defence stood Tebrij from Blackburn, since both spent time together in a German Concentration Camp. They were both released at the same time, and it was Shumka who first began to rekindle 'party' politics upon his freedom. Nevertheless, Shumka lost his appeal, since there were two fellow village dwellers in Bury who spoke against him. What was actually said I never did discover, though I did find out that he was subsequently stripped of his 'party' rights. Shumka went onto pursue a career in dentistry. I felt sorry for the way he was treated, but the incident was out of my hands.

Shortly afterwards I had a misunderstanding with Chvil, we never saw eye to eye, there was always some bone of contention or other between us. I once told him as he was a leading member, he should set an example to the others by devoting as much of his time to the 'party' as much as he spent with community affairs. He did not take kindly to this comment, so much so that he wrote his grievances against me to the regional officers, who in turn wrote me a strong letter of reprimand stating that I should not bother him in future and should show more respect.

I found this incident went totally against the grain, so to speak. On a previous occasion Chvil's brother who was also a 'party' member emigrated to Canada. At that time, the 'party' prohibited members from travelling across the ocean, members were vigorously advised to live as close to their 'homeland' (Ukraine) as possible, in the case of a war or uprising broke out, we had to be ready to defend our country. I wrote a letter to Drabat, which he didn't answer, but when meeting him later on one of his visits to Bury, he informed me that Chvil's brother had been given a special dispensation from the 'party' declaring he would be of more use in Canada than in Bury. I felt very angry with the response, Chvil's brother was a simpleton with no leadership skills whatsoever.

One of my community functions was to promote Ukrainian books and periodicals to the Ukrainian inhabitants of Bury. I personally knew every Ukrainian in the town. In Bury, most of the settlers came from Western Ukraine, one of which was Korin. I once sent him to Manchester on 'party' business, whilst he was there he met a friend from his old village in Ukraine, who spoke highly of an organisation called URDP (Ukrainian Revolutionary Democratic Party). Shortly after their meeting, he resigned from OUN, joined the URDP and later emigrated to Canada.

In Bury there were very few members of URDP. The most active member was Myronenko who later immigrated to Australia, Krawchenko, Pshenychniy a very cultured person who later died in Bury, and Oleksa Nesen, who in Heidenau was the secretary of SUM and was later found hanging in his own home. I got on very well with all of them, they bought books from me and I bought from them and donated money to their various causes.

One evening, I was called upon in my own home by Myronenko and Krawchenko. They were collecting money for a Ukrainian writer called Ivan Bahrianyi who had fallen onto hard times. I donated 10 shillings, the equivalent of today's 50 pence, and signed my name against my donation on their collection sheet. Myronenko and Krawchenko didn't call at every Ukrainian house, knowing full well who supported Bahrian and who didn't. During their rounds, one of the donors noticed my name on the collection sheet, which was quickly dispatched to Chvil. Around the same time, another collection was being carried out for ABN (Anti-Bolshevik Block of Nations) to which I donated 5 shillings, today's 25pence, thinking that there would be far more donors collecting for that cause and far fewer people donating to Bahrianyi. Furthermore, I noticed from the ABN collection list that some people had donated less than I'd done.

I admired Bahrianyi as an outstanding Ukrainian author, by that time I had read three of his books and liked him very much although I'd never met the man.

My donation was reported to the regional office of OUN and I was later summoned to explain my motive, the controlling committee headed by Lawrushkyj were not impressed, I lost my case, Chvil was triumphant again.

Chvil later invited his former fellow villager, Dutka to live in Bury. He introduced him to me as a good 'party' member who he knew very well. At that time I was in need of an assistant to mediate with the ABN so I appointed him to the task. After two weeks I realised that Dutka was lazy, always making excuses not to attend 'party' meetings and showing no interest whatsoever in liaising with ABN. I reported Dutka to the regional committee for his shortcomings but, to my great astonishment, rather than reprimand him, he was promoted as the Regional Liaison Officer to the ABN. I lost yet again !

Most of the 'party' members in Bury were former soldiers from the Ukrainian Division who had been captured during the war and had spent two years at a camp in Rimini, on the north-east coast of Italy. There were very few people like me who had arrived in the UK as displaced persons. My best fellow-worker turned out to be Skaskiw, we showed mutual respect and trusted each other.

Time didn't stand still, children were growing quickly and we desperately needed a nursery. There were now a few children, all that what was needed were carers. During a meeting of SUB one member, Mrs Ostapiuk, the local head of the Organization of Ukrainian Women, put forward the name of Mrs Zahayevych, saying they were both friends and if asked would be pleased to accept.

The problem arose that someone had to call at her house and ask her. As expected, being the head of the parents' committee, that task again fell on my shoulders. I knew that on calling at their house I would firstly have to apologise to Mr. Zahayevych for publicly ridiculing him at a SUB meeting, resulting in him losing his position. I had no choice but to go 'cap in hand' and apologise. Mrs Zahayevych accepted her new post, she loved children and never did have her own, later becoming the most popular and sought after God-mother in the town. Mr. Zahayevych, on the other hand, wasn't very impressed with my apology and demanded a public apology from me, to which I compellingly agreed and promised I would do so at the earliest opportunity.

The first nursery opened in neighbouring Rochdale, and was run by Mrs Lukianenko, the second in Bury was run by Mrs Zahayevych.

Being the head of the parents' committee took most of my time, so it was decided to appoint Chvil as the head of SUB, thereby forcing him to do some work, leaving Skaskiw to help me. Chvil agreed but he had other motives. He developed a very close working relationship with Mrs Ostapiuk, his aim was to recruit her into OUN. I don't know if she in effect did become a 'party' member, but I suspect she did, as she later became the national head of the Organisation of Ukrainian Women in Great Britain.

One of my other functions at SUB was 'welfare helper', my job description being to visit the sick in hospital or in their homes. I had so much community work 'on my plate' especially on Saturday, that I didn't have the time to visit Miss Vira Nesterenko who was a professional ballerina from Kyiv, having danced there and in other major cities of Ukraine. She worked in the same cotton mill as I did, but in her second week she began to throw spools of cotton at the foreman. She was assessed by doctors, then taken to a mental asylum where she remained. Vira had an uncle named Verbytckyj, once the administrator of the home of Ukrainian Invalids in Chiddingfold Surrey. Her uncle seldom visited her before his death. Visiting her in hospital was only possible on Saturday. On one such day I asked Mrs Ostapiuk to stand in for me and visit Vira as I had so much on that day. She agreed and went to see her, but on her return she told friends that after a visit, I'd never spoken to a doctor to ask for an update. Admittedly, I didn't hang around to wait for a doctor, I didn't have the time or patience. I confirmed my actions and said that Mrs Ostapiuk wasn't telling the whole truth, she even came out with something that I was supposed to have said, namely "If a muscovite can't guess, then he will lie". I hadn't ever heard of such a saying in my life. Moreover, and unfortunately, few people in Bury believed me. This was a blatant provocation against me, Chvil 'began to dig a whole beneath me' since I reported Dutka to the correctional regional committee. Lawrushko and Kulchytckyj came to Bury to investigate this story and spoke to Chvil, but not me the local leader, I was only informed of the outcome in the case against Dutka.

I immediately protested and with the help of Skaskiw, we compiled a letter and sent it to Drabat. My story was ignored and no action was taken against Dutka. I was informed that the ruling committee knew best which member was suited to certain functions and who was the best person to carry them out, and that applied to me too.

Another provocation against me was when, at a local meeting of SUB, Mrs Lysykanych accused me of calling at peoples' homes, urging parents not to enrol their children into SUM, the Ukrainian Youth Association, but into Plast, the Ukrainian Scouting Organisation.

Shortly afterwards, I was removed from my position of local leader of OUN and my position was filled by Stetyk. I complained again, and this time I was suspended from all members' rights until further notice.

In 1953 just before the AGM of SUB in Bury, I was summoned by Lawrushkyj to his house in Manchester. He told me to 'disappear' on the day of the AGM and that I wasn't to attend, he didn't want me to be elected on the committee. I could, remain the head of the 'Parents Committee' the administrator of the choir and liaison officer of the Former Combatants, who at that time was Kobylianskyj.

I knew the local community would be very suspicious of my absence at the AGM, even more so, because I had a couple of members of OUN living in the house. I told my wife that I had to travel to Bradford to visit my sick friend Lewycki who was seriously ill. In Bradford I couldn't keep still, I had a 'pull' to return to Bury, my conscience wouldn't allow me to stay, so I decided to return to Bury. I didn't go home, but directly to the YMCA where the AGM was being held. When I entered the hall the meeting had already ended. Most of the participants were still standing and talking amongst themselves. I stood beside them and asked if I could have a word, nobody objected.

I started with an apology to Mr. Zahayevych, I had earlier promised to him I would do so in public. I said that my motives at that time were not my own and that I involuntary listened to other people and that was why I wanted to apologise publicly today. There were some members who interpreted my speech as a joke, most wondered what had happened, yet a few of them knew full well that I hadn't been allowed to attend the AGM.

After the meeting I didn't have to wait long for the outcome, for Drabat had said at a meeting in Manchester a couple of weeks earlier, that when an outgoing member leaves the organisation voluntarily, that person needs to be taught such a lesson that would lead the member to hang himself with his own hands in his own home.

In February of 1954 my suspension from the organisation of OUN was lifted and I was given the role of an instructor for local sympathisers. I had no interest or showed much initiative in this role, I simply read a couple of boring articles by Dontsov in the church hall. The weekly Ukrainian newspaper from Germany 'The Ukrainian Independent' always contained new articles of the goings-on of the OUN hierarchy.

That summer, in Manchester, a large meeting of 'party' executive activists was held, and I as a member was also there. At the meeting, Drabat informed the assembly that a new organisation had formed in the dispora called the 'Dvikari' (the word derives from 'dvi' meaning two, the founders were L. Rebet and Z. Matlu) who had left the organisation under the leadership of Stefan Bandera and formed their own party known as Dvikari. He went onto say that, if there was anyone present who wanted to leave OUN could do so, as did Yavorskyj and others. There were no brave volunteers present, nobody stood, nobody left.

There became a period of political uncertainty in the OUN that until then didn't expect anyone to stand against their beliefs. A close friend of mine at the time Zin, who became a 'party' member back in Ukraine, brought me literature written by the Dvikari Party. He obtained this writing from Vivchar, they both rented rooms at Demyanchuk's. It turned out that Vivchar had received the papers from his friend in Todmorden, a certain Kytun I think. I read the papers with Zin at the factory in our spare time, we found a London address and that same day wrote to Matyj.

On that same day, the 10th of October 1954, I wrote a letter of resignation to the OUN addressed to Husak, the local leader, giving notice of my irrevocable decision to voluntarily leave the OUN under the leadership of Bandera. The reasons I left the party I didn't disclose or pass onto Husak. I wrote down my personal reasons and concealed them for many years, the whole text follows:

From this day, the 10th of October 1954, I am no longer a member and resign forthwith from the OUN Party under the leadership of Stefan Bandera, for the following reasons:

1. The actions of the 'party' in OUN which took place in February 1954.
2. For the unlawful and unjustified suspension of me as a member.
3. For preventing me from attending the AGM of SUB in Bury, a most heinous act that was inflicted on me both morally and mentally.
4. The lack of co-operation amongst the 'party' members, the bitter hatred especially within the party executive.
5. The 'party' under the leadership of Bandera had transformed the ideology of the OUN. When I was a young member of the 'party' my beliefs were genuine and I conducted myself without question to the cause. I accepted and believed the 'party' to be unpolitical and democratic, not a totalitarian organisation. Unfortunately, that is what it is not, rather it is the complete opposite.
6. I could never agree with the view that an idiot could rule over an educated person. One example goes back to an incident which took place in Bury. At the beginning of September this year, an audit of executive members in the district council was drawn up by Kulchytkyj, at which I was present. In my view Kulchytkyj conducted the proceedings very well, he asked each member three or four questions, but in a way that each member had to pick his questions out of 'a hat'. Every question had a number attached to it, and when a number was

called it was to be answered by the recipient. The executive committee sat to the side with me amongst their ranks. I didn't know whether to laugh or cry when I heard the questions addressed to Husak, the local leader, and Humaniuk, the financial officer, neither could answer a single question. How could I respect such a leader? How can such a leader possibly give guidance and lead a community. I can mention many more similar examples, but what would be the point, it wouldn't help, because I have come across numerous incidents to convince myself, therefore I, Ivan Prytulak 'party' pseudonym 'pryt' voluntarily resign forthwith from OUN under the leadership of Stefan Bandera.

A month later, on the 8th of November 1953 my wife gave birth to our second son, Dmytro, which happened to also be my wife Olha's 27th Birthday. Olha returned to work six weeks after giving birth. At the cotton mill we shared work on the same machines, one of us worked from 6a.m. until 2p.m. the other from 2.p. until 10p.m. swapping shifts on alternate weeks. Whichever one of us worked the afternoon shift would put the children to bed around 1p.m. before going to work. The one working the morning shift returned from work around 2.30p.m. spending the rest of the day caring for the children.

On the 7th of June 1957 Olha gave birth to our third son, Taras, again after six weeks she returned to work and we returned to our previous routine. I didn't like to work in a cotton mill, always dreaming of working in a bakery, but in those early years I had to shift baking to the back of my mind. After a couple of years, work in the cotton mills began to decline, exports were down more and more mills opened in the Far East. As a result, our overtime was cut, and this signalled the moment to look for work in a bakery and a job. I left the cotton mill and began work in a small English bakery. Now my working in a bakery, which had different hours, conflicted with my wife's hours too, which meant we had nobody looking after the children. After a short while I could see that my career change was not working out, so I left the bakery and went back to the cotton mill.

In the community, the choir ceased to exist after Hajdukevych co-habited with Musyka's wife, his immorality disgusted me. I still retained my post as the head of the Parents' Union and on the committee of Former Combatants.

I began to sing in the Rochdale choir and accompanied them on a European festival in France, including a pilgrimage to Lourdes. I took my eldest son

Jaroslaw, who was approaching his sixth birthday, and during a nightly candlelit vigil I lost him. Luckily our priest from Paris, Father Levynet, made an announcement over the loudspeakers and thankfully, shortly afterwards one of my choir members Tysaruk found him.

The conductor of our choir was Stek, until he emigrated to Canada, his position was taken over by Sverliuk . I attended choir practices fortnightly, the week I worked the morning shift. I put the children to bed at 7p.m. unattended, and caught a bus to Rochdale.

When I finally stopped singing with the Rochdale choir, I joined the Manchester choir under the leadership of Pasika. As in Rochdale, because of my party poliotics nobody befriended me except for Sverliuk in Rochdale, everyone avoided me, knowing I was a member of the Dvikari. Nobody ever confronted me or showed any animosity over my beliefs, I sang in the bass section, my voice was good, I never had problems with the conductors, I loved to sing, always attending choir rehearsals, except for the times I had to work.

When I was at home I had plenty of free time, I read, I wrote poems, I couldn't sit idly without any pastimes. At the cotton mill I worked on the same machines as my wife, Olha in her spare time would constantly walk up and down inspecting and cleaning them, whereas in my case I sat writing or reading, neglecting the maintenance of the machines. Olha found working with me hard, having to constantly bring the machines back to good running order after my shift. She was a better worker than me and earned more money, but we were lucky that both worked and didn't need any outside help looking after our children.

When I worked the morning shift I would be home at 2.30p.m. Olha would have prepared lunch, after which I brought the children downstairs, fed them, let them play until 7p.m. before I took them back to bed.

In Bury, people within the community avoided me, especially the OUN members, the only exception being Skaskiw who worked with me in same cotton mill. He always kept me well informed of the goings- on with the 'party'. Like me, he too had constant confrontations with Chvil, always disagreeing on issues, although remaining in the 'party' on the advice of his former fellow villager, Drabat. Most of the 'party' members didn't trust Skaskiw, they saw and heard the discussions I had with him and he knew he wasn't to discuss party politics with me.

The whole Ukrainian community in Bury knew that it was Skaskiw as head of SUB and myself as secretary who had bought the first Ukrainian Club in Bury, not to be outdone by the larger Ukrainian communities in the region.

When Chvil first arrived in Bury with his younger brother, he acted the big party leader, yet his brother was 'thick as a plank'. Upon their arrival there was not the same cohesion amongst the members of the party as in the beginning. Members split into two groups, those with privileges who didn't need to attend meetings, and the rest that had to. Chvil could sit at home playing chess, whereas the remainder were given political material that hardly anyone understood. People like Chvil were a hindrance to the party, doing more harm than good. I remember on one occasion, all the unmarried members were given forms sent by the executive office, with the question 'Who is ready to return to Ukraine?' There wasn't a single volunteer, yet both the Chvil brothers were unmarried. There was only one volunteer and he Kaniuk, was married, he was summarily dismissed. Two years after the younger brother Chvil emigrated to Canada, his older brother followed. Hajdukevych a former village neighbour of Drabat's, was elected the head of SUB even though he had 'taken' Musyka's wife. To win over his popularity within the community, Hajdukevych began steps into opening a bar within the Ukrainian Club. At that time I was still head of the Parents' Union, but my protests fell on deaf ears.

In the room where Ukrainian was taught to our children, Hajdukevych opened a bar. With his own hands he took down religious icons and a wooden cross off the walls to make room for his 'new bar'.

In January of 1958 a new committee was formed to run the new bar, its secretary was Ivantyshyn a Ukrainian teacher at the school. My protests were ignored, all 'party members' were informed by the hierarchy to attend and put their names forward as members, by which time they were nearly thirty.

On one occasion, still seething at his former village dweller Hajdukevych for taking his wife, Musyka threw a stone through the bar window, but missing Hajdukevych by a hair's breadth. Later he was taken to court by the bar committee and was made to pay for a replacement window.

Later that year, by which time my wife and I had saved some money, we bought a newer house for £1,200. on 130 Heywood St. very close to the Ukrainian Club. We sold our old house for £100 as it was to be demolished two years later.

At that time, as an agent of Chvyli Dnipro ('Waves of Dnieper'), I was still selling Ukrainian books and periodicals to the local community, mostly evenings during my spare time. One evening I called at the Ostapiuk's as they had bought a book from me. Mrs Ostapiuk began to boast that they had bought a bakery in Manchester, with a Polish partner and that Mr. Shumka stood as guarantor. As a baker I was very interested, asking where it was, whether and when they would they be starting to bake. Mrs Ostapiuk didn't want to disclose any information, so I didn't pursue the matter further.

A couple of days later, on my return home from my morning shift, I found Mr. Ostapiuk standing on my doorstep, immediately pleaded for my help. His Polish partner Kazimirski had fallen ill and they had nobody to carry out the work and would I help. I agreed but had to call at my wife's cousin, Olha Semehen, who also worked at the same cotton mill on my shift. The children were still asleep, and after calling on Olha Semehen, I was driven by Mr Ostapiuk to Manchester, returning late at night on the last train. There was no problem in getting leave from work, my wife and her cousin shared looking after our children and this arrangement was to last until Kazimirski returned to work. I picked up the work very quickly, Mrs Ostapiuk appointed me as the person in charge of the night shift. Apart from me worked an alcoholic from Belarus and Ostapiuk's cousin, as a helper.

Three weeks later Kazimirski returned, immediately changed into his bakery clothing and started work. That evening, once she had closed the bakery shop, Mrs Ostapiuk called me into her office, where she took care of the bakery accounts, while her husband delivered bread in their small van to local shops, two of which were Ukrainian- owned. Mrs Ostapiuk asked me to keep an eye on Kazimirski, in case of any sabotage he might carry out, he hadn't really been ill, he had been absent because of an argument he'd had with the Ostapiuks.

Kazimirski knew his work well, after all he was a professional baker, and it was he who opened the bakery. Shumka introduced him to the Ostapiuks as potential partner. That night once we'd fulfilled our orders sooner, with Kazimirski as the extra person, he asked me if I would give him a hand to bring downstairs a bed he sometimes slept on, which he wanted to take home. We loaded the bed onto the van, Kazimirski collected the van keys, saying he would return in an hour, that was at 4 a.m. Mr Ostapiuk arrived at 6a.m. looking for the van which he needed for his deliveries. Mr Ostapiuk began blaming me for allowing Kazimirski to take the van keys, but how could I prevent a partner from doing so. Mrs Ostapiuk arrived, and soon afterwards she rang Kazimirski, his explanation was that the van was his not the bakery's. In the end they managed to borrow a van from a local Jew, but they were still mad at me. I explained what Kazimirski had told me during the night of their constant arguments, something which had been kept from me, except his illness. They couldn't hold me responsible or hold a grudge against me, since they needed me to carry out the work. They would have to resolve the situation with Kazimirski themselves.

When my friend Levycki, who now owned a shop in Bradford, found out that I was working in a bakery, began to try and convince me in buying my own in Bradford. There were seven Ukrainian shops in the city but no Ukrainian bakery. When Lewycki finally found a small bakery for sale, he informed me and I travelled to Bradford to see it. On my return to Bury, I discussed my proposition with Olha. I liked what I'd seen in the bakery, I had a little money saved and our home was almost paid for.

The following Sunday I travelled to Bradford again, I met the owner and we came to a financial arrangement, even leaving him a deposit. The owner of the bakery had closed it due to his ill health, so moving in should not have been a problem. Levwycki said that he would take care of all the necessary paperwork with solicitors etc., all I would have to do was to sign the contract. After a week I gave Mrs Ostapiuk a weeks' notice, saying I would finish on Saturday, my reason being the truth, that I was about to open my own bakery in Bradford. Mrs Ostapiuk immediately appointed the Belarus as the foreman, upset with my decision, she no longer trusted me but couldn't stop me.

The following Sunday I travelled to Bradford again, having to ensure everything was in order, so that work could commence the following week. I spent the night at Lewycki's, after breakfast I walked to the bakery which was on Green Lane, not far from Lewycki's shop. As I approached the bakery, I could see a large cloud of dust covering the bakery, I was shocked to see bulldozers knocking down houses across the road from the bakery. I marched straight into the bakery to see the owner, who explained that the houses were being knocked down as they were old, and would be replaced with new houses, but the block in which the bakery stood would not be touched. I wasn't convinced, went to see Vowczyna a well- known Ukrainian, and together we found the planning department at the local Town Hall. Nobody in that department would give me any guarantee that the bakery would be the next casualty, on this advice I decided to pull out of the sale. My experience cost me ten pounds in solicitor fees, the deposit for the bakery was returned, I'd now become jobless, the Ostapiuks wouldn't re-employ me, saying they already had a replacement, I even tried my old cotton mill, though without success.

In those days unemployment benefits were hard to come by, especially when a person left his or her job voluntarily. I spent two months without any financial help from the government, even though I had three small children. Fortunately, Olha worked and with her money we managed to survive.

One day I saw an advert in the Bury Times, a bakery was looking for 'a young man'. I was in my forties, nevertheless I tried my luck. Mr Miller looked me over, after a short interview said he would let me know. In the meantime, Olha managed to have me re-instated at the cotton mill, so we again shared the same machines at Victoria Cotton Mills, my bakery days again became a distant dream.

I wasn't involved in any Ukrainian community work, in fact all my so- called friends avoided and had forgotten about all the work I'd carried out in the early days. My only pastime was singing in the Manchester choir, even there I had few friends, but soon I discovered that some of my compatriots shared my political views. The Dvikari was growing as a 'party', I began to discover new members, individuals with whom I could air my views and join in a discussion without feeling alone or ostracised. In Bury I only had two such sympathisers, who would only speak to me away from OUN members, too afraid of reprisals. The conductor in Rochdale, Swerliuk later becoming a Dvikar, Tomkiw from Bolton, Vashkovych from Manchester, who later became a member too, and in the past often came to Bury representing the committee of the Former Combatants, one such visit was to mediate in a dispute I'd had with Chvil, at that time he never took my side, even though I was right.

One day 'out of the blue' came knocking on my door Mr. Miller's son, saying his father wanted to see me. That same afternoon and he offered me a part time job, I was to start after finishing my morning shift at the cotton mill, working until six or whenever the work was completed, while on Saturday I was to start at 4a.m. working until 1p.m. At Miller's I was paid £5 for the week and from the cotton mill I earned £11 per week.

Working at the bakery had its advantages, mainly that I could take old bread and cakes home at no cost. The custom was that any two- day- old bread was sold at half price, there was always plenty for me to choose from, which also helped the family budget. After three weeks Mr Miller asked if I could do an extra two hours in the mornings, starting at 3.30a.m. until 5.30a.m., from where I went straight to the cotton mill. I couldn't refuse Mr Miller, so I worked the extra hours although I found the hours difficult, but Mr Miller paid me an extra £3 per week.

After two months working the extra hours at two jobs, Mr Miller offered me full time employment which I accepted. I again left work at the cotton mill and became a permanent worker at Miller's. With my wife's weakly earnings of £10 we were able to save extra money.

In a short space of time I had saved enough money to buy my first new car, a Ford Anglia for £650. Musyka the former choir conductor in Bury, built me a garage and sometimes I took off my 'L' plates and drove to Manchester for choir rehearsals. When it came to learning to drive a car, I was a very poor student and slow learner. I eventually passed my driving test the third time, thanks to my instructor Baleckyj from Heywood.

I worked at Miller's for two years, I enjoyed my work and I was paid well. One Monday morning before Easter a familiar face unexpectedly walked into the bakery. It was Kazimirski, we shook hands warmly like two old friends, but immediately I noticed Mr Miller's face drop. Kazimirski told me about the dispute he'd had with Ostapiuk, who in the end won. Ostapiuk sold the bakery to a Ukrainian called Pochodaj, who I knew from my singing days in the Rochdale choir.

At Miller's I spoke to Kazimirski only in Polish, although during working hours we had little time to natter, he worked at the table, whereas I worked by the oven. The only chance we had to really talk was during our break. As I mentioned I could see that Mr Miller was not happy with the situation, summoning Kazimirski into his office. I later found out that Mr Miller had told Kazimirski to leave work on Saturday. Without thinking, I stormed into Mr Miller's office telling him that I too would be finishing work on Saturday. Mr Miller tried to talk me out of my decision, saying he had nothing against my work, only didn't like us speaking to each other in Polish. I quickly retorted, ' We live in a democratic country and everyone can speak in whichever language he chooses, I despise dictatorship and nobody is going to tell me in which language I can speak'. Later, even Mr Miller's son Jimmy tried to change my mind but it didn't help, that coming Saturday both Kazimirski and I left Miller's Bakery.

Two days later both of us started working at a Jewish bakery in nearby Heywood. The work was 'nights' for which I received £24 per week. Unfortunately my job only lasted six weeks, my wife became seriously ill, so I left the bakery, not wanting to leave her alone at night.

I soon found another job, this time at a small bakery around the corner from where I lived. My earnings were only £11 per week, but I could visit my wife and youngest son Taras during my lunch hour, while Jaroslaw and Dmytro were at school.

The owner of the bakery was an elderly Englishman, who we only saw about once a week, usually on pay day. He also had other business interests. In the bakery worked two men and two women, I worked there for just four months.

That summer, once Olha felt better, we set off in our car for a summer holiday to the South of England. It turned out to be the first and last holiday for the five of us together. Out of a piece of strong canvas I had sewn a makeshift tent which, although we never pitched, we used it to cover our belongings when we emptied the car at night. I took out the two front seats and slept on the floor with Olha, Dmytro and Taras slept on the back seat together, Jaroslaw slept in the boot/trunk of the car. During our journey, we would stop in empty fields or car parks overnight. We took with us a portable gas stove on which we cooked all our meals.

One of the towns we visited was Torquay, where we spent most of the day on the beach. Jaroslaw and Dmytro noticed people on small pedalling boats in the sea, and asked if they could go on one. I allowed them and forewarned them to stay close to the shore. I saw them both nearby and after a few minutes lay on the sand, not noticing that the tide had taken them away from the shore. I suddenly heard a commotion, people were standing looking out at sea, where my two boys had drifted further and further out. At one point a young man in a small boat tried to tow them back to shore but gave up, in the end a rescue boat was sent out to tow them back to shore. At that time Jaroslaw was eleven and said that he couldn't manage to pedal fast enough and Dmytro wouldn't help.

On the way back to Bury, we stayed over at the Ukrainian Invalids Home in Chiddingfold, Surrey, sleeping on freshly cut hay. Jaroslaw had already been there in previous years with the Ukrainian Scouts, who hired a bit of land for their summer camps. The return journey took us all day, there were no motorways at that time.

Every two weeks, Iwasz, the owner of a parcel export company, specialising in sending packages to Ukraine, hired a room at the Bury Ukrainian Club. One Saturday at the end of September, Iwasz called at my house in search of me, I missed him, as I was watching a football match with my two older boys. Iwasz left a message with Olha, from Levicky in Bradford, saying I had to urgently travel to Bradford the following day. A bakery owned by two Ukrainians, who were non bakers by trade, had to close down after only five months. Their bakery was ran by a novice baker who picked up a bit of know-how whilst working at a local Polish bakery. He did what he pleased because the owners were not in a position to reprimand him. He came to work when he liked, on occasions when he had too much to drink, he never came at all, so the two poor owners couldn't put up with him anymore and closed the bakery.

Olha didn't mention the visit of Iwasz until we were in bed. That night I could hardly sleep, pondering whether to travel to Bradford or not. The following morning after breakfast, without Olha's full support, we drove to Bradford and met Levycki. After a phone call to Vowczyna, who in turn contacted the bakery owners, Bokalo and Hapachylo, we all met at the bakery.

The bakery had been converted from a corner dwelling house. The bakery itself was on the first floor, having been transformed from two bedrooms. It contained an old gas oven, which was uncannily still warm, a preparation table, one small bread mixer, twelve baking sheets and a few sacks of flour, a little sugar which was mixed with salt. On the ground floor one room was used for flour storage, and adjoining it was the bakery shop containing a few bare shelves. There was also an empty cellar.

Vowchyna tried his hardest to convince me to buy the bakery, saying it was a good potential business, needing a professional baker. Levycki, too, echoed his approval, saying Bradford had many Ukrainian shops, but no bakery, adding that the Polish community laughed at the Ukrainians, saying they had no craftsmen only farmers. During this time Olha wouldn't step foot into the bakery, saying she had a headache. After I'd given myself time to reflect, I asked the owners how much they wanted for the business. Hapachylo immediately replied 'Two and a half thousand'. I didn't want to appear to be too eager in front of Vowchyna and Levycki, so I replied, 'I will give you half'. Bokalo turned away showing great displeasure, knowing they paid far more for the bakery and didn't intend losing money on the transaction, and I was in no rush to increase my offer. Firstly, I didn't honestly have that much available money, and secondly it was a big risk. I was frightened even though

I felt a strong desire to buy it. I made a move to go outside to talk over the proposition with Olha, but Vowchyna quickly blocked my exit, determined that I agreed on a price amicably with both partners.

After a little whispering between the two partners, Bokalo dropped the price to two thousand. Vowchyna suggested that I increased my offer and the bakery would be mine, I could immediately start baking my own bread. I replied 'I honestly don't have enough money, I have three small children, but if you both want to seriously sell the bakery, I will risk one and a half thousand'. The owners wouldn't accept my last offer. Unknown to any of us, Iwasz had appeared, firstly outside talking to Olha, before joining us upstairs, he too attempted to persuade me to increase my offer. I increased my offer by £100, leaving a difference of four hundred. Levycky again started 'working on me' saying 'Why should you work for Jews, Poles or the English? Why can't you work for yourself'?

Iwasz took me to one side and advised me to buy the bakery and if I genuinely didn't have enough money, then he would be prepared to become my partner, or he could work for me as a driver, or lend me some money. In the background, Vowchyna and Levycki, were trying to convince Bokalo and Hapachylo that they would lose more money if they didn't accept my offer of £1,600.

In the end after more discussions, I became an unexpected owner of a bakery in Bradford, and would start work the following Sunday, on the 10th of October 1961.

I brought a little money with me which I was prepared to use a deposit, I urged Vowchyna to accept this in case the partners changed their minds.

Bokalo agreed to help me get started, to show me the ropes, introduce me to all the shop owners etc. I could have started work that week as Levycki suggested, but there was no flour or other ingredients in the bakery, besides I had to give my notice at the bakery in Bury. I arranged with Bokalo that he would order all the necessary ingredients required during the week and I would return to Bradford on Saturday, starting work the following night.

On the return journey to Bury, Olha was violently sick, I had to stop twice, she hardly spoke only to say 'How could you allow yourself to be talked into buying that hole'? That night I could hardly sleep, my mind was going round in circles, nothing made sense. In the morning I went to work, telling the manager during breakfast I would be finishing on Saturday, without giving him a reason.

After work I went to see my good friend Zin for advice. I explained everything that had occurred over the week-end and, after listening to me attentively, he advised me to go ahead and buy the bakery. I had £900 available, Zin was prepared to lend me the balance, saying if the business prospered I could pay him back, but if the business failed, then he wouldn't cry over lost money, he had lost far more in his life.

Our house in Bury was paid for, we decided to sell it and buy a similar one in Bradford. That week dragged, I not only counted the days but the hours until Saturday. I usually worked Saturday but not this one, after breakfast I drove to Bradford to see Levycki. He owned his own shop on Lumb Lane, were he sold meats, as he was a butcher and stocked groceries including bread, which he bought from two of the city's Polish bakeries. In his shop, I stood to his side looking how he conducted his business, and with it being Saturday the shop was busy selling mainly meats and bread. The biggest topic in the shop was when people spoke of the Ukrainian bakery which closed after such a short time. Levycki replied with delight that on Monday the bakery would re-open, introducing me as its new owner, adding that the bakery failed because the previous owners were not bakers, but the new owner was a genuine baker.

At lunch time Levycki closed his shop, we went upstairs to his accommodation, quickly had something to eat and drove to the bakery. We both spent the whole afternoon cleaning the table and bread mixer, swept the floors and I even turned on the oven, as it had stood cold all week. In the evening we returned to Levycki's house where I spent the night. The following morning I returned to Bury, collected all the money I'd saved and returned to Bradford in the evening. I called in at the bakery to turn on the oven, drove to Bokalo's house, and then returned with him to the bakery. I had become the proud owner of a bakery and I was determined to make a success of it.

CHAPTER 30
KOLOS BAKERY
BRADFORD

At 10p.m. on the 10th of October 1961 I mixed my first batch of brown bread. Bokalo had said that on a Monday we would need forty loaves of brown bread and about one hundred white loaves and that's what I made. The oven was small, only allowing fifty loaves per bake. Nevertheless, we quickly finished, then baked 150 rolls, which I had made when I worked in the Jewish bakeries and at Ostapiuk's. By 5a.m. we had finished everything, all the finished products were loaded onto the bakery van, waiting until 7.30a.m. to depart. We drove to Duleba in Keighley, to a Polish shop in Shipley, onto Bradford to Pysarchuk, Levycki, Dutka, Andrejchuk, Ernest a Polish shop, Huma another Polish shop finally Continental-English Delicatessen. These were all the shops Bokalo and Hapachylo supplied. At every shop Bokalo introduced me as the new owner of the bakery, being my first visit, out of courtesy I had to discuss one or two things, and collecting orders for the following day. I had already experienced delivering with Peter Ostapiuk, so this wasn't totally new to me.

We finished our deliveries around 11a.m. at whereupon I drove Bokalo home, returning to the bakery myself. After drinking a cup of coffee, I went to Konovalek's who owned a nearby off-license and lived above the shop. I had previously arranged with him that I would sleep in his house until I bought my own. I explained to Konovalek that I wouldn't be taking up his offer, because I had to see a flour agent and somebody else.

When the previous owners ran the bakery, Mrs Hapachylo ran the bakery shop and she volunteered her services to me. I refused her offer saying that I would sell the few loaves she sold myself. That first week I did all the baking, the driving, returning to clean the bakery, having a drink of coffee and a piece of bread, sitting on a chair and falling asleep until I was disturbed.

On Saturday when all the deliveries were complete, the bakery cleaned, I drove to Bury. I had my first proper meal in a week and went straight to bed.

The following day I returned to Bradford repeating what I had done the previous week, except on Friday after Olha had finished work in the cotton mill, she left the children with her cousin and caught a bus to Bradford. She spent the whole night cleaning the bakery, whilst I and Bokalo baked bread. After baking I went out on deliveries, Olha opened the bakery shop and sold a few loaves. About 3p.m. I drove us both to Bury, where I was too exhausted to wait for Olha to cook a meal, so I fell into bed, which I hadn't seen for a week.

During the day at the bakery nothing was baked, but occasionally, especially on seeing my car and van outside, people would knock at the door, either a customer or a representative selling his wares.

That first week we put our house up for sale in Bury, and our garage which was five minutes walk away. Our house was in good condition and sold very quickly, and with the proceeds we bought one in Bradford, five minutes' walk from the bakery.

On Sunday, I again drove to Bradford, this time I took a mattress, hoping to be able to get the odd hour of sleep. Olha remained in Bury with the children, Jaroslaw who was almost twelve, started his new school in Bolton, Dmytro approaching eight went to school in Bury and Taras at four, was too young for school.

At the end of my third week, a man walked into the bakery and introduced himself as Hutuliak, the former manager of the previous owners. He began to complain about his previous bosses, saying there were three of them, each one of them having something to say, none of them knew anything about baking bread, and he could never come to any agreement with them, this being the reason he had to leave. He tried making something new, but they wouldn't invest any money for the ingredients he needed, convinced that from flour and water only bread could be made. He also told me that he had experience, having worked in a Polish bakery for two years, and as he couldn't reason with them they argued and he left. He felt sorry for them, but it was too late. This was not the story I was told by his previous bosses, often coming in to work drunk, coming in late, and on occasions when he was too drunk, not coming in to work at all. His bosses were forced to carry out the work themselves, not knowing exactly what to do, often calling at his house in the middle of the night, asking for bread recipes and how to mix. He finished by saying that because of the previous owners he now had no work and had six children to feed.

As he lived very close to the bakery, he knew very well I was short handed, doing most jobs myself and delivering bread, so he pleaded with me to give him a job, saying he would bake nights and, knowing all the shops, deliver bread in the morning.

I wasn't sure if I was making the right decision, I knew the work I was doing was too much for me, but hearing Hutuliak's sob story, the fact that he had six children, swayed my mind and offered him the job. It was agreed Hutuliak would start work on Sunday night, I didn't say anything to Bokalo, knowing full well that they both hated each other.

I managed the first two weeks almost single handed, on the second Saturday I baked 250 loaves and 180 bread rolls, but in order to pay Bokalo his wage, I had to drive to Bury after work and collect Olha's wage so that I could pay him, as he wouldn't wait until the following week.

The money I'd collected from bread takings after the first week I used to pay for flour, as I was new in business, nobody allowed me credit, I even had to pay the Gas Board a bond of £50.

On the second Friday, I collected Olha and her 'money' both of us returning to Bradford. We both worked through the night, returning to Bury on Saturday afternoon. On the third Sunday, I travelled to Bradford, stopping off at the bakery to fire the oven and prepare my doughs. At 9p.m. Hutuliak walked into the bakery, after a short discussion I left him, in the meantime I drove to Bokalo's house and brought him back. On our return, Bokalo saw Hutuliak standing in the bakery wearing an apron. He immediately did an about-turn saying to me 'If Hutuliak works, then I go home' and that's what he did. Hutuliak stayed and helped me, we finished earlier than usual, as he could weigh the dough pieces and mould bread.

In the morning we both packed the bread orders and carried out the deliveries. On the subsequent days, Hutuliak delivered by himself. That same week Iwasz also started work, firstly in the evenings with the bread, coming back in the morning delivering in the van, while Hutuliak used my car until I part exchanged it for a larger one.

Credit was very hard to come by in the early days, the fact that my predecessors had gone bankrupt didn't help, no one gave me credit.

From the time Iwasz began work, I had more time to introduce new lines, I started making sweet crescents, small cheese rolls, apple and plum too. All the confectionery was made in the evenings before the bread, sometimes Iwasz didn't go home until midnight.

In the early days, my best customer was Duleba in Keighley, one of the reasons was that he supplied bread to Italian ladies living in a hostel.

I made an arrangement with Iwasz to put £300 into the business, thus giving him a fifth share. I paid him £10 per week and myself £15 per week. When Olha moved to Bradford permanently, I only paid her £6 per week for which she worked 12 to 14 hours daily. Her duties were helping me in the evenings with the confectionery, clean and sell in the bakery shop. With the bakery being on the first floor, every time the shop door bell rang, Olha had to run downstairs, sometimes it was just an inquiry, nevertheless potential customers couldn't be turned away, we sold about 12 loaves daily.

To be successful in business, one has to introduce new products, seek out new customers and promote the bakery. In this instance, Iwasz was very helpful, he did the weekly invoices, worked in the bakery, delivered bread and even served in the shop when needed. He was liked by all the customers, especially once they knew he was a partner in the business, some customers increased their orders. Iwasz was very honest and correct, when he collected money from customers, it was always to the penny, if there was a discrepancy, he would sit until he found the fault. Everything was correctly booked, written and accounted for.

Soon after Iwasz started work, I had to buy a new van, the inherited one was falling to bits. My old friend Zin from Bury loaned me £300 even though he never saw the bakery, his money I used as a deposit, the balance I took on finance.

Shortly after Hutuliak began working for me, Bokalo and Hapachylo began putting pressure on me to pay off the money I owed them, saying they allowed me to use the bakery before contracts were signed. I was in a dilemma, not knowing what to do for the best. In the end I used £300 from the sale of our house in Bury. When we finally bought a nearby house, our shortfall forced me to take a small loan. On the 1st of December 1961 we received the keys for our first house in Bradford.

Before we moved into our house, we lived in the attic above the bakery, with Dmytro and Taras. Fortunately, winter was approaching, otherwise the heat would have been unbearable, the noise from the gas burner was so loud, conversation next to it was almost impossible. Jaroslaw began a new school in Bolton a month before I bought the bakery, I decided it would be best if he stayed there until he finished his first term, meanwhile he lived at Olha's cousins house in Bury until then.

The bakery contract was ready shortly before Christmas. I paid Bokalo and Hapachylo all the outstanding money I owed them, and so became the owner of the bakery.

On Friday nights I never baked more than 300 loaves, though on the last day of baking before Christmas I managed to produce 500 loaves. As the oven capacity was only 50 loaves at a time, it took me over 10 hours to bake the 500 loaves.

After Christmas the bread orders slowly grew, I began to introduce new lines, 'Vienna Bread' plaited bread and a few English items.

In spring I took on another driver, Krawczuk who used the van while Iwasz drove my car. We began delivering bread to neighbouring Huddersfield. We worked many hours, one of the hardships being finished products had to be carried downstairs, raw materials upstairs. The bakery floor had no room for storage, all finished products, flour and everything else stored on the ground floor. Every time I had to carry a basket of baked bread downstairs, I would routinely carry a bag of flour upstairs on my return.

After a great deal of hard work we somehow managed a year in business, whereas my predecessors had only lasted five months. Nobody counted their hours of work, the most important task was to fulfil our orders, sometimes later than we would have liked.

One person who didn't survive the first year was Hutuliak, I replaced him with a Yugoslavian baker who previously worked for Polish bakeries.

At the end of our first year, Iwasz and I totalled all our outgoings and incomings, leaving us a paltry £73. Iwasz decided that there wasn't enough money in the business to support two families, so he voluntarily left. I returned his £300 for which he was grateful, and I was happy to be able to return it.

When Iwasz left me, his work was carried out by Krawczuk who, unfortunately wasn't as versatile and wasn't suited to production. I paid him £11 per week, and again I had to use my car to cover Iwasz's deliveries, not to mention all the accounts.

That was not the end of my immediate problems. I suddenly noticed a drop in orders with the Ukrainian shops, except from Pysarchuk and Levycki. One day

Krawczuk returned from his run with a basket of bread, when I inquired what had happened he replied 'Mr Prytulak, the bread is from Mrs Andrejchuk, who said that people don't want to buy Dvikarski bread (being made by a Dvikar, the political party I supported) because it crumbs easily and on the following day it's as hard as stone'.

To remedy the situation, I began adding vegetable oil to each bread mix, but it didn't help sales.

When I first arrived to Bradford, I was almost immediately hounded with letters from members of the OUN party, but Iwasz always stood by me, defending me, never repeating what people said about me, sparing me the immoral accusations from the people who tried to mentally break me.

During my second year, I worked much more than in my first, not because of an increase in production, but because I didn't have a good baker to help, having to do most of the work myself.

I was baking nearly 2,500 loaves a week, which was a large amount being handmade, mostly single-handed. One day I accidentally sent Dutka two loaves less than he ordered, on noticing the shortfall, he quickly telephoned me and said 'If you desperately want to make your first million, you should go and rob a bank, not bake bread'. He added 'So that you don't make any more mistakes, I will order a round figure of ten loaves daily'. I always supported fellow Ukrainians in any way I could, but his derogatory remarks and insulting manner, prompted me to stop his deliveries completely.

With the confectionery side picking up, especially the sweet crescents, I bought a crescent machine, which saved us pinning out dough pieces, the machine made the finished article. I also employed a lady part time, she covered the work that Iwasz used to do in the bakery, her name was Lida Orlov from Belarus.

I also began to bake 'Vienna Bread' a light crispy loaf. Admittedly, it could have been better had I had a better oven.

In my second year both Easter's coincided, that is according to both the Julian and Gregorian calendars. I made Pasky (Easter Bread) the previous year, one of my Ukrainian customers Boychuk, liked them very much, I even baked him more after Easter.

My bread sales overall had dropped by around 200 loaves weekly.

At Whitsuntide I was approached by a Pole, Mr Pilny who owned a few shops in the city, he was interested in buying confectionery. At that time I made sponge cakes and other similar items which were quite popular.

In July of that year I had a motor accident, damaging my car beyond repair. The following day I bought a Bedford van, which had collapsible seats behind the driver.

That summer I began to deliver bread to Mr Szlapak in Bury, to compensate the loss of sales in Bradford, there were various forms of slander being spread within the Ukrainian community. But I didn't give up, even though I struggled with bakers and drivers, I was forty seven at the time, working all hours God sent. Many times my baker didn't turn up for work, I had to turn to Olha, making her help me through the night, otherwise the bread orders wouldn't have been fulfilled, whereas on Fridays I used Jaroslaw.

One day whilst I was delivering bread to a Polish shop in Halifax, I noticed rye bread on the shelves, made by a Jewish bakery, which interested me, for back home in Stanislaviw I used to make rye bread, we only used white wheat flour for rolls.

From that day on, I began making inquiries as to where I could obtain rye flour, asking two of my flour suppliers but they didn't know. I approached the Jew who supplied me with vegetable oil, he later passed on an address. Jaroslaw who began to help me with secretarial duties, wrote to this company and within a week I had rye flour.

I found it very difficult to make a rye bread, every Saturday after work I would experiment, but it wasn't easy, it took me three months before I was satisfied with the finished product, prior to that, the local Ukrainian farmer, Kozar received a steady supply of rejects for his pigs.

On the 9th of September 1963 I baked six rye bread, which had the taste and look I still remembered. I took them downstairs to our bakery shop, at which time stood two Ukrainian ladies talking to Olha. I cut a loaf and invited both ladies to taste, immediately they nodded with approval, so the following Saturday I baked 9 loaves, giving them out to Ukrainian shopkeepers. My samples were appreciated and liked, so each Saturday I increased by six.

At the end of that month, Krawchuk left the bakery, alleging I'd offended him by saying that I worked harder and better for a Jew, than he worked for me. Needless to say, he was a slow worker. In his place I employed a Hungarian called Luysa. Around that time my Yugoslavian baker left, in his place I took a young un-skilled Italian called Roman, we called him 'Romo'.

I had the opportunity to buy 30 kilos of caraway seeds, which I used in rye bread, from Pysarczuk, thinking that I would never use them in my lifetime. I was soon proved wrong to my satisfaction, in later years I would buy half a ton at a time.

On the strength of my rye bread, my weekly production rose to 2,600 on a Friday I had orders for over 500 loaves. Each bread piece I weighed by hand, moulded into shape, Romo was only able to place the bread onto a peeler (wooden shovel) as I inserted it into the oven.

Towards the end of October 1963 a large bakery in Bradford called Busby's stopped producing Vienna Bread, and on the strength of that, other shopkeepers mostly Polish owned, namely, Slavia Stores, Huma, Europa of Keighley, began to buy my Vienna bread and rye bread.

My driver Luysa left after a couple of weeks, so I employed a Ukrainian, Zasedko. I always had problems with drivers, more than with bakers, I could bake myself, but it was too much to do both jobs, especially as I was baking 120 rye bread weekly and 50 Vienna Bread daily.

That year, Christmas Day fell on a Wednesday, I started baking at 6p.m. on the Sunday before, finishing at 6p.m. on Tuesday. I worked nonstop, my order for Tuesday was for 1100 loaves, and the only help I had was an unqualified Italian, I had to bring in my wife and son, otherwise I wouldn't have managed.

After Christmas Zasedko left my employment, in his place started a Pole called Kisela, drivers gave me the most headaches.

Once the Polish shops began to buy my rye bread, I couldn't cope, I began to make rye bread twice weekly, I was getting busier with orders for rye bread, white bread, brown bread, rolls, Vienna bread, plus confectionery. Bread production was increasing weekly, as was weekly turnover.

On Friday I would finish work at 1p.m. Romo worked from 9p.m. till 7a.m. at which time Olha took his place, and together we finished the bread production, after which I prepared a mix of confectionery, going to bed about 3.p.m. returning three hours later, ready for the following day's production. That's how we struggled, me, my wife and children.

Before Easter that year, I received orders of 600 rye bread, I couldn't physically cope with such a large order, I had to cut down everyone's order, I also had to bake Pasky. When I started work at 6p.m. on Thursday I worked until 5p.m. on Saturday, I was forty eight years old, and although it was beginning to take its toll, I was determined to succeed.

On the 3rd of August 1964 Olha went on holiday to Rome for a week with our two youngest children. That week Kisela became ill, in his place I employed Hashoshyn and Dubey. Without Olha, I found work that week very difficult, I even thought of getting rid of some of the smaller shops, or buy a new oven.

The same Jewish baker who found me a mill manufacturing rye flour came to my rescue again. He found me the name and address of a London company, who acted as agents for German ovens. Jaroslaw wrote them a letter and after a few days we received a brochure. Three years previously, I bought a bakery with all its equipment for £1,600, and now a new oven was about to cost me £1,800.

On the 21st of August 1964 Romo went on holiday and ten days later on the last day of August Jejna started work for me as a driver. I paid him £15 per week as he'd already worked as one in a English bakery. When Romo went on holiday, it was without my consent, I drove to Halifax to his sister's where he lived and asked her when her brother would return. She replied she didn't know, but on his return he will go to the bakery. Olha had to work nights in his place for nine weeks, and fortunately a young man by the name of Biloshtiak was on his way to America from Poland. He stopped off to see his father in Bradford, and whilst doing so, worked in the bakery for us.

By the end of my third financial year, bread production rose to 2,880 weekly, included in that total was 850 rye bread.

When Olha worked nights with me, the children had to look after themselves, Olha would return home to make breakfast for the children, Jaroslaw was the hardest to wake, he helped me in the bakery after school, sometimes not finishing until midnight, then having to do his homework. Olha would sleep for a couple of hours, before returning to the bakery at noon, making me lunch and carrying on with her normal duties.

On the 26th of October 1964 Romo returned from his holiday in Italy. He never admitted, but I think his family retained him in Italy to help with the harvest. I was compelled into accepting him back, as it was difficult to find a night worker. With Romo returning, Olha could return to her day duties, and work during the night became easier.

Around that period I employed a part time driver named Jacubiak, who later in life became a church deacon.

After Hotuliak left my employment, he spent a little time unemployed, later approaching the owner of the Polish Bakery Prima, saying that he could bake them similar rye bread as I made. When I experimented with rye bread, I always made everything alone. True to form, I never even dreamt for one minute of making rye bread whilst Hotuliak worked for me.

One weekend I was in Bury visiting my old friend Zin, boasting that bread production had increased from the first year, adding that the Banderites had stopped spreading malicious gossip since I introduced my rye bread. I even mentioned that I had put down a deposit of £600 on a new oven. Knowing that I now had money, Zin asked for the £300 I borrowed from him, which I did, without interest. He was happy I was able to repay him, he knew very well about the propaganda against me.

After Iwasz had left, I stopped taking a wage from the business, only giving my wife enough money for housekeeping. I didn't smoke or drink, I never thought about a holiday, thinking myself lucky at the end of the week on Saturday, that I could get at least one good night's sleep and rest.

On a Sunday mornings I drove everyone to church, where I had the opportunity to meet and speak to someone, buy a Ukrainian newspaper, before returning home for lunch. Sunday afternoon was the only time I had to do the bakery accounts and invoices, with Jaroslaw's help. By this time Jaroslaw also knew how to mix bread doughs, he would walk to the bakery and mix the first two doughs, allowing me to have a couple of hours of sleep before my week began again at 10p.m.

Someone in Bradford found out that I used to sing in the Manchester Ukrainian choir, and so I was invited to join the Bradford choir. I agreed, but only attending rehearsals on a Saturday evening. The choir was led by Mr Hawryliuk, who died in 1983. Although I loved to sing, my singing with the

Bradford choir soon came to an end. The rehearsals were always late, either through waiting for the conductor, or for other choir members travelling from neighbouring towns to arrive. Most of the singers didn't mind sitting around, socialising and drinking, but my time was precious, I couldn't afford to sit around without purpose.

From the time I began to manufacture rye bread, my profits continually increased. After the first year with Iwasz, out net profit was £73, the second year without Iwasz it was £700 and after the third year it increased to £3,000. I had saved enough money to buy a new oven, one which hopefully would bake my bread evenly. Unfortunately I had to travel to Germany in order to see the oven. I left Olha in charge, I had taught her how to mix the bread doughs, Jaroslaw answered the telephone and took bread orders, Romo took charge of the oven.

On Saturday I flew to Munich, where I spent two nights with friends, the Kozak family, and on Monday I travelled to Nuremberg where the ovens were built. I liked the oven immediately and ordering one, returning to Bradford the following day.

During that period I produced a thousand loaves of rye bread weekly. I still made white and brown bread, though their sales dropped slightly, but I wasn't concerned as rye bread was three pence more expensive and easier to make. When moulding white and brown bread, a person could only make one at a time, whereas moulding rye bread, because they were round, two at a time could be moulded.

On the 15th of March 1965 the oven arrived with an engineer. Work on the old oven finished on Saturday, it was left open overnight to cool. The next day on Sunday we began to dismantle it, by Monday we began to erect the new oven and by the following Saturday, we began baking in the new oven. It turned out to be very economical compared to its old predecessor, it had five decks, giving a baking capacity of 100 loaves compared to 50 from the old one. Baking, too, was a lot easier, inserting bread was done on a rolling canvas, and all the bread was evenly baked.

As a result of the far superior looking bread, production increased immediately to over 3,000 weekly. That Easter we made over 4,000 bread of which 1,800 were rye bread.

No matter how tired I was, from the very beginning I kept a diary, making notes of my production, staff changes etc. Every week I would total the production with Jaroslaw, and every time we beat a previous target, he would enter 'Record'.

With the new oven, even our 'Vienna Bread' improved, it was evenly baked and crispy, and on a Friday I baked over 80 loaves.

With the increase of production, a new problem arose, we had to expand the bakery in order to accommodate all the extra bread we were producing. Firstly, I closed the shop, added new shelves and converted into a finishing room. I had to store the flour in the cellar, which was not very practical as it attracted rats.

Secondly, the bread mixer I inherited with the bakery had a mixing capacity of 50 bread. Now that we increased the oven batches to 100 I needed a larger bread mixer. The bakery floor, which was built for domestic use, wouldn't safely hold the extra weight. My only option was to position the mixer on the ground floor, in a small room which was originally the kitchen. I mixed the white and brown doughs downstairs, after which small dough pieces were carried upstairs by Olha and the children. I still mixed the rye doughs in the bakery, as the consistency was softer and couldn't be risked carrying upstairs.

In the end I decided to build an extension, adding a room on the first floor. Before I did this, I went round to the next door neighbours, who constantly complained about the noise coming through the walls, preventing them from sleep, and asked if they would sell me their house, they refused outright.

I received planning permission quickly, even so bread production was increasing continuously, the shops in Huddersfield complained that Jejna didn't arrive until lunchtime. So to try and speed up production I employed an English baker.

On the 20th of September 1965 I had built new steps from the ground floor to the first.
I noted in my diary 'Built new stairs for the benefit of my staff, so it will be easier for them to carry rye loaves and to send me to my grave quicker'.

As the extension was being built, I knew I had made a mistake and started to look for larger premises. I looked at old factories and warehouses, none of which were suitable for a bakery. One day my old partner Iwasz dropped in, I explained all my problems, the bakery being too small, I needed another oven with a capacity of at least 200 loaves. After listening, Iwasz said there was an old co-operative building on the next street which had been bought by an electrical winding company, and was now for sale. I asked Iwasz to find out on my behalf, who owned the building.

Two days later Iwasz came back with the address of the owner of the building, adding that if I required a partner, he would gladly step in. Without thinking I immediately agreed, knowing him as well as I knew my own pocket, I also knew that it was too big a project for me to undertake alone.

The following day I went to see the owner of the building. I walked into the building noticing an office which I entered, whereupon the secretary asked me to wait in the corridor. After waiting a length of time, I entered the secretary's office and asked how much longer I had to wait. The secretary rang the director's phone on her intercom and he appeared instantly. His first comment was 'Do you know how much this building costs? Do you have enough money? His reply was very demeaning, probably because standing before him stood a visibly overtired, untidy tramp, he probably didn't even have the inclination to talk to me. He had seen me earlier waiting in the corridor, but completely ignored me, and added 'The building together with 22 lock up garages costs £12,000. When you have the money, I will then talk to you, at the moment I am busy'.

I returned to the bakery feeling humiliated and rejected, I didn't have that kind of money, nor did Iwasz. A couple of days later, I received a gratifying letter from a finance company, writing that, as I had been a valued customer in the past, they would be happy to offer me a loan. When I phoned them and gave them the amount I required, their reply was negative.

Someone advised me to ask one of the flour millers I dealt with. At that time I dealt with three, I asked all their sales representatives the next time they appeared in the bakery. The first flour rep I asked said that his company didn't as a rule give loans, but he would ask his manager. The other two said there was a possibility, and they would be in touch. After a couple of weeks, the first miller I asked said no, the second kept stalling. The third company Spillers said, before they could give me a decision, they had first of all to view the prospective building.

I returned to the building to see the director and asked if there was a possibility of viewing the building. He agreed, and on the designated day a director from Spillers attended with his local rep. After viewing the building, with which the mill director was happy, we agreed that I would only buy the building for £8,000. The garages at the rear of the premises would be sold as a separate entity.

One of the conditions of the loans, was I had to arrange for a surveyor and valuer to inspect the premises. The valuer sent his report, writing that the building was only worth £7,000, and when I reported this to the building's owner, he again ignored me and wouldn't talk to me. I waited three weeks for a reply and finally went to see my solicitor. I explained everything to him, adding I liked the building very much and wanted to buy it. My solicitor advised me to wait, but I was worried that somebody in the meantime could offer the full asking price. I returned to see the building's owner and offered him an extra £500 to which he reluctantly agreed.

Spillers conditions were that I couldn't take on a partner, all my flour I had to buy solely from them until the loan was repaid, unless they couldn't, as was the case with rye flour.

I explained everything to Iwasz, all the conditions of the contract between me and Spillers, which he totally accepted, and we have remained friends till this very day.

I had around £3,000 of my own money, but I would need this to renovate the building I'd just bought. The present owners of the company repaired electrical motors, consequently the interior of the building was quite dark and greasy, I would need a considerable amount of money to bring it up to food standards.

On the 27th of December 1965 I gave a deposit of £1,000 even though the extension on my bakery wasn't completely finished. That winter was so severe, it was too cold for the builders to work, the final wall wasn't bricked, only temporarily boarded. That Christmas I was extremely busy, unable to cope with demand. On Wednesday I baked 2,000 loaves and the same on Thursday, I had to work 48 hours nonstop.

After Christmas I caught the 'flu' but had to work through it all the same, there was nobody else who could stand in for me. I felt physically drained, my assistant Romo had the flu too, and stayed home all week, Olha worked three nights, Jaroslaw the remaining three. I took on an old Polish baker called Veber on a part- time basis, he spoke a lot, but did little.

My rye bread was becoming more and more popular, I couldn't cope with all the work, so I stopped baking sponges and other little cakes, which took up too much time, it was far easier and more profitable to make rye bread.

I began to have more and more problems with Romo the baker, he would turn up for work one day then miss two, I couldn't sack him without a replacement, I only had one ill-fated Englishman and old Pole. I had to be patient, he gave me no other choice, every time he did come to work, I was happy, it was easier for me. In the end, my patience broke and I sacked him on the 1st of June 1966.

The following week I found a Ukrainian worker, named Chaban, who had never been inside a bakery, let alone work in one. He showed plenty of effort and willingness to work, so much so that after his first week both his hands had swollen, keeping him at home the following week. He remained in the bakery's employment until he retired.

Around the same time I employed a part- time driver called Lawriw, a very honest and punctual man. I also employed a lady to help Olha with the cleaning, a Mrs Iwasiw.

The new premises 128/132 Parkside Road, Bradford.

On the 1st of July 1966 I received the keys to my newly acquired building, four days later I signed the contract. I approached a few building companies for quotes to renovate the interior of the building. They all wanted so much money, I refused them all. Somebody advised me of a Ukrainian builder who worked on his own, his name was Ilko. We met, agreed on a price which was half the amount I'd been quoted earlier. He quickly started work and whenever he didn't have a labourer, I supplied him with one.

I again had to travel to Germany to buy another larger oven, this time with a capacity of 200 loaves. I paid the company a deposit of £1,000, the remainder on a interest free loan until the oven was paid off. I also bought two mixing machines from Jimmy Miller in Bury. He left his father's bakery business and set up on his own buying and restoring second- hand bakery machinery. For two of his reconditioned machines I paid £600.

That summer, during and around the time we had to move from the old bakery on New Cross St, to the new premises on Parkside Road, 'an Angel dropped in from Heaven' in the shape of a Ukrainian bakery manager from Warsaw. He had come to Bradford to visit his sister, but her financial status was quite critical, so rather than sit around, he went out to seek work. He had called on a few Polish shops in the city that gave him telephone numbers of the two Polish Bakeries, neither of which offered him work.
He telephoned me saying his name was Stefan and spoke to me in Polish. When I asked him his surname he replied 'Prokopuf' I said 'There is no such name in the Polish language, maybe you are called Prokopiw?' He admitted that was true. I sent Jejna my driver to pick him up. He worked for me not in the bakery, but in the new premises, painting and helping Ilko. Stefan Prokopiw worked for three whole months. He spent one month with his sister, telling her he was returning to Poland, the other two months he lived in my house, I gave him a room and food, he did everything I asked him, sometimes on a Friday in the bakery. Besides his food and lodgings, I paid him £15 per week, we were both very happy.

Another man who helped me a great deal was Dubey, a bus driver, who would stand in for a driver when needed, helping Ilko in the new bakery and later he painted the whole building on the outside.

Once the bakery floor had been tiled, Jimmy Miller delivered the two machines and advised me where to position them. Seeing me in my new bakery, which was bigger than his father's, was a tremendous and unexpected surprise, for five years previously we both worked for his father, and he knew very well why I left, for merely talking to a fellow worker in Polish. Mr Miller promised he would visit me one day, but never did. I suspect he probably felt too ashamed of why I'd left his employment.

Six weeks later, the new oven arrived from Germany, all the parts were placed on the newly tiled bakery floor. In Germany, I'd made arrangements with the factory, that the bakery engineers would install the new oven a week before we moved production to Parkside Road. Once the oven was erected, the engineers dismantled the smaller oven the day after production ceased in the 'old bakery', reassembling it in the 'new bakery'. This way disruption was at a minimum, production stopped on Saturday in the 'old bakery' and commenced in the 'new bakery' the following day.

With great difficulty, I finished five years of trading. My fifth financial year of trading showed a loss of £379. This amount was offset by all the money I paid out for Ilko's materials and additional helpers, I also paid out a further £5,018 in loan repayments for the bakery and new oven.

On the 7th of November 1966 worked commenced at 128/132 Parkside Road. I also took on a young Ukrainian as a driver, Wasyl Mycio, who remained in the bakery's employment until he retired.

Work in the new bakery went well, everything was on one floor, there was no need to carry flour and raw materials up a flight of stairs, or carrying bread downstairs. I had three workers, two Englishmen and a Ukrainian layman. M.Karpynec starting a week later, who turned out to be the most false and two-faced worker I'd ever had in my employment. A week later I started another worker, Arkady Hawrylenko, who'd came to Bradford from New York, after realising his 'real' biological mother lived in the city.

Once the interior of the bakery was finished, I was left with a debt of £12,000. My old baker friend Veber came inquiring about work. When I told him that I had enough workers and didn't need anymore because I hadn't the money to pay them, he retorted, 'Take a rope and hang yourself'. Although at that time I didn't offer him a job, he often popped in for a chat, I always gave him a free loaf and he did work for me in the future on a casual basis whenever I was desperate.

In the new bakery production kept increasing, Olha made the confectionery in the afternoons, Jaroslaw would help her on his return from the Bakery College in Leeds.

Every month I managed to pay Spillers £100 for the building loan and another £100 per month for the oven. It was difficult to pay off loans, at the same time feed and clothe a family of five. My outgoings were almost larger than my income and I needed to find new customers. I proposed to Jejna that he tried to find new customers in Leeds, or in Lancashire, a shop in Bury, Shlapak's had asked me a few times if I would deliver bread to him. Jejna showed no interest or had any inclination to find new routes, saying that he already had so much on, he didn't even have time to stop for a cup of tea. His attitude angered me, so one day I drove and parked near his house, and sure enough, a few minutes later he stopped outside his home in my van. He spent a whole hour inside, before he sat back in the van and finished his run. I returned directly to the bakery and said nothing to him when he returned. When he did return an hour or so later, he walked towards the kettle ' singing' his familiar words, I've not had time for a drink since early morning'.

Once Jaroslaw passed his driving test, he started to deliver bread once a week in my car to Bury. When orders increased and my car became too small, Wasyl Mycio took over the run after finishing his first local run. Slowly, as word spread that I was sending bread to Bury, we began to include shops in Rochdale and Manchester, gradually expanding even beyond.

I was now baking 5,000 loaves weekly, as well as rolls and confectionery. Whenever there was a hike in the price of flour, I bought 20 tons at the old price, as I had plenty of space in the new premises.

During my sixth financial year, my accounts never showed a profit, only a loss. And yet, I always ensured I paid off my loans on time. Every time flour went up in price, bread prices would rise, in turn increasing my takings. My rye bread was becoming more and more popular, I was approached by a Polish wholesaler, Yorkshire Delicatessen, who began to buy my bread, delivering it with their produce, to the Midlands and even London. A Polish shop in Preston owned by Kasperec came once a week buying produce in the area and my bread.

On the 7th of July 1967 I sold the old bakery as a building for £1,500, thereby helping me to finance my new house which cost me £4,000 and selling the old one for £1,800.

That summer I took my first holiday with Olha and Taras to Spain. I left Jaroslaw in charge, who was nearly 20 years old, and Dmytro nearly 16.

On my return, I could sense that Jejna was not happy, he had plenty of time, but showed no effort to increase his workload. After a couple of arguments, Jejna left on the 27th of August 1968. In his place I employed an Englishman, but I soon noticed he was stealing bread so I sacked him and replaced him with Jaroslaw Horobecz and Roman Pysarchuk.

It was always difficult to find a sound and reliable driver, someone who was willing to start work at 4a.m.

It was also difficult to find a suitable baker, who would be willing to work nights. At the same time, I also had to be careful who I employed, I was afraid that someone would steal my recipe for the rye bread. Many people came supposedly looking for work, Poles, Germans, their only interest being to steal my recipe. My recipe was only known by my family, and as long as they kept it for themselves and safeguard it, they would have a good life.

Dmytro, my second eldest son, on finishing school went to Bradford College and did a two year part- time bakery course, I now had two of my own professional bakers. Taras, the youngest, didn't have the desire to become a baker. Instead, he chose to be a chef but, after spending about a year working in various hotels and restaurants, disliked the unsociable and split hours in the catering trade, returned home and decided to become a baker after all.

Rye bread continuously rose in popularity, on the bakery forecourt stood three vans, of which two were assigned with full time drivers and one operated part- time. In the bakery, including Jaroslaw, I had six bakers working nights. I kept up with my loan repayments every month, carried out all necessary repairs and even built a garage adjoining the bakery building.

With rising production, I decided to buy a 'dough divider', a machine that cuts pieces of dough into pieces, the dough pieces still had to be checked on the weighing scales, but it made the work quicker and easier.

On the 17th of June 1968 I employed an old Irish baker who was already 55 years old, and everybody called him 'Paddy'. He worked with us for 14 years, retiring on his 70th birthday.

On the 9th of October 1968 I finished seven years of hard work, noting in my diary 'Finished seven years of trading, but will I survive another seven'? I was still £6,500 in debt.

On the 25th of October 1968 I was approached by Morrisons Supermarkets to supply their city centre store. In quick succession we supplied a total of five of their stores in the Bradford area, the only drawback being that everything had to be wrapped.

New customers constantly approached me from near and far, staff turnover also changed both with bakers and drivers. Arkady Hawrylenko started and left me five times. I always took him back, he was a good worker, though sometimes he could be lazy.

After my eighth year, my accounts showed a loss of £707 but that year I repaid nearly three thousand pounds of debt. To celebrate I flew to Rome to attend the blessing of the new Ukrainian Cathedral Saint Sophia.

The following winter Bradford was hit by a flu epidemic, affecting most of our bakers and drivers, except for myself and Pysarchuk, the rest were off for three or four days at a time. There were days when I had to cope with only two bakers, which was very difficult especially on Friday and Saturday, baking 1000 rye loaves each day. On top of the flu outbreak, we had a heavy snowfall, causing severe delivery problems with the drivers.

In Bradford we had a Polish firm that owned shops and other enterprises, even partnerships in one of the Polish bakeries. One of their employees by the name Mietik Kostuch came to work for me as a driver. He turned out to be a very honest person, didn't mind getting up early and, after finishing his deliveries, he would help around the bakery doing odd jobs, for which I paid him extra. He worked seven years for me, until he was commandeered by a Polish bakery in Nottingham.

The bakery building was originally built by the Co-operative Society, during which time it was split into three segments, the largest the middle was the grocery, to its left was the greengrocery, and to its right was the butchery. To the rear of the building stood an outer wall, with enough space to manoeuvre a horse and cart, which were used 'post 1920s' to deliver coal that was stored in a cellar at the rear of the building. Over the years most of the yard was 'filled in' with extensions, as so happened that year in 1970, when a room was built to store baked bread, years later it was converted into a 'walk- in' freezer.

On the 15th of April 1972 Jaroslaw married Roksanna Babuniak, the younger daughter of Mr. Jaroslaw Babuniak, the conductor of the Ukrainian Choir 'Homin' in Manchester. Jaroslaw had found a newly built house in a small cul-de-sac which he bought. On looking at Jaroslaw's house, I saw a larger house around the corner with a big garden, something Olha had always wanted, so I bought it.

At the end of June, I took a holiday with Olha to Spain. On our return, the bakery had stopped working nights, something I'd pre-arranged with my sons. I didn't want to be around when the switchover took place, knowing there would be repercussions. Even so, I received many complaints from customers, most of them saying the bread wasn't as fresh as it used to be. After a few weeks the complaints subsided and the bakery continued to bake bread during the day.

Working days instead of nights was much easier, all the bakers had a good night's sleep and everyone felt healthier. We planned our work so as to finish work before 10p.m. that way people without cars could still catch a bus home. The more work we had the earlier in the day we started. I personally came into the bakery around 4a.m. to open the bakery for the drivers, whereas working nights there was no need to do so. I stayed in the bakery until 1p.m. and was replaced by my sons who began production with the bakery staff, which they now managed without my help. On Fridays we baked 1800 rye bread and Saturdays 2000 customers began to get used to bread not being as fresh.

At the end of that financial year 1972, I finished with a profit of £6,390, my debt was now down to £500 and customers owed me £1,000. My profits increased every year, even though Ukrainian shops were closing in Bradford, as did Pysarchuk, Lewycki and Dutka. Polish shops too, especially on the outskirts of the city began to close, being replaced by Pakistani and Indian owners, who mostly didn't care for continental bread. Supermarkets became more and more popular, they had the largest selections and the cheapest prices.

In the summer of 1973 I bought a bread slicing machine, as more and more people were demanding sliced bread, and it turned out to be a large success. I also had to replace the first German oven I'd bought, it was seven years old.

Unfortunately, I replaced it with a British built one, because it was £2,000 cheaper, but later it transpired not to be as good as the German oven.

My twelfth financial year finished with a profit of £5817 despite paying £4,000 for the new oven in the summer. The following spring I bought a bread moulding machine for the white and brown bread, thinking that with staff shortages a machine could be the answer to my problems. As it turned out, the machine became 'a white elephant' since the finished product wasn't the same as from 'a handmade loaf'. As a result, the machine was only used in dire emergencies, spending most of its life tucked away in the corner of the bakery. I tried a machine I was told would mould rye bread, that too proved to be a failure, at least in this case I didn't buy it, only used on trial.

My thirteenth financial year finished with a profit of £3,500. I felt happy at that time, having paid off all my debts, and people owed still owed me £2,000.

CHAPTER 31
HOLIDAY IN AUSTRALIA

After Christmas of 1974 I decided to have a holiday in Australia. It was a country neither of us hadn't visited and it was also an opportunity to visit my newly found cousin who lived in Northam 100km from Perth.

On reaching Australia, Olha almost immediately became ill, she was never in good health, always visiting doctors in Bradford and Leeds, with back problems, but whoever she saw couldn't give a correct diagnosis. My cousin showed great concern, quickly making an appointment with his own doctor. Upon examining Olha, his doctor swiftly came to the conclusion she had kidney stones, which was the result of her intermittent back pain and an operation to remove them as soon as possible was strongly recommended. The doctor gave Olha medication to ease the pain, the next day she was sent for an X-ray, which confirmed the doctor's analysis.

Our holiday in Australia was not only to see my cousin, but to see some of the country too. At my cousin's it was unbearable with 40oC heat, there was no air- conditioning system in the house, stepping outside I could only do so early in the morning. Olha constantly sat in the shade by the house, sleeping was almost impossible too.

In Northam I was introduced to a Ukrainian by the name of Jarymovych, who agreed to take me into Perth on Sunday to attend mass at the Ukrainian church. Someone had informed the priest before the service about me, who during his sermon mentioned that a member of this congregation had just arrived from England. After the service I was immediately surrounded by 'ex pats' one of which I recognised from Manchester Mr Lehkyj. We arranged that next Sunday I would travel to Perth with Olha and book us into a hotel.

Our stay in Perth coincided with the celebrations of 'Malanka' a dance and social event to bring in the New Year. In the Ukrainian Community Hall, my escort Lehkyj, noticed I was talking to the head of the community a Mr Gutej, when it came for all the people present to take their seats, Lehkyj whispered in my ear 'Did you know the man you just spoke to is a Dvikar, he won't even allow me to launch SUM in Perth, Gutej is such a bad head, his committee is full of Dvikari, not allowing others to join, not allowing SUM to be launched, saying there's no need because there is Plast, the Ukrainian Scouts.

The next day on Sunday, I again went to the church alone as Olha wasn't feeling well. After the service Lehkyj approached and invited me for lunch. He still assumed I was a Banderite and treated me as such, so I quickly declined, saying I left my ill wife alone in our hotel. Without further ado, he drove me to my hotel, we both walked to my room, where I found the door locked, and yet I remembered on leaving I had only closed the door without locking it. I started knocking, but there was no answer, I began to get into a panic, thinking to myself 'do I have to break the door down'. It was Sunday, the reception area was deserted, I left the building into the street when, all of a sudden, I noticed Olha slowly making her way towards me. I gave her a good telling off, explaining all the predicaments she'd put me in. When I had calmed down, I told Olha to change her clothes, we then left with Lehkyj to his house where his wife had prepared lunch and were warmly entertained. After a few hours, I asked Lehkyj to drive us back to our hotel which he did. At the hotel I found a telephone directory and rang Gutej, within a few minutes he was at our hotel and took us back to his house. On reflection, I had lunch with a Banderite, and later supper with a Dvikar.

Although we only spent a few days in Perth, every evening we met new people, who would take us to their homes, were we discussed many subjects and shared our thoughts.

I found the Ukrainian community atmosphere completely different from that in England. It was apparent that in Australia there were a much higher percentage of educated people who ran the communities and true democracy was very evident. Each community post was filled by a competent person, who carried out their duties accordingly. It was difficult for people like Lehkyj with his limited education, to put across his political views. The committees were made up of people who could and did carry out the work required. The committees were formed by people, who were elected by the people, not by a 'political party'.

When we returned to my cousin's, we had already spent three weeks in Australia. Our ticket was for six weeks but because of my wife's ill health, we decided to cut our holiday short and already had our return flight booked.

The day before our departure, Mrs Jarymovych prepared a buffet in her home. In attendance was the Ukrainian doctor who diagnosed Olha, Father Ihor Shputkowski from Perth, my cousin and his wife Myken and a few others. We were well entertained and time flew, until it was finally time to say goodbye. I thanked Mrs Jarymovych for her hospitality and apologised for having to cut our holiday short because of my wife's health, as I would have liked to see more of Australia. Mrs Jarymovych replied 'Why? Everything is possible, Olha has good medicine, if she lasted three weeks, I am sure she can last another three, giving you time to visit all the cities you wish'. I replied that I had already booked our flights for the following evening. Mrs Jarymovych intervened 'flights can be easily changed, as long as Olha agrees'. Mrs Jarymovych sat next to Olha trying her best to convince her to change her mind saying 'It would be a shame for the sake of a little pain, not to be able to see more of Australia. After all, who knows if you will ever get another opportunity in your lifetime'?

The following morning I went to the travel agent in Northam where I had booked my return tickets, saying I had to cancel them because my wife is too ill to travel. He picked up his telephone, spoke to someone, replaced the receiver and said that everything was sorted. When I asked how much I owed him, he said nothing. I then said 'I want to book a flight to Adelaide as soon as possible, from there onto Melbourne, then to Sydney, back to Perth, and finally to London'. He stood staring at me and said 'Is that for one person, or will you be travelling with your wife?' I replied 'With my wife, she's ill I can't leave her alone'. He then asked 'When do you want to fly?' I replied 'even today if possible'. I was asked to wait whilst he made more telephone calls. After about half an hour he approached me and said, 'At 3p.m. come to see me here and collect your tickets, at midnight be at the airport in Perth, your flight departs at 2a.m. for Adelaide'.

Everything happened so quickly and unexpectedly, that I didn't have any contact addresses in Adelaide, I had one address I was given by Mr Fesych in Bradford, a parcel for his son, but as I'd changed our travel plans, I went and posted his parcel instead, without making a note of the address.

We arrived in Adelaide early in the morning, from where we took a taxi, telling the driver to take us to a city hotel. On reaching the hotel, I didn't like the look of it and asked the taxi driver to take us to another which he did. A little lower down the same road, stood an impressive looking hotel. We were given a room on the first floor, with a balcony overlooking the courtyard. Olha wasn't feeling well, so I left her lying on the bed whilst I left the room to explore. In the corridor I noticed two chambermaids, with a foreign look about them. When I asked where they were from, one of them replied, 'I am Polish and she is German' I then asked if there were any Ukrainians amongst them, the Polish lady replied, 'Our manageress is Ukrainian' pointing towards her from the balcony, she was watering a flower bed in the courtyard.

I didn't wait, I went straight downstairs to find the young Ukrainian manageress. I spoke to her in Ukrainian addressing her by name, which startled her. I explained to her that two of the chambermaids had told me about her, and I was very proud to learn that a Ukrainian lady was passing out instructions to others.

After a brief talk she invited us for tea, whereupon she advised me to get in touch with the head of the Ukrainian community, a Mr Pasichynskyj, her former Ukrainian teacher, also admitting that he often reprimanded her in his classes.

After breakfast I telephoned Mr Pasichynskyj's number and his son answered, saying his father was at work and advised me to go to the community hall at 6p.m. where I could find his father, as it was the 22nd of January celebrating 'Independence Day'. (This date was originally used to mark the declaration of the Ukrainian People's Republic on 22nd January 1919). I couldn't wait that long, so at 5p.m. I sent for a taxi and on arrival there were many Ukrainians milling around talking amongst themselves. The majority of people came in their own cars, some were dressed in embroidered national costumes. I approached a nearby group of people and asked where I could find Mr Pasichynsky. I was told that he hadn't yet arrived, but when he did they would inform me. Around me there were many interesting conversations, until someone called for people to take their places, as the programme was about to start. I had to find a seat and wait until the interval before I could see Mr Pasichynsky.

The programme I found very interesting, which consisted of an informative reading, recitals, a soloist singer and local bandura players, the Ukrainian National instrument. During the interval I quickly moved to the front of the hall, again asking a gentleman for Mr Pasichynsky, who introduced me to him. Mr Pasichynsky apologised for not meeting me earlier, saying he had to quickly glance at the local Perth newspaper, which had printed an article about today's events. We didn't talk very long, as he was singing with the local choir after the interval. He invited me to take his seat between the priest and Mr Turak.

After the academic programme finished, Mr Pasichynsky came to my side as asked where I was staying, when I said in a hotel, he replied 'It would be a shame and embarrassment for the Ukrainian people of Adelaide if you stayed there, because we people here will willingly invite you into our homes'. Before I could say another word, he picked up a microphone and made such an announcement. Mr Turak quickly intervened and said 'This guest is mine and he will stay at my house'.

I later had the opportunity to meet many more people of Adelaide and after many interesting discussions I left to return to my hotel. The following morning Mr Turak came and drove us to his house were we stayed for almost a week.

Mr and Mrs Turak both worked, they left us alone in their home in the mornings. Their garden was a cornucopia of fruit trees, branches so heavily laden, and their fruit was almost touching the ground, there were plums, pears, apricots, apples, oranges, lemons, tomatoes, everything the heart desired.

After Mr Turak finished work, he drove us around the whole of Adelaide, showing us many interesting places such as the Plast Camp, he introduced us to many Ukrainian families. One evening he took us to a local football match, were a Ukrainian team played against an Italian team. Mr and Mrs Turak's hospitality was overwhelming, the week we spent was soon over, and we had to move on to our next destination of Melbourne. In his generosity, Mr Turak offered us the address of his daughter but, as I had the address of Mr Boluckha that been given to me by Mr Kaminsky, I declined. Mr Turak drove us to Adelaide Airport from where we flew to Melbourne.

On arrival at Melbourne Airport, it was Saturday, I picked up a telephone directory and found the number of Mr Boluckha. On dialling, the phone was answered by an elderly lady who said he was away for the weekend and would not be returning until Monday, whereas the day after we had already booked a flight to Sydney. I still had another address which was given to me by Mrs Nina Kovalenko from Bradford, who had a daughter in the city.

Firstly, we booked into a hotel, by which time it was noon, had something to eat, and later caught a taxi to Nina's daughter. Our taxi driver easily found the address and soon we met her. To our disappointment, she said she was out of touch with the Ukrainian community, but explained how to find the Ukrainian Club.

That evening we were taken again by taxi to the given address. On entering the Ukrainian Club, there wasn't a soul to be seen. I walked around the building until I heard the sound of a typewriter. I knocked on a window, alerting a man who opened a nearby door and invited us in. I asked him if this was the Ukrainian Club, to which he replied it was. 'Then why isn't there anybody here except for yourself?' I asked, he replied, 'Today is Saturday and there's no specific function, that's why nobody is here'. Another man suddenly stepped into the room and the first man introduced him as a new immigrant from London a Mr Boretkyj. He began to reel off newly arrived people from England, one of whose names was Vasyl Hutuliak who used to work for me. I was very interested in seeing how Hutuliak lived in Australia, having seen his hovel in Bradford, so I asked for his address.

We arrived at Hutuliak's house. He opened his door, then shouted 'Eva! Come and see who is here'. It was a great surprise to them, seeing us on his doorstep. They invited us in for supper and both were perfect hosts. That evening he drove us back to our hotel, returning the following morning for us and our suitcases. We left our suitcases in his house, and he accompanied us to mass at the Ukrainian Catholic Cathedral. That afternoon he drove us to another Ukrainian Club, and on the following days to many of his friends' homes, giving us an idea of how the Ukrainian community lived in Melbourne.

As in Adelaide, in Melbourne the Ukrainians lived quite well. Out of all the homes I visited, the poorest of all was my cousin Vasyl Prytulak in Northam and Vasyl Hutuliak in Melbourne, neither of whom owned their homes, while the rest we saw did, and most of their houses had large gardens with orchards. Our overall impression was that they lived a better life than we did in England.

The few days we spent in Melbourne quickly passed. On Tuesday, Hutuliak drove us to the airport, even taking the afternoon off work to do so.

In Sydney I had an address of a member of OUN who I had once met at a conference in New York. At the airport, I telephoned the office where he worked, to be told that Mr Prykodko had gone to Melbourne. I scratched my head thinking who to ring, I took the telephone directory again looking under the letter 'U' and found the number of the Ukrainian Church. The telephone was answered by Father Shewtiw, who I didn't know personally, but heard many stories about him, as he used to be the Parish priest in Bradford before I lived there. After introducing myself, he asked where I was presently, whether I had a pen and paper, and then he began to give me instructions, saying that following them would be the cheapest option to reach the church. We took a bus to the centre, from there by train and within the hour Father Shewtiw met us as very welcomed guests. He gave us a tidy room, told us to freshen up before taking us to the adjoining convent where the nuns would serve us lunch.

Father Shewtiw devoted much of his spare time, showing us all the major attractions of the city, even organised a day out by the sea. We were in Sydney around the 19th of January, which in the Ukrainian Church Calendar is dedicated to the annual blessing of the house, in biblical times John the Baptist blessed Jesus in the river Jordan. This was a very busy period for Father Shewtiw. The following morning I escorted Father Shewtiw to the bank, followed by the publishing house, which all took some time. Meanwhile, that morning Olha wasn't feeling very well so she lay down to rest. She soon became bored, got up and walked to the garden and sat on the grass. A neighbour, noticing a strange woman on the convent premises, telephoned the church. One of the young priests went to investigate and, on seeing Olha, fetched her a blanket. On our return to the convent there was no sign of Olha. I walked over to the nuns, they had not seen her. Father Shewtiw, not knowing about my dilemma with Olha said, 'Call your wife for supper, I must set off a little sooner today with the Holy Water'. I replied that I didn't know where my wife was, which must have sounded odd to our host.

In a panic, Father Shewtiw jumped into his car and drove to the local police station, in case an accident had been reported.

All of a sudden another ex- Bradfordian arrived, a Mr Hamaniuk, with whom we had previously arranged to spend an evening together. He too joined me in search of Olha, but she was nowhere to be found.

Just before sunset, as it was getting cooler, Olha woke from her slumber, placed the blanket under her arm and walked towards the vicarage. As I noticed her I asked where she had been, to which she replied 'The young priest knew where I was, he even brought me a blanket'. Unfortunately, the young priest didn't wait for supper, hurrying to carry out his duties with the blessings.

I had heard many stories in Bradford about Father Shewtiw, but only bad ones, hardly anyone praised him, especially the 'party revolutionaries' because he quite often chastised them. I had met many priests in my lifetime, Father Shewtiw in my view and opinion was one of the best.

Whilst in Australia I had the opportunity to see three churches, outside the church in Sydney was inscribed a plaque which read 'This house of God was built with the diligence of Father Ivan Shewtiw'. The evidence was plain to see, a newly built church, at the side a vicarage, a children's nursery of a very high standard, a sports ground, a large garden and a nunnery, which was an old building, but Father Shewtiw showed me plans for a new building to be soon erected. There was also a church bank, turning over millions of Australian dollars. When I asked Father Shewtiw where all the money came from, he replied, 'Our people are very good and generous, they have money and are willing to donate to a good cause, one must know how to best live with them'. His testimony shows that he did.

In Sydney I found a few immigrants from England. On one occasion I was even subjected to a bit of a lecture from one man. When I asked him if he knew a Mr Myronenko, who was from Eastern Ukraine, he replied 'Here we don't have people from the East or the West, only people from Ukraine, and yes I do know him' at which point he gave me his address. I knew Myronenko from Bury, and I also knew he belonged to the 'Ukrainian Revolutionary Democratic Party'. In Sydney he was held in high esteem, he invited us to the community home, showed us all the rooms, explained everything as we went along, where what was taking place, and added ' Here, we only have one community, even though it's large, we celebrate every National Feast day together. We don't ask anyone about their beliefs, we all live very well, in harmony like a large family'.

I visited many households with Myronenko, and was convinced that Ukrainian life in Australia was far superior to that in England, a totally different atmosphere. I asked many people that same question, including Father Shewtiw, and the answer was always the same, 'In Australia we have a large percentage of educated people, whereas in England you have one educated person per thousand'.

The evidence was clear. Unlike Australia, in England we celebrate our national poet Taras Shevchenko on the 22nd of January, at different venues, by different political factions, and so on.

When in good company time flies. Father Shewtiw drove us to Sydney Airport in his own car, and we boarded a plane to Perth. We didn't return to my cousin's, instead we spent two nights in a beach hotel, recharging our batteries before our flight to London on the 7th of February.

On arrival at London, I went to the nearest telephone box and called the bakery. Jaroslaw answered and said that yesterday they had received a telegram from Poland to say that Olha's mother and sister were there for two weeks and would like to see her. Jaroslaw advised me to go directly to the Polish Embassy in London for a visa.

We collected Olha's visa at the Polish Embassy, but decided she couldn't travel to Poland without any gifts, so we returned to Bradford and, after a couple of days, though still in poor health, Olha bravely set off to cold, freezing Poland.

Olha flew to Warsaw and from there to Wroclaw, the weather was -20oC, everything was covered in snow. In Wroclaw she travelled all night by train until she finally reached Byszyce, where her mother and sister Hanya were staying. She had several mishaps en route, in one case going to the wrong town as they sounded so much alike.

Olha spent 10 days in Poland, sleeping on an uncomfortable sofa in freezing conditions, but at least she met her mother and sister, which was worth the pain.

The day after she returned from Poland Olha went to see her doctor, accompanied with the letter from the Australian doctor. Finally on the 18th of March she had her long awaited operation.

CHAPTER 32
BACK IN BRADFORD

Three days before Olha's operation, Mr and Mrs Turak visited us from Australia, we all travelled to the hospital and left Olha alone.

Whilst Olha was in hospital I had a couple of errands to attend to in the city centre. I parked my car in Forster Square and went about my business. On returning, I reversed my car and accidentally hit a passing woman carrying two shopping bags. I must have hit her with considerable force as she fell to the ground, her shopping scattered all over the car park. The lady shouted when the car hit her and I immediately braked, stepped out of my car, helped the lady to her feet, picked up all her shopping with the help of a passer-by, and then invited her to sit in the car, where I asked if there was any need to call an ambulance. I was more frightened than the woman, thinking the worse about us both, but she said only her leg hurt and asked if I would drive her home, from where she would decide what to do.

I was in more shock than my victim. Once we sat her down in her own home, I pleaded with her not to tell anybody about the accident, and if she didn't feel up to work, to take a few days off for which I would compensate her. She took down the registration number of my car, I gave her my name and address and drove home. I didn't tell my sons or wife about the accident.

That accident cost me a little money, at least I was relieved that I caused no permanent damage to the lady. She only had a bruise on one leg, but stayed off work for two weeks. I compensated her loss of income and gave her some bread, inviting her to come to the bakery anytime, which she did for a short period.

That summer we built another extension, business was on the increase and we needed the extra space.
When Dmytro reached twenty- one years of age, I cut down my work load, allowing myself more free time. At that time I was the head of the 'Plast Pryat' (civilian helpers or Friends of the Ukrainian Scouts). We were renovated the old Catholic Church Hall, which the scouts later used for their meetings. I offered very little physical help, mostly financial and overlooking the work.

A few months later, my cousin from Australia visited us with his wife, en route from Hamburg in Germany. Her mother had been gravely ill, and died a week later. After burying her, they visited us in Bradford on the way back to Australia.

At the end of the World War Two, Olha and I both wrote letters to our mothers in Ukraine. Olha had left two sisters behind, one of whom spent 12 years in Siberia for helping Ukrainian partisans. After we settled in England and had a little money, we would periodically make up parcels, mainly of material and clothing, to send to our relatives in Ukraine, as did most of our fellow compatriots.

CHAPTER 33
BACK TO THE USSR

In 1976 Olha, together with her cousin, travelled with Intourist (the official state travel agency of the Soviet Union, founded in 1929 by Joseph Stalin. It was responsible for managing the great majority of foreigners' access to, and travel within, the Soviet Union) to the Soviet Union. There were several combinations offered through Intourist at the time, always including Moscow, but some of the tours included Kyiv which Olha and her cousin took. My mother constantly begged me to come and visit her, one last time before she died, she was 83 at the time.

I was afraid because my brother Vasyl belonged to the partisans until 1946. At that time the Russians promised no repercussions against them, telling them to return back home to their families. My brother didn't trust them and stayed hidden in a den which he built in a nearby wood. Somebody in the village, however, informed the authorities. My brother and some of his fellow partisans returned to the village at night for food. One night the secret police, the so-called NKVD – from the Russian 'Narodny Komissariat Vnutrennikh Del' translated as 'People's Commissariat of Internal Affairs, surrounded their den and ordered them to surrender. Rather than give themselves up to the enemy, they blew themselves up with grenades.

The secret police brought the mutilated bodies into the village and herded all its inhabitants to see. My mother and her daughter- in- law Malanka, Vasyl's wife were included. My poor beloved mother recognised the body of her son, but restrained herself and wouldn't admit to the on looking secret police.

The mutilated bodies lay in front of the church for three weeks, the secret police called upon their informers from neighbouring villages, hoping somebody would recognise them, but nobody did. In the end the villagers were allowed to bury their dead. This incident took place in the village of Kaminne in 1946.

This tragedy was told to me by my dear mother, God Bless her soul, in Kyiv a year later, when I finally plucked up enough courage to take a similar trip to Olha's the previous year. Most were too frightened to talk about the tragedy, until my poor mother had to once again suffer, reliving the day she saw the mutilated body of her son.

Before Olha and I left for Ukraine in 1977 I only told my son Dmytro and close friend Kowalysko. I told Jaroslaw and Taras that I was going to Germany, because my old friend Slywchuk was seriously ill.

We departed from London directly to Moscow by a Soviet aeroplane, even though it was winter, every seat was taken. In just under three hours the plane was on its descent, as one stewardess gave us a brief history of Moscow over the intercom. As she was finishing her written speech, the plane suddenly touched down on the tarmac of Moscow Airport.

The bulk of the passengers on the flight were Russian. They quickly passed through airport security, but when it came to my turn, the security officer began to turn each page individually of my British Passport, where he saw visas stamped from Germany, Canada, USA and Australia. On the aeroplane, each non- Soviet passenger was given a form to fill in asking, 'Where are you going? How much money do you have? Have you visited the Soviet Union before? Name, address, place and date of birth etc. My name speaks for itself who I am. At the desk I was shaking, not from the cold, but from fright. The passport controllers in Moscow have all the time in the world, I've never experienced similar controls, the length of time it took to be processed, checking one page then another, going back to the first page, going to a colleague, what a procedure. I was at my wits end waiting all that time, but in the end my passport was handed back to me, I noticed some other fellow passengers going through the same routine.

After undergoing passport control, we had to reclaim our baggage. I landed upon a woman who wouldn't stop talking, telling her that most of the items were presents for my family. She didn't confiscate anything, but looked at our Customs Declaration Form and asked why we hadn't declared your 'Shubu'. I had never heard of that word before, until she turned and pointed at Olha's fur coat, so I had to add the coat onto the form.

Finally, after going through two such security checks, we boarded our shuttle bus which was to take us to our hotel. It turned out that there were only seven of us, three students from Australia, two elderly people from New Zealand and the two of us. The coach took us to our Moscow hotel named 'Hotel Ukraine'.

The hotel was large, clean and the staff treated us respectfully. Most of the guests we found to be German. Every part of the hotel was meticulously clean, all the staff were smartly dressed in their uniforms, the food served was mainly 'European', the crockery was made from porcelain and the cutlery from silver, everything sparkled.

Our room was quite large, but it was cold during the night despite the central heating. I asked the maid to turn up the heating or give us extra blankets, but she didn't, she was probably expecting a tip, fortunately we only stayed three nights in Moscow.

Our days were spent sightseeing, we saw the Red Square, a couple of churches and museums. Because of the severe frost, Olha wouldn't venture out of the hotel, except for the first night when we went to a theatre, the second to a circus.

The Australians always latched onto me, as I could make myself understood, they didn't speak any Russian. I tried to explain various things to them as best as I could, translate and became their guide.

In one museum I saw golden chalices and paintings from Ukraine, works of art from all over the world. The Russians had much wealth on show, which they had claimed over the centuries, and which very few other countries could equal.

All the time I spent in Moscow, each step I took was with caution, always expecting the worse. There was plenty to see and do, but my thoughts where elsewhere.

On Tuesday afternoon we left Moscow and flew to Kyiv. Our baggage was not checked, only our passports, though not as vigorously as in Moscow, allowing us pass through much quicker. We landed at 9 p.m. and were in our hotel and hour later. Our hotel was named 'Intourist'. I later understood most hotels were fully booked due to a party conference.

A few weeks prior to our departure to the Soviet Union, both Olha and I wrote to our families informing them the date of our arrival and at which hotel we would be staying. The bus stopped at our hotel, the Australians alighted first as they had less luggage. Olha and I always spoke in Ukrainian to each other and as we stepped off the bus I noticed three men dressed in black fur hats and long coats standing by the entrance, but we didn't exchange greetings. Once we were in the hotel foyer, I noticed a group of people standing to one side, among them stood my dear old mother, holding a small posy of flowers. Next to her stood Olha's mother, both her sisters, my two brothers, my brother Peter's wife, my late brother Vasyl's son Peter, Dmytro's daughter Luba, my cousin Natalka and husband, and my cousin Taras. The three men standing outside of the hotel were, Taras, Dmytro and Natalka's husband. We placed our cases on the floor and greeted our families.

Our little group was filled with happiness and tears of joy, after we all had greeted each other. I stepped over to the reception desk to register, I now had or organise accommodation and a meal for my large family. It was getting late, outside the bitter frost bit deep and sharp, I had to do something fast. Natalka showed me the manageress's desk. I approached the desk, overcome with joy and fright and spoke to the lady in English, to which she replied in Ukrainian, 'Mr Prytulak, surely you haven't already forgotten your mother tongue?' I felt so embarrassed and began to appeal to her to find me rooms for my family, whereupon she agreed. I then asked if we could have a meal altogether, to which she also agreed.

In the dining room the waiters hurriedly joined three large tables into one, and out of the blue there appeared a fresh vase of flowers, candles, crockery and cutlery. Natalka took charge of the drinks, ordering two bottles of champagne, spirits and wine. I stood to my feet and proposed a toast to both our mothers' health. No sooner had everybody stood up than, without thinking, I began to sing 'Mnohaya Lita' (Happy Birthday), to which everyone joined in, even the resident Polish band. It was difficult to start a conversation, everyone wanting to say something, before I knew it, the manageress approached me to say that we had to finish as it was midnight and the staff were scheduled to go off duty.

The manageress had prepared three rooms for the family. Nevertheless, everyone clambered into our room where our festivities continued. The family had brought all sorts of cakes and meats, Olha and I brought a bottle of Scotch, they brought Russian vodka and that's how we continued. At one point I proposed to both mothers' that they retire for the night, but my mother replied, 'No son, I just want to see you, you all talk, I will just listen and look at you, because it might be my last time I see you'. We all sat around until 5a.m. at which point I stood and said that I was tired and would like to sleep for a couple of hours. Everyone stood without protest and retired to their allocated rooms.

That morning, after breakfast, I walked to the manageress's office, presenting her with a couple of packets of English cigarettes and pair of ladies stockings. I paid her for the meal and accommodation which was quite cheap. She also revealed to me that she was Russian, born in Ukraine and married to a Jew.

Some of us ventured into the freezing cold, to see the Ukrainian capital Kyiv. Besides myself, Natalka and her brother Taras, who was a teacher, the rest remained in the hotel, talking to their heart's content, especially Olha, who had seen Kyiv the previous year.

All the trees where white, not from colour but frost, it was not just the trees, but I too felt the frost biting my nose and ears. We survived half a day fighting the elements, in which time we saw the Pecherska Lavra, known as the Kyiv Monastery of the Caves, and the Golden Gates. In the afternoon we visited a 'Beryozka' a store selling luxury goods, accepting only foreign currency, where we bought a few gifts, later dropping into a small restaurant for afternoon tea.

I noticed a mammoth difference between the hotel in which we stayed and hotels open for the general public. Our hotel's staff, the food, of a far superior standard, as to the toilets, they were an embarrassment to even mention.

All our family left us on Thursday by train to Lviv, whereas Olha and I flew that evening to Leningrad (now St. Petersburg). The following day we were taken to the Hermitage Museum, which contains one of the world's major collections of paintings. The nucleus of its collection was the art collection of Catherine the Great. Amongst the stolen treasures I noticed where valuable paintings, chalices, swords and old military uniforms, that the Bolsheviks had stolen from Ukraine. The Russians take great pride in showing the world their mass of treasure, or, rather, booty, bringing thousands of tourists annually from all over the world.
In Leningrad most of the tourists we saw were German, and when they entered a church, the men took off their hats, the Russians didn't.

We returned to Moscow by train, travelling all night in sleeper wagons. We didn't feel comfortable and slept very little, mostly due to the cold. In Moscow we were driven to a hotel where we were given breakfast, after two hours we were taken to the airport. Some of our group especially the Australians, wanted to see the Red Square, I went along with them, but we ran out of time to see anything else.

At 1 p.m. we were sitting nervously in our airplane seats. Once we were airborne and only then, some of my fear left my body and I was able to breathe a sigh of relief, some of the passengers left their emotions on tenterhooks until we landed on the tarmac in London, clapping with joy and great relief.

Looking back on my trip, I was very pleased I'd made it, especially being able to see my mother, the capital of Ukraine and hearing many stories about my late brother Vasyl and his heroic death. I didn't advertise my trip, kept it only to my closest friends, I felt no need to give the Banderites any unwanted ammunition, which could prove detrimental for my business.

After about a week, one of the Australians in our group, who was a big fan of 'Coronation Street, the British soap opera, travelled from London to Manchester. Then, realising Bradford was only 35 miles away, decided to surprise me with a visit. I gave him the bakery address, so he walked in and was met by Jaroslaw. He told Jaroslaw about our recent holiday, even showing him photographs. Jaroslaw explained that he had just missed me, I had finished for the day, but rang me and asked me in a joking manner, 'How was Germany?' Jaroslaw asked him to wait while I got ready and drove back to the bakery.

CHAPTER 34
BRADFORD, THE PATRIACHE AND MORE

My business was doing very well, turnover increased annually, the government gave the baking industry subsidies, which helped us tremendously. My fourteenth financial year grossed me £70,000 from which left me with a profit of £10,000. I still had a little debt for the oven, I bought a new van that year too, overall my business was good, I certainly couldn't complain.

In 1975 began a big movement for the 'Patriarch'. I once read in the 'Ukrainian Thought' that we had a Patriarch, and I didn't know when this had happened. I was an ardent reader of the Ukrainian Thought, yet I couldn't recollect ever coming across such a topic. I went to see my old friend Kowalysko and asked him what all the commotion was about. He explained that theoretically there was no Patriarch, although some Ukrainian bishops were demanding that Cardinal Joseph Slipyj be conferred the title of Patriarch. To have a Patriarch the ruling Ukrainian Church had to go through a minefield of Episcopal legislature. In the meantime, the Banderites took it upon themselves to misinform and misled the Ukrainian communities with their revolutionary stance on the matter.

Meanwhile, another good friend of mine, Wasylko, informed me that one of our members wanted to buy a hotel in London. Not having enough of his own funds, he was looking for a partner. Knowing I had money, Wasylko advised me to buy. I drove down to London for an inspection and after seeing it, thought it would be possible with a partner to buy this hotel. Unfortunately, the owner a Mr Shved was in ill health and it became more and more difficult to communicate with him. In a short space of time, Mr Shved died, leaving the dealings between Mr Tarnawsky and Mr Boretkyj, who didn't have the ready funds, and began stalling. Another buyer stepped in, offered more money and bought the property.

I travelled to London three times, always at the weekend. On Sunday I went to the Ukrainian Catholic Cathedral where, to my surprise, I noticed that people were donating no less than a pound in the collection boxes. Indeed, I saw very little small change. On my return to Bradford, I mentioned this incident to a few people.

A couple of weeks later a meeting discussing the Patriarch, was held at the Ukrainian Club on Claremont in Bradford. Out of interest I decided to attend this meeting and listen to any news, a couple of similar meetings had already been held previously, probably when I was down in London. I came a few minutes before the meeting commenced, to find the hall full of around 300 people. I managed to find an empty stool at the back of the hall, Mr Maksym Bakhmat presided over the meeting.

What I heard at that meeting was beyond belief, I was supposed to be amongst people in the Ukrainian Cultural Home, in the presence of a few young people. Those young people had probably never heard some of the vile, repulsive words in the Ukrainian language, how some people uttered derogatory remarks about the parish priest Father Kushko, and the Ukrainian Bishop Horniak. I was embarrassed to sit and listen to all the filth that was thrown around and was ready to leave in disgust. Without an inkling of warning, a certain Mr Sadiwnyk stood and demanded that I, the local baker, explained myself and declared in public if it were true that I'd said it didn't matter if people placed money in the collection boxes, because I was financially able to support the priest and the nuns, because if it were true, the people who supported me in business activity could just as easily boycott me. The whole hall erupted in support of Mr Sadiwnyk. I promptly stood up and attempted to reply, but the herd of people didn't stop heckling and shouting at me, even though Mr Bakhmat tried to calm them down. In the end I shouted back at them, warning them that if they didn't stop bellowing I would leave the building altogether. This seemed to have worked, so I slowly made my way to the front and said.

'First and foremost, I have never made such a comment, those were blatant lies against me. I attend church and will carry on going to church, I always gave money in the collections boxes and will carry on doing so. So who then should give to the church? The unemployed? Children? Old Aged Pensioners? Or me a businessman? If someone doesn't like my bread they don't have to buy it, you can eat stones,' In anger I was about to say 'eat shit' but refrained in the last second. I walked to the back of the hall, returned to my stool, and when I did stop talking, there were a couple of brave people who clapped.

That incident didn't affect my business in the least bit, there were still a core of Ukrainian people who had their own minds and didn't allow themselves to be persuaded by the Banderite doctrine, nor did they listen to their propaganda. The Banderites tried to ruin me in other underhand ways which invariably failed and did me no harm. They were also under a false illusion that all Ukrainians ate my bread, which wasn't true, most of my trade at that time was with the Polish shops, who didn't care much about Ukrainian politics.

At one time there was a rumour that I had died, another that I was so ill that a doctor was constantly by my bed. One Sunday somebody called the Fire Brigade to the bakery. The following day, two detectives asked me who I suspected, the police wanted to be aware of any such people, in case similar incidents were repeated on other Ukrainian churchgoers in Bradford. The police were determined to find the perpetrators, but I said nothing, I honestly didn't know who undertook such activities. Fortunately I was left in peace, no such occurrences were ever repeated again.

Personally ,nobody gave me any problems, but what went on in church every Sunday would be an embarrassment to write, and which reflected badly on my nerves. In the church I often helped the cantor to sing. On Christmas Day after the service, we began to sing a Christmas Carol, but were rudely interrupted by a section of the congregation singing their own 'patriarchal song' in a wild and loud tone, I sat and no longer sang. The following Sundays I stood at the back of the church and when the wild outbursts of singing commenced I left the church.

Ever since my childhood days, remembering the old man lying next to me in hospital after I had broken my arm, who taught me to pray, and later at the hostel run by the nuns and priests, who gave me food, shelter and an education, how could I possibly turn my back on these people, how could I blatantly turn away from these people who taught me God's ways and how to respect the church?

My health suffered during those turbulent times, often experiencing severe stomach pains, irrespective of what I ate. I visited my doctor for a consultation, who prescribed me medicine, but that didn't help. My wife didn't know what to cook for me, I didn't know what best to drink, coffee or tea, both disagreeing with me. My illness even drew me to the thought of suicide, such was the pain. I often thought of driving my car into a wall, ending the pain, but someone advised me to see a specialist, saying it was impossible that there were no cures for my stomach pains.

I took my friend's advice and saw a specialist, who asked me many questions, after which he booked me into a hospital for a thorough analysis. Tests showed no obvious detrimental malfunctions in my body, but I still experienced the same pain. Two weeks later, the specialist called me back and gave me an X-ray and I was told to call back in two days for the result. The specialist explained to me that I had an ulcerous stomach, which was brought on by anxiety and that I wasn't to show any form of anger or worry, and the best advice would be to leave Bradford completely, the further the better, and not to return to the bakery at the first sign of trouble.

How could I carry out the specialist's advice? I loved my business too much, and in addition I started to build the bakery's third large extension. Even though there was a small contingent of people who boycotted my bakery, our trade kept improving, hence the new extension.

Since the specialist confirmed I didn't have a serious condition, that I only needed peace and rest, his words lifted me mentally, though physically I still felt the pain.

In 1978 I again visited Ukraine with Olha, but this time I didn't hide the fact that I was visiting as a tourist, no longer afraid that I would be boycotted, or falsely accused of any turn of events.

CHAPTER 35
GOOD-BYE MOTHER

On this occasion, we travelled with Mr Paul Walowka and his wife Eva. All four of us drove to London in their car, from where we flew directly to Kyiv.

On arrival at Kyiv Airport, we saw a large queue forming at passport control. Our entire group were escorted into a large courtyard, surrounded by four tall walls, overhead we could only see darting swallows and swarms of flies. In the courtyard there were no benches or seats, giving the impression we were 'prisoners of war'. We were made to wait over an hour, some of the women were bitten by mosquitoes, and there was even visible blood on their bare legs. It wasn't until all the smokers had lit their cigarettes that the smoke finally dispersed the biting mosquitoes.

When we were finally called into the main building to Passport Control, we were detained another three hours, we had landed at 5p.m. but arrived at our hotel four hours later, subsequently missing our evening meal.

The Walowkas were met at the airport by Paul's sister and her daughter from Lviv, Eve was met by her two sisters, one of whom came with her husband and two children, eight of them in total. Both Paul's and Eva's families waited patiently at the airport in separate formations, not knowing each other. I was the first person who came out into the main public area from the baggage area, when suddenly a small boy aged about ten, clutching a bouquet of flowers, approached me and called out 'These are for you Granddad'. I was startled, as I wasn't expecting anyone, so I asked who he was waiting for, to which he replied 'Walowka' I could see the boy's confusion, as both Paul and I had grey hair. The boy wasn't the only one who didn't recognise his relatives from abroad, Paul's sister didn't recognise her own brother, nor did Eva her sisters.

Four of Walowka's party travelled with us by bus to the hotel, the other four by taxi. We went through all the usual formalities at reception, I was given a room on the fourth floor, the Walowka's on the fifth. All eight of Walowka's family followed him to their room, but visitors were refused entry by the floor receptionist. Paul left his luggage in his room and with his family came down to my floor.

Fortunately, our floor receptionist said nothing as everyone entered my room. After a few minutes, I left my room with Eva and went to see the floor receptionist, asking her if it were possible for all the family to have something to eat together in my room, because we hadn't eaten all day, to which she replied 'I know nothing'. We returned to my room to find Eva's sisters emptying their bags of food and drink, I soon noticed that it was after 1a.m. I went back to see the receptionist, this time asking if it were possible for my guests to stay in my room, as it was too late for them to find a hotel. She replied, 'I've told you once before, I know nothing'. Without saying another word, I placed a pair of ladies stockings on her desk and left.

Five minutes later, the receptionist entered my room, Paul poured her a generous glass of vodka, which she downed in one and left. After another half an hour, she returned with a large flask of tea, at that point began to talk to us, she could see that the children were already asleep on the sofa, so she left and returned with a few blankets. Luckily I had an adjoining room, so we all managed, four of us on two beds, the two children on the sofa, the rest on the floor.

The following morning after breakfast, I too had visitors, my brother's son, his wife and their two children. That day we didn't travel with the main tour group. Instead, we went to the park on the banks of the river Dnipro where we spent the whole day. The Walowkas did the same with their family, we all met back at the hotel that evening.

Outside the hotel, Paul's niece informed me that she had found a hotel on the next street for them, advising me to do the same for my family. I followed Paul's niece to the hotel she found by the name of 'Moscow'. I proceeded to the reception, seeing a young good-looking girl, and on the counter in front of her stood a plaque with the inscription 'A.Bodnarenko' whereupon I spontaneously broke into Ukrainian, but she replied in Russian. When I asked her why she didn't speak to me in Ukrainian, she replied with indignation, 'Can't you see where I work'. I then asked if there was a vacant room for Volodymyr and his family. She again replied angrily 'Why doesn't he speak himself if he wants a room?' She then turned to Volodymyr and asked him for his ID document, and then handed him a registration form.

Our guests spent two nights in Hotel Moscow, during the day we all organised our own excursions. On the first day, Paul's niece knew Kyiv well, so she proposed we hire a bus, as we were a large group. We followed her to the nearby bus station, where she requested a 'Ukrainian speaking' guide. She was told that if the majority of the passengers were Ukrainian, then we would be assigned one. Unfortunately, besides our group, there were two girls from Lviv, the rest from Poland, Germany and Russia, so we had to listen to a Russian speaking guide, showing us around our Ukrainian capital. I sat close to a couple of the ladies, who interpreted everything for me.

Kyiv had a total different look in the summer, as opposed to my last visit in winter. I have had the opportunity to see many capitals, but nothing could measure up to the beauty of Kyiv. The city was lined with tall green trees, shading the pavements, along which well- dressed people went hurriedly about their business. I saw few older people, most of them were young and female. In the park, on the banks of the river Dnipro, opened out a paradise, the fragrant smell of linden trees in full blossom.

I urgently wanted to at least dip my toe in the river Dnipro, I had to cross the river by a bridge to the other side, where it was safer, the scene looked more like a beach, with hundreds of people bathing on the river banks.

Two days quickly passed in Kyiv, in the afternoon my family returned home, and we took the overnight train from Kyiv to Odessa. On arrival at our hotel, we discovered that one of Paul's suitcases was missing, which he reported immediately. The receptionist made many phone calls, but the suitcase didn't show up. All the contents of the case belonged to Eva, who had to borrow many items from Olha to get by.

The hotel in Odessa was of a high standard. Whilst there we attended a Ukrainian concert, which was held in a beautiful auditorium, as tourists we were always ushered to the best seats and without having to queue.

On the first day, we were shown the usual local attractions, which included a short cruise on the Black Sea. We also visited the city's bathing beach, but didn't enter the sea, as we didn't bring our swimming costumes with us, but I managed to at least 'wet my toe' in the Black Sea.

At the beach, we broke away from the main party and made our own way to an 'open market' where we saw an abundance of garden produce, fruit, vegetables, eggs, butter and cheese, honey and cream, even live chickens, many of the traders invited us to taste their produce. There were no queues or shortages, such variety displayed in ample quantities. Prices were, however, higher than in the government- controlled shops.

Odessa, like Kyiv was in full bloom, trees everywhere, even grape vines climbing up building walls, sometimes to the second and third floors.

From Odessa we caught an overnight train to Chisinau, the capital of Moldova. First light gave us an insight into the land and how in was cultivated, there were few ploughed fields, the landscape was a mass of orchards, no wonder whenever the train stopped at the larger stations, local women were waiting with baskets laden with cherries, which we paid for with 'roubles' the Russian currency. The cherries were so cheap, fresh, juicy and so tasty, we found the whole area to be covered in field upon field by orchards, all growing a wide variety of fruits and grapes.

In Chisinau we were accommodated in a beautiful new hotel, which wasn't quite finished, so we ate our meals in the hotel across the road. Shortly after our arrival, we were taken on a city tour and saw the man-made lake which enhanced the city. On our return to the hotel, my cousin Natalka from Nadvirna was already waiting.

Whilst in Chisinau we attended a Sunday Mass, presided by three priests and accompanied by the mixed church choir.

Another two days quickly passed and I had to say goodbye to my cousin, who returned to Nadvirna by bus. Our group this time flew to Lviv, arriving early evening and being met by a light drizzle.

At the airport was a large group of family waiting for the Walowkas, so many of them that three taxis had to be hired, and six of them travelled in our bus. At our hotel, Olha's sister Hanya, was also waiting for us. As soon as all the formalities were taken care of, both families walked to Paul's brother's house, where a veritable feast had been prepared for us. On entering the house, I noticed a covered table the length of two rooms set for about thirty people, and on it, an unbelievable spread of food and drinks. Paul's sister who we met in Kyiv with her daughter, spent two days baking and cooking this banquet. After we all finished eating, which was washed down with plenty of alcohol, our guests began to sing and we joined in. They sang many new songs, unheard by us, but they also sang older songs familiar to us. We carried on singing and drinking until 11p.m. when it was time to leave, as the hotel gates closed at 11.30p.m.

Once we returned to our hotel, the Walowkas had a second surprise of the day, waiting for them in their room was their lost suitcase. It later came to light that they had to pay postage for it to be returned.

The following morning I woke early, nervously anticipating my own visitors. I walked out of the hotel into the courtyard and saw two men accompanying an older woman. My eyes filled with happiness as I knew it was my mother, she was with my brother's son Petro and my friend Slywchuk's brother's son. I took my mother into my arms, slowly escorting her to my room on the first floor. Olha's sister was waiting for us, revealing a large basket of food and cakes, even a roast chicken, which she had brought from home.

After breakfast, I left with Olha and her sister to the 'foreign currency' shop, where we stocked up on presents for the family. On our return Hanya packed away everything in her bag, ready to leave again, this time to her village with Olha, my mother and myself. My brother's son and his friend were to stay behind in the hotel and wait for our return. I didn't even have time to inform the Walowkas of our plans for the day, leaving a message for them with my nephew.

Outside the hotel Hanya found a taxi driver who was willing to take us all to her village, but insisted on payment for the journey in advance. No sooner had we taken off, the taxi driver began throwing the car around the side streets, that my mother yelled at him to stop, for she felt sick, fortunately Hanya had an empty bag which she gave to my mother, the driver totally ignoring my mother's pleas. As we drove out of the city onto a straight road, my mother felt a little better, until we approached their village of Kaminka Strumylova, when the roads again became more twisted, my mother began to yell again. The driver reduced his speed once we were in the village, the road took us past a homestead, then onto a very narrow road which was under water. The driver asked Hanya if the water was deep, she replied that other cars drove through the puddle. The driver began to accelerate, the water half covered the wheels and car floor began to let in water. Thirty metres later the large puddle was no more, nevertheless the taxi driver didn't manage all four wheels onto dry land, the rear wheels were stuck. The driver again accelerated robustly, this time all four wheels were on dry land. After another twenty metres another puddle emerged, by it stood two piles of wood chippings, which was to be used for traction the following day for a wedding party. The driver wouldn't go any further, we walked the rest of the way to Hanya's house which wasn't very far, while the taxi driver reversed his car towards the homestead.

At Hanya's house, my mother immediately lay down on the sofa, as she wasn't feeling very well . We were greeted by Maryna, Olha's oldest sister, who said that her mother was getting changed. So as to save time, I asked Hanya to show me around their smallholding. In the yard were several ducks and geese and their droppings, a barn in which they kept two cows and a pig, it also housed an electric threshing machine which she demonstrated by putting in a bundle of straw, shooting chaffs of it a metre high.

Once I'd seen the garden and orchard, I returned to the house, where Maryna and two cousins were preparing a table of food enough for a wedding. I had to remind them that we could only stay for an hour, for two years previously when my son Dmytro visited the village, he was confronted by the police, and I didn't want a repetition. Olha's mother finally entered, briefly greeted us, and then went on about her business feeding the small chicks. I noticed her giving them pieces of bread pasted with cheese.

The meal preparations were taking forever, I was beginning to feel agitated and couldn't hold back, so I again reminded them that we couldn't wait any longer, and if they wanted us to eat some food, then we must all sit at the table and start. We all sat, except for Olha's mother, who still had to feed the dog, he was first and the rest of us had to wait.

All this time, my mother lay on the sofa, I began to pour everyone a drink, leaving out my mother because she wasn't well, at which point my mother sat up and said to me, 'Pour me a drink son, allow me to drink once more to your health'. I poured my mother a generous glass and we toasted together.

All the food that had been prepared earlier remained untouched. Personally I wasn't hungry, and secondly I was afraid. Every minute I sat there I envisaged someone bursting through the door and arresting me. I asked Hanya to escort us to the bus, which annoyed everyone present, including Olha, but I stood firm, insisting that we had to leave.

My mother cried that she wouldn't return to Lviv by taxi, especially today when she still felt poorly, the others advised her to rest for a couple of days before returning.

Suddenly I was faced with a difficult and awkward moment, Olha and I both had to leave, but before leaving we had to say goodbye to our mothers, which was to be our last time. I approached the sofa on which my mother was lying, I knelt and kissed her, and then I walked to Olha's mother and the remainder of the family. Olha and I both stood and turned to face the front on the house, where we saw our two mothers following and blessing our safe passage. I will never forget the picture of my mother standing by the house blessing us, it will always be in my thoughts. My mother died on the 18th of

February 1984, at the age of 98. Olha's mother had passed away six months earlier.

I walked with Olha through the homestead, where I noticed a woman sweeping the yard, with a brush made from the branches of a birch tree. Hanya soon caught up with us directed us onto the tarmac road. I asked her where's the bus stop was, but she replied there wasn't one, the bus would stop if we raised our hand. We waited and waited, the bus never came, but unexpectedly a jeep appeared carrying milk urns. Hanya flagged it down. The driver agreed to take us, but after a couple of kilometres we stopped, when I asked why, the driver said the petrol had ran out of one tank and he had to switch over to the other. I froze with fright, I could only see military vehicles in the homestead, and no civilian owned cars. Luckily the switchover didn't take long and we were on our way. We reached the market in Kaminka Strumylova, where we caught a bus to Lviv.

That same day the Walowka's had their own programme. His brother hired a minibus, which took the whole family to the cemetery where Paul's mother was buried. They later called at the houses of his brothers and sisters, before meeting up with us again that evening.

It was the 12th of July, the Saint's Day of Peter & Paul, and as on the previous day, we were all invited to Paul's brother's house, for food, drinking and singing, which lasted into the early hours of the morning.

My brother's son Petro returned home the following evening with his friend. We in turn flew from Lviv to Moscow. We were driven to a hotel in the city, but only stayed a few hours, before our flight home to London that evening. At Moscow Airport, two young Jews were detained, apparently they had kept a diary of all the places they visited. What happened to them later, I didn't find out.

Thankfully, we returned to Bradford safely, to our daily routine, the same work and familiar problems.

CHAPTER 36
RETIREMENT YEARS

The bakery was running smoothly, despite there having been a year when I experienced a faction of Ukrainians boycotting my bread. In 1978 I bought two new ovens, the larger with a capacity of 390 loaves costing £25,000 while the smaller with a capacity of 260 loaves cost £18,000. Despite unforeseen difficulties, I managed to give a deposit of £14,000, and the ovens were paid for within two years. In addition, we spent £12,000 on a building extension.

I had to work hard for my money, twelve to fourteen hours daily, weekends too, not only myself but the whole family. We didn't work set hours, everybody worked until all the orders were fulfilled.

I didn't have much free time, on Sunday morning I would go to church, the afternoons were occupied with the bakery accounts. I never complained about my work because I loved my job and was very pleased with the fact that my rye bread was in such demand. I was also pleased that all three of my sons took an interest in the business and on the 3rd of August 1981 I formed a partnership, giving them all a stake in the business.

After my 60th birthday my health worsened, and on the advice of my doctor, I needed to be stress free and away from Bradford and the business. One Sunday I read an advertisement of new homes being built in Littlehampton. The following day I rang the agent who sent me brochures and information. Two weeks later I drove down with Olha and Dmytro for an assessment. It was a peaceful location, close to the sea in a much sought-after area, especially for the London pensioners.

Within a few months I had sold my house in Bradford and on the 18th of April 1979, taking a little furniture and clothes in the bakery van, we moved into our new home. My health began to improve, albeit slowly. I did very little, went for walks and read. On the other hand, Olha soon began to get bored, there were no Ukrainians to talk with, the neighbours were very good, though whenever we spoke to them, it was always over the garden fence.

From time to time on Sunday, we would catch a train to London, to attend mass at the Ukrainian Catholic Cathedral. After the service we met with familiar people, spending the whole day in London, returning home in the evening. In the summer months, we quite often travelled to the Ukrainian Invalid's Home in Chiddingfold, Surrey, which was a short distance away from Littlehampton.

Having spent so many years in Bradford, it turned out to be difficult to let go completely, so we would periodically leave our house in the care of our neighbours for two or three weeks, returning to Bradford, where we stayed with our son Dmytro, who at the time lived alone in his house.

We carried on living this way for two years, commuting between Bradford and Littlehampton. When Olha was alone in Littlehampton, she always complained, especially about the lonely nights. I had plenty of books to read, I wrote a little, time passed very quickly for me, and when I became bored or worried what was happening in the bakery, I jumped into my car and drove to Bradford.

After two years of being pestered and listening to Olha's complaints, one day I came across an advertisement selling properties in Spain.

We soon sold our house in Littlehampton and bought an apartment in southern Spain. I enjoyed the new environment, the sun, the beach, so after a couple of years sold the apartment and bought a house.

Today, my sons pay me a weekly rent for the bakery, and I am pleased they are healthy and working together. The business I built from nothing has prospered and has grown from strength to strength. Our bread is available all over England and is the envy of many of my compatriots. As long as my sons live in harmony and look after their business, they will have their lives secured. In the meantime, I will spend the rest of my years with my wife in Spain.

THE END

OUR FATHER, WHO GAVE US OUR DAILY BREAD

THE SON'S STORY

My mother was admitted into a nursing home in 2010 after being diagnosed with Dementia. Shortly afterwards, while clearing space in a cupboard in the house next door to the bakery, which she and my father stayed in England until his death in 1999, I stumbled upon a large brown envelope. Inside it I found over 100 sheets of paper typewritten in Ukrainian text which I at once knew for certain was my father's autobiography. I was well aware of its existence even though my father had never discussed it with me, and yet sometimes he would do so in the presence of his friends, knowing full well I was within earshot of the conversation.

At that particular time, I was commuting between England and Cyprus. Rushed off my feet and too busy to sit and read it, I took it to Cyprus with me, knowing I would have more time to read it there.

One day I summoned up courage and began to read the hardships my father had endured during his childhood and teenage years, I was totally surprised and felt increasingly compassionate reading about the difficult years of his early life. When my father was alive he talked very little about his childhood. I knew his father had died very early in his life, and that my father became a baker, that he was conscripted into the Polish Army, later captured by the occupying German forces, shipped off to a concentration camp for a couple of years, and later to be released and spend the rest of his time in a Displaced Persons (DP) Camp in Heidenau, Germany, before eventually settling in England.

In the 1980s I was attending a bakery exhibition in Hamburg, northern Germany. While in the area, with prior arrangement with my father, I visited the same bakery he worked in after the war. I met his old boss and his wife, at that time in their seventies, who treated me very hospitably. I spent a couple of days at their bakery, run at the time by their son who, my father once told me, was still in his pram after the war. I also met and spoke to a man about my age, whose Ukrainian parents stayed in the village after the camp was disbanded.

I finished reading the 100 or so pages, knowing there was likely to be much more elsewhere. It wasn't until a couple of years later, while sorting through old bakery documents and ledgers in the bakery attic that my younger brother Dmytro came upon the remainder. I don't know how many copies my father typed. As I was rearranging the papers in chronological order I found many duplicated pages. I overheard snippets of conversation between my father and a couple of his friends, when he tried to publish his autobiography, but because of high costs gave up on the idea. I also remember his cousin by the name of Natalka, who met my father in Ukraine in the 1970s and 1990s. She later visited England with her son Volodomyr Dubiak. He travelled to England himself a couple of years later by bus and returned in a fully laden car which my father had paid for. I know my father gave him a copy to have published in Ukraine. I later found out from Volodomyr that he had all the typewritten pages bound into book form by a printer.

Once I'd received and read the remainder of the pages, I was shocked to discover that 'we didn't really know our father', there were so many parts of his life he'd never spoken about to his children, other parts he'd omitted in his autobiography, some good, some not so good, some of which our mother revealed after his death whilst she was still of sound mind. Mother would never have dared mention to me or my brothers when he was still alive what she later told us after his death. To some extent, it was only when I turned the last page of my father's story that I began to fully appreciate the trials and tribulations of his life. I felt proud of his achievements, especially in the early years of his bakery business, something that I personally wouldn't have undertaken. And I recalled that, while growing up, I too had witnessed similar hardships with my own eyes and experienced some of the things he'd been through. I felt I owed it to him to publish the story of his life and leave a record for future generations to read. I have read many various books in my lifetime, some of them autobiographies, and I feel his story is both interesting and moving, shocking in parts, eye-opening in others, well worth writing in the first instance, translating and finally leaving the reader to draw his or her conclusions. At this point I must also add and express my sincerest thanks to my oldest and dearest friend Alex Kirichenko, who has helped me enormously in putting this book together.

I also felt duty- bound to write at least one chapter about my father, the side of him that I knew best as I was growing up. Some people might think it unfair, insensitive or undeserved to write about certain events of his life, but in writing his story I began to understand much more about him that I didn't know before. At times, while translating, I felt I was entering his body and mind, living through his life as if it were my own, providing me with a better understanding of what made him 'tick' and the reasons behind his actions.

As a person, he rarely showed any fatherly love, keeping his distance. In later years his gratitude invariably took the form of financial reward. To be on my father's side everything had to be done his way, he would rarely see reason, especially coming from me, his word was final, to go against him made you his enemy. I have seen early photographs of me sitting on his knee, his eyes filled with pride, but as the years went by all I could see in his eyes was scorn. I read of the times he was re-united with his own mother, how he revered her presence, even though as a child she had kept him tied to a table as if on a leash. I can only remember one occasion when I was seven years old, after I'd showed him a good school report, he put his arm around me with pride and joy. I don't recall ever seeing him hold my two children, a handshake was our only physical contact whenever he returned from one of his trips to Spain, and even then only if he was in a good mood. Sadly, my mother was much the same, very often I thought it was because of the hard attitude my father had instilled into the household. During his surprise 80th birthday celebrations, my brothers and I presented him with a gift, he extended his arm towards me which I shook, I moved closer to him and put my arms around him; a rare embrace that turned out to be the last in our lives.

As children, my brothers and I received no pocket money, even as we became older we were seldom given anything by our father, we had to earn it like he had to. On the other hand, he showed a generous side to strangers, which at times I resented, especially since nothing ever came easy to us. Admittedly, when the bakery business was successful, he allowed us interest free loans to pay for our houses and cars, but he kept a tight rein on the business capital until his death.

How far back does my memory stretch? I remember living in our first house at 68 Wyndham Street in Bury, I remember some of the lodgers who shared our home. I remember going to see Queen Elizabeth 11 in Bury town centre, on her two-day visit to the mill towns of Lancashire in 1954, being lost during the event and brought back home later by a policeman. In those early years, living with my parents, I of course accepted the order of home life as any other child would, not knowing or understanding any better or worse. My memories were clearer once we moved into our second house at 130 Heywood Street, the smallest bedroom of the three being occupied by a lodger, until my youngest brother Taras was born in June, 1957.

When my brothers and I were at home in the sole presence of our father, our mother was at work in a cotton mill, the atmosphere in the house was very tense. Our father usually sat at the dining table reading, we three boys sitting on a sofa trying to play very quietly, we dared not make any noise, we knew the consequences only too well. We had a television set in the room, but had to ask permission to switch it on; if he was in a bad mood we didn't even bother asking. Whenever the television was on, we needed permission to switch channels, even though in those days there were only two channels, BBC and ITV. At around six o'clock when the news was broadcast, no matter what we were watching, our father stood up and switched it over to his desired channel.

School holidays were something most children looked forward to, not in my case though. The night before my father would set me a task. He had stacks of exercise books, and whilst he was at work I had to write many chapters of text before he returned from work, only then could I go out and play with other children. When our father worked in the cotton mill, he brought home rolls of old leather machine belts, discarded by the factory. Some of the leather was used to repair our shoes, as in those days most shoes had leather soles. He also cut off lengths which he used to 'tan our backsides' especially mine whenever I stepped out of line.

I wasn't a spoiled brat or a problem child, mischievous yes, but with our father I felt that he sometimes looked for an excuse to scold and hit us. It wasn't until much later that I began to understand more, especially after writing about his early years in Bury and knowing what he'd lived through in the Ukrainian community. In retrospect, maybe he did, rightly or wrongly, beat us purely to offload his anger and get rid of his frustrations. After my father's death, my mother once told me that he also used to beat her, but I don't remember ever seeing this happen. Apparently, in those days it was a very common occurrence in Ukrainian and other eastern European households.

Once we moved to Bradford, his form of punishment changed. In September of 1961, I started the Isis School in Bolton, (named after the Egyptian goddess) which, incidentally, was the best school I ever attended. Unfortunately, it only lasted one term, and occasionally I was given a lift to Bolton by Mr. Zahayevych. My parents and brothers moved to Bradford in November of that year, whereas I stayed with my auntie, my mother's cousin in Bury until Christmas.

In January of 1962, shortly after my twelfth birthday, I started Fox's School of Commerce, on the recommendations of my father's partner Volodomyr Iwasz. That school was the worst I ever attended. Not surprisingly, I left as soon as I could, three months before my sixteenth birthday. Being the eldest, my father would force me to help in the bakery after school. As I became more proficient, I would sometimes work until 11p.m. then return home to do my homework before going to bed. Leisure time after school was non –existent. Many times I had to stay behind on a Friday night if a worker failed to turn up for the night-shift. I even had to work on Saturday morning from 7a.m. until 1p.m. cleaning the bakery floor on my hands and knees, scraping pieces of hardened dough which had bitten into the asphalt and covered floor throughout the week. I also washed down the tables and mixing machines, for which I received the equivalent of 50 pence, providing I didn't sleep in and did a good job. It goes without saying, if my father found fault, I wasn't paid. When I was twenty one, he introduced a 'bonus' system. Later, as my brothers became of age they became recipients, which all sounded very good and promising. Our father was, however, an expert in finding fault with us, fabricating an excuse not to pay us, and was equally good at disappointing us when he so wished.

There just never seemed to be much respite for me. Even on Sunday afternoons I had to help my father with the weekly invoices. In those days there were no computers or calculators, we used 'ready reckoners' and manually operated adding machines instead. When I was about 13 years old, one of my duties was to go to the bakery every Sunday evening at around 8p.m. to mix a batch of brown dough, followed by a mix of white dough, and after finishing I would return home. My father came in around 10p.m. or thereabouts with Romo or whichever helper was helping him at the time.

I hardly saw anyone outside of school, perhaps on a Saturday evening at the Ukrainian Scouts meetings. School holidays, Christmas and Easter, was always spent at the bakery. By the time I was fifteen, I could perform almost every task. As my brothers Dmytro and Taras became older, they too were brought into 'the fold'.

In the mid-1960s, my father owned a Vauxhall Bedford van that had windows to the rear of the driver and a collapsible bench, making extra floor space when it was used for bread deliveries. The Ukrainian Catholic Church in those days was still on Fairfield Road, and our father used to drive us to church almost every Sunday. In Bradford, at that time, were three Ukrainian nuns who lived on the other side of the city. One Sunday after mass, my father approached them and offered them a lift to their home. This turned out to be a regular occurrence, and I often wondered to myself why my father revered the nuns so highly. Everything came to light when I was translating his childhood years, of course it was the nuns and priests in Ukraine who sheltered, fed and educated him, and this was his way of repaying his gratitude fifty years later. He then began leaving a weekly box of bread to the priests and nuns for many years. Every Ukrainian Christmas he donated free rolls to the church. These were later blessed by the priest, and this symbolic bread was broken into pieces and shared amongst families on Christmas Eve. This donation is still carried on even today, not only in the Bradford church, but also the Manchester one, and even the Ukrainian Cathedral in London.

When I left school at fifteen, I enrolled into a full-time bakery college in Leeds. I travelled back directly to the bakery after lessons and helped out in the bakery, more so during college holidays.

I completed the two-year course, achieving a City & Guilds Certificate in Baking. I asked my father how much he would pay me as a full- time worker. His answer was a lot less than any other member of staff received. In anger I went to work at Silvio's Bakery, where I received more money than my father was prepared to pay me. After about a couple of months he must have felt embarrassed that his son was working for someone else. So, swallowing his pride, he offered me the same money if I came to work for him.

Like many young men in the 1960s I was a smoker but never dared to smoke in my father's presence, as he was vehemently opposed to smoking. One morning after finishing a night shift at the bakery, I was two months short of my eighteenth birthday, I began to make my way home. I walked past my father who, noticing a bulge in one of my pockets, told me angrily to empty both, thereupon revealing a packet of cigarettes.

With hardly a word exchanged apart from a few puzzled glances, I followed him into his car and we drove home. In the house he searched for a suitcase and told me to pack it with my clothes which I did. He reached into his pocket, took out twenty pounds and said this was for the eighteen years he had known me. My father returned to the bakery in his car, I walked to the nearby bus stop, caught a bus to the city railway station, from where I caught a train to London.

In all the time I spent in London I never once got in touch with my family. I returned after almost a year, to be told by my father that I couldn't smoke until I was twenty one. My father died when I was forty nine, by which time I was married with two children and two grandchildren, but I never attempted to smoke in his presence.

Our father was never gratified to hear of our achievements, nor would he shower us with any praise, no matter what we did to please him, there were even times when he showed signs of jealousy. One significant occasion he omitted from his autobiography was the 10th anniversary celebrations of Kolos Bakery, on the 10th of October 1971, held at the Ukrainian Club, Claremont, Bradford.

Several months prior to the date, I started to plan a surprise party for my father, with the help of my future wife Roksanna and her parents Jaroslaw & Tamara Babuniak who arranged the buffet. Specially printed invitation cards were ordered, and these I distributed to our customers who, one by one, were sworn to secrecy, not a word was to be uttered to my father. On the day of the party, I had previously arranged with Mr & Mrs Zahayevych to call at my parents' house and entice them to the Ukrainian Club, which they did dutifully. I would have given anything to capture the look of unadulterated shock on my parents' faces as they walked into a hall full of Kolos customers and friends.

The bakery's next party was to celebrate its 25th anniversary, which was held at the new Ukrainian Club on Legrams Lane, in Bradford, on Sunday the 5th of October 1986. I am not sure when my father finished writing his story, I believe it might have been around 1984, two years before the event. This celebration was done on a much grander scale and was such a success that people talked about it for years. I remember my father giving a speech, and one of the unforgettable things he said was that very day marked the first time in his life he'd eaten 'Chicken Kyiv'. We even had a cake baked for the occasion, a replica of the bakery from photographs, which was baked and decorated by Mrs Lida Kolomyetch from Bolton.

Over the years since that memorable 25th anniversary, the bakery has featured in many television and radio programmes, has been written about in books, magazines and newspapers, has inspired high street supermarket chains and retail stores to stock of Kolos breads on their shelves, and has satisfied the taste buds of successive generations of clients and customers. It is primarily thanks to the courage, endeavour and enterprising spirit of our father that Kolos grew to become a highly successful family business.

In his autobiography my father wrote about his trips to Ukraine, the second being in 1978. He wrote about meeting his brother's son, his wife and their two children. As I grew older, in the back of my mind I began to harbour suspicions of my father having a 'secret family' in Ukraine, confirmed later by my mother after his death. Mother told me that when they first met, he'd told her he was a bachelor, though later admitted otherwise. My mother also told me that whilst they were living in Spain, two of his grandchildren from Ukraine came to stay with them.

Going back to my father's trip in 1978, I found it strange that part of his family had travelled so far to visit him in Kyiv. Why was that? After all, they lived in the same region hundreds of miles away from Kyiv, just as the remaining relatives of both families did. The only conclusion I can come up with today is that my father must have been too embarrassed to meet them in my mother's mother presence in Lviv. Indeed, whilst sorting through my parents' belongings, I fell upon a photograph of my father making a speech at a graveside in Ukraine. The photograph soon jogged my memory. I remember my father making a hastily planned trip to Ukraine, saying it was to the burial of his cousin, when I suspect it was in reality his son's funeral. The photograph was dated 29th of May 1998, only months before his own death the following year.

Shortly before publishing this book, my brother Dmytro received a surprise phone call at the bakery from my father's cousin's son Volodomyr Dubiak. I later found Volodomyr through the internet and since that day we've had many interesting conversations.

I was intrigued about my father's 'secret family' and Volodomyr told me about the photograph dated the 29th of May 1998, which he himself took at the graveside of my father's first son. Volodomyr answered a phone call from my father, asking him to meet him at Kyiv Airport the following day, which he did. They both drove directly to a hospital in Ternopil, and my father was able to share the last few hours of his son's life. He was buried the day after.

I also found out through Volodomyr that my father married a girl from a neighbouring village, and that when he left for war in 1939 the girl was pregnant. What again puzzles me is that my father returned to his village in January of 1942 by which time his son would have been 2years old. Why did he leave his young wife, who apparently never married again, and his young son?

Over the years, like others of my generation born of Ukrainian parents who, as former DPs eventually settled in the free and democratic world, I have heard of many stories about what people had to endure before, during and after the war years to survive. In the years before the Second World War, it was customary among country folk to be married by their early twenties if not their late-teens. My father was twenty-three when WW2 broke out. Many of his generation of DPs fled the Soviet Communist yoke, having survived the Holodomor (famine) in Ukraine in 1932-33, witnessed the Stalanist purges and forced deportation to Siberian camps in the late 1930s, as was my mother's sister Hanya, who spent 12 years there for helping Ukrainian partisans. Many people ended up in a German concentration or POW camp, or were rounded up at gunpoint, uprooted and forcibly transported to work as slaves in German armament factories, farms and fields, as my mother did, while others had to live by their wits to get by and survive one terrible ordeal after another. There were women who smuggled their own children into foreign countries, passing them off as their brothers and sisters.

Looking back today to the not so distant past, the bakery's most prosperous years flourished after my father had finished writing his autobiography, when he was spending most of his time in southern Spain, visiting us a few times a year, and after his death.

In 1998 I was interviewed for a television series about various specialist food manufacturers. That same year I received a letter to say that we had been selected. Two months later a film crew descended on the bakery and spent two and a half days filming. They filmed all the different stages of production and conducted a televised interview with me and my two brothers. The series was called 'Taste with Jancis Robinson' and was screened on BBC2 and still can be seen on YouTube. We were even filmed attending the Ukrainian Catholic Church in Bradford, and on their last night my wife Roksanna organised a buffet for our family and the film crew in our home.

During the course of the evening, Jancis Robinson conducted an impromptu interview with my father, asking him a few questions and saying how proud he must have felt to see his sons carrying on the business, to which my father astonished everyone with an unexpected blunt criticism of me and my brothers. Naturally this was good television and was included in the broadcast the following year on the 8th of June 1999, with over 2 million viewers.

Sadly, my father never lived to witness the greatest accolade of his business life. He passed away on the 11th of February 1999. More recently, my mother too sadly passed away in a nursing home on the 26th of May 2018.

The documentary producers couldn't include the detail of my father's death in the ten minute documentary, but on the night of broadcasting, it was mentioned by Moira Stuart a former news reader with the BBC after the programme.

In the end, my brothers and I have remained eternally grateful to our father who gave us not only 'our daily bread' but a good trade and business too. Over the years he provided jobs to the scores of staff who in return gave him good service. He also helped the Ukrainian Catholic Church, the Ukrainian Scouts, various charities and individuals, some known to us and I am sure there were plenty unknown.

Ivan Prytulak's life was certainly a true 'rags to riches' story. From his impoverished and humble beginnings, he nurtured his beloved bakery despite his many disappointments and became one of the most successful Ukrainian businessmen of his generation in England.

Jaroslaw Prytulak has pleasure in inviting

Mr. & Mrs. ....

To attend a Surprise Party of

The 10th ANNIVERSARY of KOLOS BAKERY

to be held at The Ukrainian Club
Claremont, Off Morley Street, Bradford
On SUNDAY 3rd OCTOBER 1971 at 6 p.m.

Cabaret   *Dance*   *Buffet*

Celebrated on Sunday the 5th of October 1986

25th Anniversary cake baked and decorated by Mrs Lida Kolomyetch of Bolton.

Left to right at the main table: Angela (side) Taras who died on
18/09/2009
Roksanna, Jaroslaw, Ivan, Olha and Dmytro Prytulak

Ivan with Olha, at Ivan's surprise 80th Birthday Celebrations

Ivan Prytulak, his fulfilled dream

Printed in Great Britain
by Amazon